A Casebook of Public Ethics and Issues

William M. Timmins

Brigham Young University

Brooks/Cole Publishing Company
Pacific Grove, California

To my wife, Theda Laws Timmins,
and my children: Mont, Ruth, Clark, Laurel,
Sally, Rebekah, and Nicolaos

Brooks/Cole Publishing Company
A Division of Wadsworth, Inc.

© 1990 by Wadsworth, Inc., Belmont, California 94002.
All rights reserved. No part of this book may be reproduced,
stored in a retrieval system, or transcribed, in any form or
by any means—electronic, mechanical, photocopying, recording,
or otherwise—without the prior written permission of the
publisher, Brooks/Cole Publishing Company, Pacific Grove,
California 93950, a division of Wadsworth, Inc.

Printed in the United States of America
10 9 8 7 6 5 4 3 2 1

Library of Congress Cataloging-in-Publication Data
Timmins, William M.
    A casebook of public ethics and issues / William M. Timmins.
      p.   cm.
    Includes bibliographical references.
    ISBN 0-534-12612-X
    1. Political ethics—United States—Case studies. 2. Business
ethics—United States—Case studies.   I. Title.
JK468.E7T56   1989   89-38155
172—dc20   CIP

Sponsoring Editor: *Cynthia C. Stormer*
Marketing Representative: *Adam Steele*
Editorial Assistant: *Mary Ann Zuzow*
Production Editor: *Marjorie Sanders*
Manuscript Editor: *Alan Hislop*
Permissions Editor: *Carline Haga*
Interior Design: *Lisa Thompson*
Cover Design: *Stephanie Workman*
Art Coordinator: *Cloyce Wall*
Typesetting: *Bookends Typesetting*
Cover Printing: *Philips Offset Company*
Printing and Binding: *Arcata Graphics/Fairfield*

One of the most enduring legacies of the Watergate scandal has been the increased attention given to the question of ethics in government. We saw the development of the Federal Election Commission, which embodied and institutionalized campaign reform. We have seen the creation of rules of conduct in both houses of Congress, and seen them expanded and institutionalized in the Ethics in Government Act. We have seen the emergence of citizen-based "watchdog" organizations, and the emergence of investigative reporting in the journalistic community. Phrases like "advisory opinion," "conflict of interest statements," "blind trust," "divestment," "special prosecutor," and "whistleblower" are now well established in the government vocabulary.

Every four years, the Presidential Commission on Executive and Legislative Salaries proposes increases for top government officials, unleashing a torrent of discussion and criticism of "outside income," "honoraria," and "perquisites of office," and we see members of Congress wringing their hands over so-called self-serving votes that might bring down the wrath of their constituents on their heads, regardless of any factual justification.

There are perhaps no more difficult personal questions facing those who serve in high public office today than what is the current definition of ethical conduct, and what are the standards against which they will be judged in office.

The debate continues on ethical conduct and what is and is not appropriate for elected and senior government officials. Because the issue is so subjective, I suspect that it will never be fully resolved; honest individuals can and do disagree on moral judgments, and true consensus is difficult to achieve. The result of such debate in a legislative body is usually the lowest common denominator or the simplest, most expedient solution, and that rarely yields the best result.

That is precisely why I have always felt that the key to ensuring ethical conduct on the part of elected and high-level appointed officials is to have the most complete disclosure possible. I have sufficient confidence in the voters that they will be able to judge effectively for themselves whether or not any public official's conduct is ethical if they are given the facts. If they are not satisfied, they have recourse to the ballot box.

To be sure, as a society we have established certain standards of conduct over the many years of our civilized existence that are shared by the vast majority of individuals. Many of the standards we have codified as law and provided penalties for their violation. The challenge is to define standards for public service on the basis of those existing standards that may be shared by many, but have not yet been accepted as law. Perhaps only more time and more experience will enable our society to meet that challenge.

The basis of that experience is the vast array of individual cases that arise and the various outcomes of those individual cases. For that reason, Dr. Timmins has performed a very valuable service in bringing together this casebook.

Nothing will more clearly demonstrate the difficulty in resolving ethical issues, or more meaningfully instruct students in the field of ethical studies than the process of wrestling with specific factual situations and arriving at conclusions about the issues involved.

Senator E. J. "Jake" Garn
United States Senate

My first introduction to some of the complexities of ethical behavior came in the late 1930s and early 1940s, a time of great social upheaval in the United States. Millions of men and women found themselves criss-crossing this rich and vast land seeking an opportunity to rebuild their lives and to find meaningful work. My father and mother owned a modest home in the Avenues section of Salt Lake City. One of my jobs each spring and summer was to whitewash a picket fence that formed one boundary line of our family home. Every time I'd whitewash the fence I realized someone had marked some strange symbols on the pickets in charcoal, pencil, or crayon. It frustrated me. Years later in college I read articles on these strange symbols and learned they were a universal hobo language. Roughly translated, the marks on the fence meant, "good meal, will let you work for it, won't call the cops." Hobos were the transients—quite different in many ways from the street people of today, but sharing some of the same human needs. I realized after reading these articles that our home was visited nearly daily by men or women who came to our back door. Politely they asked if my mother had any work they could do to earn a meal. My mother always handed them a broom or a rake and assigned them to a task while she fixed a meal. She always fed them well. They always did a good job. No one ever bothered our home in any way. I came to realize this was the heart of ethics—care and concern about the dignity and worth of others, now when it is needed, not eventually or later on.

Years later I served as chairman of the bioethics committees at two large hospitals. Our committees were charged with drawing up rules and procedures on withholding life-saving or life-extending care. We were confronted with some very difficult ethical decisions, sometimes so hard to reach that they produced tears, even for grown adults.

I also served on an earlier task force of the American Society for Public Administration (ASPA), which drafted a code of ethics for public administrators. This was not an easy task. We met over a couple of years and read through a mass of materials from other professional occupations. Ultimately, ASPA adopted this draft code and started a long-range discussion effort to implement it in a meaningful way.

I also served as an officer in a number of businesses that required us to sign codes of ethical behavior. Yes, we all took these quite seriously. The corporate culture of these companies was such that you knew that signing a promise to be ethical was not just a gesture, it was an understood way of doing business, all the time.

It is from these perspectives, as well as twenty years in the classroom with hundreds of graduate students, that I present this casebook on ethics. It is designed to provide instructors with a wide selection of real-life cases organized by broad clusters that relate to current issues. Each chapter includes a brief introduction, raises an ethical issue, and details the case. Instructors demand cases that have depth, require hard analysis, provoke discussion and debate, and tie into the broader personnel administration and human resources management agenda. Every case herein has been tested in the classroom and in executive development courses, some over several years.

The *Casebook* is designed for students at the undergraduate and graduate levels in ethics, public and private administration, and organizational behavior. Students also demand cases that are challenging, real-life, and require tough analysis and discussion. These cases have long been popular with students who've used them—but the same cases have proven powerful and been well-received by executives in seminars, management training classes, and conferences; executives have recognized them all as meaty, tough cases, with lots to chew on.

The *Casebook* provides a set of assignments for each case. Again, every assignment has been classroom tested, often, and has demonstrated that it pays off in worthwhile learning. The approaches suggested vary widely—debates, simulations, role play, research papers, problem solving and skill building, and structured interviews. Instructors using these assignments have been uniformly pleased with the results and very positive about the variety of analytical methods. Grading will be easy—instructors need only to decide the weight of the required elements.

In addition, the *Casebook* provides a useful set of references for several cases— not extensive reading lists but highly recommended key sources.

Every case in this text has been published elsewhere by the author himself, usually in refereed journals. Each case has been revised and edited after a public response— indeed, some of these earlier publications have drawn scores of letters over time. The author is grateful for the permission to revise and use these cases (credits appear at the end of the cases). I am also grateful to the reviewers who offered helpful suggestions: Gayle Avant, Baylor University; Terry Rhodes, University of North Carolina, Charlotte; Allen Settle, California Polytechnic State University, San Luis Obispo; and Leonard Stitelman, University of New Mexico.

The *Casebook* does not attempt an exhaustive bibliography on the topic of ethics—that is not its purpose. Still, the following seminal sources will provide teachers and students a thought-provoking beginning.

John A. Rohr, "The Study of Ethics in the P.A. Curriculum." *Public Administration Review* (July/August, 1976): 398–406. Rohr listed dozens of sources "to suggest a method for integrating the study of ethics into a public administration curriculum."

Susan Wakefield, "Ethics and the Public Service: A Case for Individual Responsibility." *Public Administration Review* (November/December, 1976). Wakefield argued that only individual responsibility can "serve as the first line of defense against unethical behavior."

Professional Standards and Ethics: A Workbook for Public Administrators (Washington, D.C.: American Society for Public Administration, 1979). ASPA defined a number of key questions, key principles, and some self-diagnostic questions on ethics.

Whistle Blowing (Washington, D.C.: American Society for Public Administration, 1979), 1–7. ASPA stated a proposed course of action.

G. Homer Durham, *Good, Evil, and Public Administration* (Provo: Brigham Young University Press, 1974), 1–6. Durham argued that the "effectiveness of codes of ethics depends on . . . fundamental beliefs."

N. Dale Wright, ed., *Papers on the Ethics of Administration* (Provo: Brigham Young University Press, 1988). A series of thoughtful essays that "return to the familiar theme that organizational ethics is dependent on personal ethics."

Our thanks to the following publishers for permission to reprint herein or adapt the author's following works as part of the *Casebook: Fire Chief* magazine; the Inter-University Case Program, Inc., Syracuse, N.Y.; *Arbitration Journal,* a publication of the American Arbitration Association; *Assessor's Journal,* a publication of the International Association of Assessing Officers; *Public Administration Quarterly; Public Personnel Management,* a publication of the International Personnel Management Association; and BYU *Exchange.*

The contents of the *Casebook* are as follows. This material fits a single-semester course format or can be used in a two- or three-semester ethics class series.

Part I, Personnel Administration and Ethics, presents issues that arise within organizations. Chapter 1 discusses drug testing, based on the case of an alcoholic worker. Chapter 2 applies day-to-day management rules to the ethical issue of not telling the truth and getting caught in the lie. Chapter 3 deals with censorship, rule making, and discharge procedures, and Chapter 4 discusses comparable worth. In Chapter 5, the right of public employees to strike is analyzed. Chapter 6 focuses on employee fitness programs and whether the pressure for health-cost containment gives employers the right to enforce employee fitness.

Part II, Ethics and Politics, brings ethical issues into the political arena. Chapter 7 discusses interference with free local elections by public employees trying to protect their jobs. Chapter 8 presents a political smear campaign, and Chapter 9 discusses conflicts between political appointees and careerists.

Part III, Ethics and Public Economics, focuses on money-based decisions in the public sector. Chapter 10 deals with the ethical issues involved in downsizing, Chapter 11 presents the ethics of tax incentives and waivers, Chapter 12 points out the impact of privatizing public jobs, and Chapter 13 discusses inter-local contracting agreements.

Part IV, The Ethics of Health and the Workplace, illustrates how personal decisions affect and are affected by administrative decisions. Chapter 14 raises the dilemma of bioethics: the right to live and the right to die. Chapter 15 presents the issues society confronts in dealing with child care on the job. The exchanging of gifts, and whether it's mandatory or voluntary, is investigated in Chapter 16. And the controversial issue of smoking versus nonsmoking in the workplace is raised in Chapter 17.

These are cases full of the gristle and grit of life. Ethical behavior is, by definition, the right behavior, but it isn't always easy to know what that behavior should be. It is my fond expectation that these cases will help future public administrators, if only in some small way, to achieve more ethical behavior.

William M. Timmins

Code of Ethics for Government Service

This Code of Ethics applies to all government employees and office holders. The Code was agreed to by the United States House of Representatives and the Senate as House Concurrent Resolution 175 in the second session of the eighty-fifth Congress.

Any person in government service should:
Put loyalty to the highest moral principles and to country above loyalty to persons, party, or government department.

Uphold the Constitution, laws, and legal regulations of the United States and all governments therein and never be a party to their evasion.

Give a full day's labor for a full day's pay; giving to the performance of his duties his earnest effort and best thought.

Seek to find and employ more efficient and economical ways of getting tasks accomplished.

Never discriminate unfairly by the dispensing of special favors or privileges to anyone, whether for remuneration or not; and never accept, for himself or his family, favors or benefits under circumstances which might be construed by reasonable persons as influencing the performance of his governmental duties.

Make no private promises of any kind binding upon the duties of office, since a government employee has no private word which can be binding on public duty.

Engage in no business with the government, either directly or indirectly, which is inconsistent with the conscientious performance of his governmental duties.

Never use any information coming to him confidentially in the performance of governmental duties as a means for making private profit.

Expose corruption wherever discovered.

Uphold these principles, ever conscious that public office is a public trust.

PART I

Personnel Administration and Ethics   1

1 Employee Drug Screening and Ethics 3

Introduction   3
Alcoholism in the Workplace   3
Employer Options for Effecting Change   6
   Progressive Discipline and Drug Testing   6
   Employee Assistance Program   6
   Alcohol Treatment Program   6
Progressive Discipline in Action   7
Drug Testing Doesn't Deter Drug Use   7
Reviewing EAP Contractors and Programs   7
   Identify the Problem   8
   Define the Problem   8
   Analyze the Problem   8
   Generate Alternative Solutions   8
   Select the "Best" Solution/Strategy   9
   Implement the Solution   9
   Evaluate the Solution   9
Monitoring and Control of EAPs   10
Assignments   12
References   12

2 "We Were Just Doing Her a Favor by Not Firing Her" 14

The Facts   14
Assignments   16

3 The Ethics of Censorship, Rule Making, and Discharge Procedures 17

The Case 17
The Real Issues 19
Assignments 25
Notes 26

4 The Ethical Issues Behind Comparable Worth 30

The Importance of Comparable Worth 30
A Sex-Neutral System in Practice 31
Assignments 37

5 The Right to Strike by Public Employees
An Ethical Dilemma 39

A Right to Strike? 39
Seven States 41
More Not Less 42
Assignments 43
Notes 43

6 Ethical Issues of Employee Fitness Programs 44

Fitness Program Examples 46
    Cardiovascular 47
    Muscular Strength 48
    Flexibility 48
Summary 49
Assignments 49
Notes 50

PART II

Ethics and Politics   51

7 Interference with Free Local Elections 53

Incorporation Is Proposed 54
Incorporation Versus Other Proposals 56

Proponents Are Heartened 56
The Deputy Sheriff's Plan 57
Opposition on Two Fronts 59
Legal Opinion on Union Activity 61
The Opponents Take a Poll 61
The Early Stages 62
The Role of an Expert Speaker: Dr. Smith 63
Surprise Media Campaign Stresses Taxes 63
The School Issue 65
Last-Minute Confusion over the Issue of Public
Employee Activism 67
Post-Mortems on the Election 68
Assignments 69
Notes 69

8 Political Smear Campaigns 70
The Original Dispute 70
The Arbitration Process Examined 74
Assignments 77
Notes 78

**9 Conflicts Between Political Appointees
and Careerists 81**
The Sources of Conflict 81
Assignments 83
Notes 83

PART III

Ethics and Public Economics   **85**

10 Ethical Issues in Downsizing
Or, Cutting Back 87
The Case of a Declining Workload 87
Some Additional Factors 88
Problem 88
Assignments 88

11 The Ethics of Tax Incentives and Waivers 90

Boston and the Property Tax   91
Taxation and the Prudential Center   91
Tax Concessions and Compromises   95
Property Tax Inducements and Questions   98
The Economics of the Tax Concession   99
Assignments   100
Notes   101

12 The Ethical Issues of Privatizing Public Jobs 106

Career Disruption and Dislocation   106
Morale and Productivity   107
Relocation and Reciprocity   108
Erosion of Civil Service and Merit Systems   110
Trust and Credibility   110
Assignments   111
References   111
Notes   112

13 Ethics and Inter-Local Contracting Arrangements 114

Reciprocity Provisions   114
Some Conclusions   122
Agreeing on Requirements   124
Response Time   126
Assignments   129
Notes   130

PART IV

Ethics of Health and the Workplace   131

14 Bioethics
The Right to Live and the Right to Die 133

Bioethics in American Life   133
Bioethical Committees in Hospitals   136

Assignments   137
Notes   137

15 Child Care and Ethical Issues   138

The Importance of Day Care   138
Day Care in the Public Sector   139
Assignments   149
Notes   150

16 Public Employees and the Exchanging of Gifts   152

A Survey on Gift Exchanging   153
Summary   159
Assignments   159
Notes   160

17 The Ethics of Smoking Versus Nonsmoking at Work   161

Smoking on the Job   161
Survey Methodology   162
Survey Findings   165
Summary and Next Steps   170
Appendix—Survey Responses   171
Assignments   175
Notes   175
References   176
    Books   176
    Articles and Related Publications   176

PART I

Personnel Administration and Ethics

The six cases in Part I deal with ethical issues involving lone individuals as well as groups: an alcoholic executive secretary and a labor union in which a large number of public workers take concerted action, for example. One case deals with sex discrimination and wage determination; another shows that less-than-honest decision making by supervisors can haunt management later. Major roles are played by a diminutive librarian who takes on an entire county government and by a class action capable of shutting down a city or county government. The suggested class assignments include constructing ordinances or statutes that reflect the ethical issues raised by the cases and preparing interviews with guests who are asked to explore specific ethical dilemmas and conflicts.

CHAPTER 1

Employee Drug Screening and Ethics

Introduction

This case is presented first because it integrates issues of human resources and personnel administration with the ethical problems it raises. It is a real-life case to which the actual solution is provided—normally the cases are left unresolved. This case, however, brings together a number of topics that students may not initially see as related policies and procedures, but that clearly are—job performance and an employee's leave records, for example. Students are asked to write a research paper, to interview guests, to debate ethical issues, to defend a choice of options, to explore the side issues the case raises as well, and also to see how problem resolution creates opportunities for improvement of an administrative system.

Programs like the Employee Assistance Program (EAP) discussed in this chapter have become popular with both employers and workers. In this case, an EAP deals with hiring practices, privatization, testing for drug use, progressive discipline, and the discharge of an alcoholic executive secretary. Many ethical issues are apparent. Students are encouraged to look for a fair and equitable application of a work rule to an employee who is a drunk.

Alcoholism in the Workplace

"Alcoholic!" The word hung in the air. Brighton looked again into the gray eyes of the Employee Assistance Program coordinator. The county Brighton worked for had used this EAP consulting firm for many years. Their contract was no longer competitively bid because the firm was so efficient and their services so satisfactory that the county commissioners no longer even looked at other bidders but routinely extended the contract every five years. Brighton had never used EAP services before, that is, until now . . .

Brighton's job was near the top of the county's Administrative Services Department. He was now only two steps below a commissioner. The excellent pay, the satisfactory perks, and the opportunity for service (and yes, power) were what he had worked to achieve for over fourteen years with several different county units. He had also completed an Executive MPA by going two evenings a week for more than three years at a nearby private university. All had gone well until his executive secretary quit.

Although Brighton depended heavily on his secretary, he had nevertheless encouraged her to try for her new job. Because of his county cabinet membership, he had known long in advance that the new position was opening. It was perfect for her and was several pay grades more than he could offer. He did not really want to lose her—she was an excellent worker—but Brighton had a well-known reputation for helping his people and looking out for their interests. In fact, people aggressively tried to work for him. Those who performed well quickly found themselves on a fast track upward. Brighton enjoyed having a gifted team of high achievers.

Britainy, Brighton's new executive secretary, had been hired through the county's internal bidding and posting program. Executives like Brighton were required to recruit internally for fourteen calendar days before they could select someone from outside the county. As he always tried to do, Brighton had meticulously checked *in person* with every reference. Britainy sounded almost too good to be true from the start, and Brighton had never even looked outside the county. The county personnel office had ranked the top twelve county employees who were bidding by typing scores, Lotus and WordPerfect skills, General Aptitude Test scores, and other factors such as veteran's preference. Britainy was among the top three, and after an interview with her and his reference checks, Brighton offered her the job and negotiated a starting date a few days before the incumbent secretary left so that Britainy could be at least partially acclimated to the new position and its duties.

His plans went awry from the beginning. Britainy was sick the several days prior to her official start, so no introduction to the job by the woman she replaced was possible. In fact, Brighton now reflected somewhat angrily, Britainy was sick a lot. In the first six months there was not a week she (or a friend) had not called in on a Monday morning to say she was sick. And after long weekends or holidays, you could make book on her being absent one or two extra days. When Britainy *was* there, however, she was superb—well-groomed, attractive, extremely pleasant, and able to crank out prodigious amounts of high-quality work. Brighton had begun to shift some of his work onto her shoulders—she prepared his weekly meeting agendas, did the agency's budget summaries, even space utilization studies. She loved it—she called it job enrichment; Brighton called it delegation. Indeed, he would have turned many other important tasks over to her and hired her a secretary of her own for routine work—if she was not sick so often.

Just days ago, Brighton finally called Personnel, and that office sent him to the EAP coordinator. Reviewing the official leave record on Britainy with her, Brighton realized Britainy's leave card looked like a checkerboard. As he thumbed through some of the other leave records, something he had never done before, it struck him forcibly that the county's sick leave conversion policy (conversion to cash at retirement, extra days of paid leave at Christmas) was obviously accomplishing its objectives with everyone but Britainy. (Brighton had assumed her accumulated eligible leave days when she transferred into his division.) Imagine his surprise when the EAP coordinator said to Brighton, "Britainy's sick leave is *predictable*," and proceeded to explain.

In minutes the coordinator showed Brighton the *pattern* of Britainy's sick leave use—and there was a consistent pattern. His real shock came as an answer to "Why?" The coordinator said that Britainy was an alcoholic and that her job performance demonstrated how drinking was damaging both her productivity and Brighton's as well. It took only a few minutes to verify these facts independently.

During the next hour with the EAP coordinator, Brighton learned a great deal. For the first time he realized why the county had such an EAP effort (which in this case was contracted out), why the commissioners felt so positive about the present EAP firm's skills (the county regularly verified the firm's ongoing performance and continued the noncompetitive award of the contract), and what he had done wrong in selecting Britainy. A question he would *always* ask from now on in checking references was whether the candidate was known to have an alcohol or drug problem. Brighton was himself a social drinker and had never before had an alcoholic working for him. The question of alcoholism had never arisen in his reference checking in previous years.

One of the books the coordinator gave Brighton to read was the current edition of the *Supervisor's Safety Handbook,* published by the National Safety Council in Washington, D.C. Here Brighton learned that one out of every ten American workers is alcoholic and another ten percent has a serious drug addiction problem—that is, one out of every five has a problem with controlled substances. Until now, he reflected, he had been lucky in his employees.

The county had covered much of this in the basic training courses for managers that it offered, but somehow Brighton had missed the module about alcoholic workers. Subsequently, the EAP coordinator and the training director revised their training efforts and began to track managers who missed any modules and to provide follow-up training—not surprisingly, quite a few other managers had also missed several modules. This single effort by itself greatly strengthened the county's in-house managerial training program.

Brighton's next response was anger toward the supervisor he had called to check Britainy's references before hiring her—and toward the county personnel office, which ranked the list of twelve in-house candidates he had initially relied on in his selection.

The supervisor admitted she had known of the drinking problem—but was delighted to get rid of Britainy in what was, for the supervisor herself, the most painless way. She had cajoled, threatened, and counseled Britainy for years, but any change in behavior was only temporary. This supervisor rationalized her behavior toward Brighton by saying, "You didn't ask me about a drinking problem." Personnel began to offer managerial training in reference checking both for those doing the checking and those being asked for a reference. Subsequently, the county would not give out information on present or former county employees to persons either calling or writing. The process of reference checking became highly centralized in the personnel office to reduce the possibilities of litigation. All inquiries were directed to one person with knowledge of the legal ramifications of reference checking. The county did provide inquirers with annual sick leave use figures on former workers, however, leaving them to draw their own conclusions. Brighton's blaming of Personnel was probably fruitless. Personnel offices rarely acknowledge their own shortcomings or imperfections. As noted, the county increasingly emphasized the legalities of reference checking in its managerial training, and, most useful to those like Brighton, who did the actual hiring, added a weighted column to the other columns on the list. This column ranked employees who were bidding in-house and noted any vexing issues of attendance, punctuality, and so forth. Nearly all managers who had to hire people openly expressed great satisfaction over this one change. Personnel analysts complained at first that the new computations were just more work, but in time they came to appreciate the new column because it made their jobs more analytical and less clerical. The commissioner over Administrative Services won a national county innovation award, and of course he took full credit for the idea and its implementation, using the award in his reelection campaign. (He would never bother to try to explain the innovation itself to voters, since he hardly understood what it was all about.) He was reelected that next year. Of course, none of this changed Britainy's being a drunk.

Britainy had an alcohol problem. The issue, however, is not her *drinking,* but its impact on her *job performance.* She used excessive sick leave: The county defined "average" as 2.2 days per year, and she was several deviations beyond the average.

Employer Options for Effecting Change

The EAP coordinator explained to Brighton that he had several possible courses of action to deal with his problem.

Progressive Discipline and Drug Testing

One option was progressive discipline, followed by discharge if needed. Brighton must give his executive secretary a specific warning that he would fire her if she abused sick leave even once more; track her job performance; monitor and document her behavior; grant her a hearing before taking final action; and discharge her if she used leave wrongfully. Brighton could also have Britainy undergo drug testing. The Drug-Free Federal Workplace Act and the Drug-Free Work Force Rules of the Departments of Defense and Transportation as well as specific state statutes and related county ordinances (plus the personnel office's own policies and procedures manual), all identify what is lawful drug testing. All spell out the need for accuracy in drug testing and interpretation of results; laboratory selection and quality control monitoring; implementing a comprehensive substance-abuse program; providing employee assistance (designing and implementing the county's program and monitoring its effectiveness); defending terminations for substance abuse; and testing of employees in "sensitive" jobs.

Employee Assistance Program

A second option was to put Britainy into an Employee Assistance Program. She would go on extended leave from her job, paid and then unpaid when her accumulated leave became exhausted. The county and its medical plan insurer would pay for alcohol treatment, which costs perhaps $10,000 to $15,000 or more, annualized, just for the treatment. Usually only highly valued workers and those with long tenure are deemed worth such an "investment."

Alcohol Treatment Program

A third course of action was to grant Britainy unpaid leave but hold a similar job for her for up to six months *if* she voluntarily entered an alcohol treatment program and succeeded. The costs would not be the county's responsibility.

Progressive Discipline in Action

After some thought, Brighton chose the first course of action. He told Britainy he liked her but needed full performance at her peak powers and couldn't wait any longer; he showed her the grim statistics, which she did not challenge. He then put her on immediate notice: One more time and I will fire you.

It would be pleasant to be able to say that the threat of losing her job had a salutary effect on Britainy and that she quit drinking. This is real life, however, and booze in her case is a disease, an addiction. Her drinking predated her employment. (That is, the county is not liable even in part because it may have driven her to drink.) During the weekend she was predictably drunk and came to work drunk on Monday rather than be absent. Brighton called the personnel office, which sent a person to verify Britainy's condition. Security was called; she was escorted off county premises in as tactful a way as possible—after being fired. Britainy went through a series of jobs with other employers, and her drinking became worse. Ultimately, she began attending Alcoholics Anonymous meetings. It has been years now since she took a drink, but she will always be a drunk. She is no longer an executive secretary, but has an honorable job that seems satisfying. She has no bad feelings about Brighton. Brighton remembers her prodigious talent and is a bit introspective. What if . . . ? The woman who replaced Britainy still works for him, but now as his administrative assistant. This very morning someone called to ask about her for a position. He does not want to lose her, but he recognizes that a wonderful opportunity may be opening for her and that she is certainly ready for a promotion.

Drug Testing Doesn't Deter Drug Use

The county found that shortly after starting its very successful drug-testing program (in full compliance with applicable laws), the pass rate was already *very high.* Testing is not a good deterrent to drug abuse, however. Measuring job performance is the only way to successfully deter drug usage. Personnel department members think that sometimes people are too creative at beating the tests.

Reviewing EAP Contractors and Programs

As noted, every five years the county commissioners review the measurable EAP objectives and look at the contractor's compliance and track record. They remain fully satisfied and continue to contract for the service. The EAP contractor makes a reasonable profit and works hard to keep this contract. Many employees with serious problems have been helped. The program is very popular with workers and their families and strongly supported by the unions.

It sometimes takes a lot of time before EAPs get organized. This is especially true once an agenda is selected and the EAP team begins to research a topic. Following is a suggested set of steps for EAP personnel to follow in pursuit of a solution to a given problem. These seven steps (not necessarily always in this order, but typically so) are powerful problem-solving tools.

Identify the Problem

It is best if the problem can be stated succinctly in five or six words. This permits everyone to communicate more clearly and keeps the focus on the real issue at hand. John Dewey, the great educator, once wrote, "A problem well stated is half solved." How true. A long, drawn out statement of a problem, even a complex one, suggests that the EAP team members are still not entirely sure what they are trying to accomplish. Two key substeps are to identify what should be and identify what is. That is, when and if the problem is solved, what would be the ideal result? Then document what is—where you are at this moment. The difference or "gap" is what you are trying to resolve. Some research suggests that this vital step is almost universally ignored or shortchanged. EAP staffs grow impatient and want to move on—"Let's explore some solutions." That means trying to solve a problem before really knowing what the problem is.

Define the Problem

Defining the problem is best done in two substeps: (1) define constraints, and (2) specify measurable objectives. Research shows that many EAP teams go all the way through solving a problem and are then told, "But there is no extra money," or "We can't get that material until the next fiscal year." How much better to have all constraints up front. The success of a solution depends on knowing in advance what the constraints are. Specifying measurable objectives means that the EAP staff writes multiple outcome or performance specifications for the problem. If you are going to reduce absenteeism (the problem), by how much? By when? Who will monitor the program? How will you actually measure the success of your solution? If EAP team members say the problem is to provide debt counseling, they will be able to determine success only if the goal/outcome is measurable. Many excellent books are available on writing measurable objectives.

Analyze the Problem

In analyzing the problem, the EAP team tears the problem into pieces. Many of the pieces of the problem the team will know all about, and thus it can work on the pieces it knows little or nothing about. There is no magic to this process of analysis. It is a systematic study of a problem already identified and defined. Still, it is interesting to observe how often an EAP team will jump to the solution stage of the process before really analyzing the problem. The analysis itself leads to solutions as team members become better acquainted with the problem.

Generate Alternative Solutions

Too often EAP teams depend only on brainstorming to find solutions to the problem(s) they have identified, defined, and analyzed. There are many other sources of solutions, however: expert opinion, consultants, review of the literature, site visitations, and pilot testing, among others. But if the EAP team is going to use brainstorming, let me suggest five substeps. Too many EAP teams violate both the spirit and the letter of every one of these proven substeps. Applying them results in rich dividends.

- **Use a heterogeneous team.** Mix the brainstorming team members (newcomers, old-timers; blue-collar, pink-collar; young, old) to avoid "groupthink" and stereotypical ideas.
- **Strive for quantity, not quality.** Anything goes, any idea should be raised. Determination of the merits of each idea is saved for later. Set goals of thirty or fifty ideas and see how quickly the team can exceed those numbers. Any idea should be listed.
- **Defer Judgment.** Don't let team members evaluate or criticize proposed solutions. The team leader or facilitator must prevent anyone from evaluating ideas because creative juices dry up quickly when the team discusses the merits of ideas. Don't allow this; keep the process moving along so the number of ideas continues to increase.
- **Incubate.** Whenever possible, let the team think about the problem over a weekend, overnight, over a lunch period, as long as possible. Evidence suggests the best ideas emerge after a period of incubation. The human brain has a remarkable facility to solve complex problems after a period of quiet contemplation or meditation.
- **Refine.** After generating many ideas from a variety of sources, the team (or a few designated members) should refine the ideas into solution strategies; that is, reduce the many ideas to a few broader strategies. Almost always thirty to seventy ideas reduce themselves (by bunching or chaining related ideas together) to around five to nine mutually exclusive alternative strategies that can stand alone or solve the problem by themselves. This substep typically generates the best and brightest of ideas. The handful of strategies is now ready for vigorous comparison.

Select the "Best" Solution/Strategy

Here the team uses cost-benefit analysis to compare each mutually exclusive strategy. Some traditional criteria are costs, ease of implementation, and political feasibility, but the best way to carry out this step is to compare each strategy against the multiple measurable objectives written when defining the problem. Those were the original objectives; why not use them now to determine the best solution/strategy?

Implement the Solution

Here a careful plan is developed to close the gap between what should be and what is. This action plan determines who is responsible for each task and when each task must be accomplished. It is a detailed plan for the next steps. The EAP team must be confident of top management support, union support, and so forth, if the plan is to succeed. Too often, EAP teams skimp on such details. "We never seem to have time to do it right, but we always have time to do it over," is a familiar complaint.

Evaluate the Solution

Murphy's Law being true, any plan will need revision as it develops, and so EAP planners must provide for step-by-step evaluation of the action plan. Yet, too often little or no provision is made in advance for serious program evaluation. Again, if the measurable objectives were carefully written, it is easy to evaluate success. Otherwise you are just "muddling through."

EAP plans that follow the seven steps discussed earlier will do a better job of solving problems than EAP plans that don't. Research demonstrates that a systematic way of approaching an EAP agenda pays off in more and better ideas and more workable solutions. Teams should be encouraged to use these action steps to develop their next agenda. Be patient. Some of these seven steps may take a little practice, but they are easy, practical, and powerful when properly followed.

Monitoring and Control of EAPs

Monitoring and control are among the most neglected aspects of EAP administration. Monitoring is the accumulation of data on the operations of a given workplace. Control is the use of the accumulated data to correct or change the system.

Examples of control systems are daily or weekly logs, absenteeism records, periodic records, health-cost containment reports, and tables of output measures. Nearly every management system relies on several controls for feedback and correction, especially small organizations in which managers are intimately involved in day-to-day details.

Monitoring and control systems have five primary objectives:

- Resource utilization
- Program accomplishment
- Security
- Quality
- Human development

Although most EAP managers recognize an objective for a control system such as "Program accomplishment," few normally cite the purpose of "Human development." It is well to regularly reflect on all five of these objectives in designing and evaluating programs.

The characteristics of effective monitoring and control systems may be summarized as follows:

- They are designed to deal with and reflect the specific activity.
- They report deviations promptly.
- They are forward looking.
- They point up exceptions at critical points.
- They are objective.
- They are flexible.
- They reflect the organizational pattern.
- They are economical.
- They are understandable.
- They lead to corrective action.

Whole books could be written on some of these characteristics. For instance, "economical": Many people can cite examples of monitoring and control systems that cost more than they could possibly benefit in frustration, wasted effort to accumulate raw data no one used, reports so late in the cycle they were useless, and so on. Business and government leaders would be well advised to periodically check their own various monitoring and control systems against the characteristics of effective systems given above and revise controls as necessary.

To help ensure effective control systems, EAP managers should adopt certain behaviors. Among them are to

- Maintain an adult view of controls
- Encourage subordinates to participate in setting standards
- Introduce flexibility in the control system
- Be sensitive to personal needs and social pressures in administering controls

Sometimes a manager adopts a parental role in control systems—"I told you so," or "Gotcha," or "How many times have I warned you." Or a child role—tantrums, blaming others, outbursts of yelling. How much better the adult role—"What happened?" "Why?" "How can I help?" "What should be done now?" "What can we learn from this?" The same principle applies to the other behaviors EAP managers should adopt.

Finally, if managers do not act as they should, what behaviors and feelings may be expected from employees, public or private? We may expect the following:

- Failure to accept objectives as legitimate
- Feeling that standards of performance are too high
- Believing that measurements are inappropriate
- Fearing negative feedback
- Perceiving the source of control as illegitimate
- Playing games with the controls
- Engaging in sabotage or negative behaviors

Managers may hesitate to admit that workers would—or could—act in such irresponsible ways, yet any experienced manager has seen some of these negative and destructive employee behaviors and feelings. Experienced consultants have heard enough horror stories to fill books. Managerial misbehavior may well result in employee misbehavior.

Two short examples here may suffice. In a state agency, management felt workers were wasting time. Rather than institute a time management program or involve workers in the problem-solving process itself, management instituted overnight a time log requiring workers to report activities by a series of codes, every fifteen minutes (for example, "#OD3, restroom," "#OD4, break time"). Workers met in halls, elevators, the coffee shop, and at their homes, to plan ways of sabotaging the new system. It became such a game that work almost came to a standstill while workers found creative ways to manipulate the new control system. Management quickly capitulated, by necessity.

A hospital installed a log system to control access to supplies in order to contain costs. No employee input was sought and no pilot test was carried out before several thousand pads of checklists were printed. Within a day it was obvious that some key functions had been overlooked. By the end of the week the new form was perceived as hopelessly incomplete. Eventually all the forms were thrown out—using them as scratch paper had been a continuing reminder of management's folly.

In summary, every organization must rely on monitoring and control systems. Such control systems should fulfill a number of purposes. Effective control systems share common characteristics. Managers should act in certain ways, or we may reasonably expect employees to respond in predictable ways. Managers should routinely review these factors as they accumulate data on EAP operations and use this data to correct or change their EAP systems.

Assignments

1. As a class, or as teams, discuss the three options Brighton had. Which would you have selected? Why? Debate the issue. Discuss ethical issues in general.

2. As a class (or as teams) research federal laws (say, the Drug-Free Workplace Act) or one of the many state drug-screening employment laws. Report on ethical issues, procedures, problems, pending cases, and so forth.

3. Where possible to arrange through an employer, personally take a drug-screening test and report on "invasion of privacy" or other feelings you had during the process.

4. As teams, secure a company's or agency's Comprehensive Substance-Abuse Program, analyze it from the ethical behavior perspective, and report in a written research paper your team's critiques and evaluation. (Suggested length: fifteen to twenty pages.)

5. As teams, invite the coordinators of one or two Employee Assistance Programs (EAPs) from public or private organizations to class and hold a structured interview in front of the class. (Notify guests of questions in advance; invite them to bring materials—guides, handbooks—for distribution to class members.)

6. See if one or two people who have been helped as individuals through an EAP will share their experiences with the class. However, be careful to avoid highly personal questions or surprises. Be sure the guests know in advance what will be asked and are willing to respond.

7. Invite an Alcoholics Anonymous spokesperson to explain the program to the class. (Some of AA's skills and techniques are among the most effective worldwide.)

References

Behrens, Ruth A. *A Decision Maker's Guide to Reducing Smoking at the Worksite.* Washington, DC: The Washington Business Group on Health, 1985.

Carnahan, William A. *Legal Issues Affecting Employee Assistance Programs.* Arlington, VA: The Association of Labor–Management Administrators and Consultants on Alcoholism, Inc., 1984.

Coelho, Richard J. *Quitting Smoking: A Psychological Experiment Using Community Research.* New York: Peter Lang, 1985.

Copus, David A. *Matters of Substance: Alcohol and Drugs in the Workplace.* 2nd ed. Washington, DC: National Employment Law Institute, 1989.

Hawks, Richard L., and Chiang, C. Nora, eds. *Urine Testing for Drugs of Abuse.* Rockville, MD: National Institute on Drug Abuse, Monograph 73, 1986.

Myers, Donald W. *Employee Assistance Programs: Drug, Alcohol, and Other Problems.* Chicago: Commerce Clearing House, Inc., 1986.

Rutkowski, Arthur D. "Feature: Comprehensive Substance Abuse Program, Policies, and Employment Assistance Program for Union and Non-Union Employees. *Employment Law Update.* Evansville, IN: Rutkowski and Associates, 1986.

Timmins, William M., and Timmins, Clark B. *Smoking and the Workplace: Questions and Answers for Human Resources Professionals.* Westport, CN: Greenwood Press, 1989.

Walsh, J. Michael, and Gust, Steven W., eds. *Interdisciplinary Approaches to the Problem of Drug Abuse in the Workplace.* Washington, DC: Public Health Service, DHHS Publication No. [ADM] 86–1477, 1986.

CHAPTER 2

"We Were Just Doing Her a Favor by Not Firing Her"

The Director of Nursing was truly shocked. "Grievance!" he sputtered. He had tried to do one of his school nurses a favor by laying her off instead of firing her. And now she had filed a formal grievance, and he was advised he would be a witness at the arbitration hearing. Perhaps he and the school district should simply have fired her outright and not tried to be nice to her. Ethically, it did not trouble the director one iota that he had chosen the wrong means to achieve a proper end, but now his choice had apparently backfired on him.

The Facts

Mrs. S. has been employed more than twenty years by the Granite School District (hereafter, the District) as a nurse, nurse coordinator, and other similar positions, continuously since 1962. Approximately two years ago she became a Title I Nurse and last year a Chapter I Nurse, changes in nomenclature due to the sources of federal grant money. On February 11, 1983, the district (by letter from Director of Personnel, Dr. Blair H. Brewster) notified Mrs. S. that her "continued employment in Granite District is in question at this time" and that her employment would probably be discontinued because of an "anticipated cut in Chapter I funding." On March 23, 1983, Mrs. S. was advised by Brewster, "This letter serves as official notice of non-renewal of your contract for the next school year" because of "the uncertainty of funding of the program in which you are employed." This notification was in basic accord (the district alleged) with Article 21, Paragraph 21.6, Non-Renewal of Contract (subsection 21.6.1, Preliminary Notice, and 21.6.2, Non-Renewal Notice) of the 1982–1983 *Professional Agreement* between the district and Granite Education Association, Inc. (hereafter, GEA). GEA is a teacher's union.

Mrs. S. sought an informal hearing as provided for in Paragraph 21.7 of the *Professional Agreement* and then a formal hearing as provided for in Paragraph 21.9, Formal Hearing for Regular Contract Teachers. That formal hearing was held May 5, 1983, with William M. Timmins as the arbitrator.

Some ten years prior to her termination, Mrs. S. had returned to school and received a master's degree in Educational Psychology. (The award of this degree presumably is evidence that she completed all university prescribed courses and practicum requirements for such a degree.) Subsequently, she applied to the Utah State Board of Education for a Basic Professional Certificate as a counselor. Her certificate as a counselor was later renewed in July of 1981 and was valid through 1986.

Article 21, Suspension, Termination, and Non-Renewal of Contract, contains a key section, Paragraph 21.11, Reduction in Staff, that reads as follows:

> If for any reason it should become necessary for the district to decrease the total number of its employees at the close of the school year, the superintendent may release as many teachers or other professional personnel as he deems necessary. Comparable vacancies in the areas in which the affected teachers are qualified shall not be filled until these teachers have been placed. Teachers to be released because of such decrease in staff shall be notified in writing of such release by April 1.

Mrs. S. contends that her counselor's certificate from the state board means that she is qualified under Paragraph 21.11 and that she should be placed as a counselor before anyone else is appointed to fill existing comparable vacancies that are posted (see Article 17, Posting of Vacancies, Transfers and Promotions, of the *Professional Agreement*). Mrs. S. is convinced the positions of nurse and counselor are comparable (as per Paragraph 21.11) because both apply to her as defined in the *Professional Agreement* under Article 1, Definitions, Paragraph 1.1, Teacher, and Paragraph 1.3, Regular Contract Teacher. Mrs. S. had long ago completed her required provisional service and was a regular contract teacher as defined in the *Professional Agreement.* To her it is irrelevant that for the last two years her salary has been budgeted by the district under Chapter I funding. Mrs. S. believes the district should either transfer her to a nurse position elsewhere in the district or, if that is not possible, follow the *Professional Agreement* in Paragraph 21.11 and place her as a counselor or in another comparable position for which she qualifies. Mrs. S. argues that "nurse" and "counselor" are comparable vacancies as defined under Paragraph 21.11 because she *is* qualified as a counselor by her possession of a currently valid certificate from the Utah State Board of Education. She argues that Paragraph 21.11 does not say she must be best qualified, only qualified. GEA introduced a number of Notice of Vacancies issued by the district. Based on the stated qualifications and requirements on three or four of these official notices, Mrs. S. would be qualified as a counselor because she had a valid secondary counseling certificate. GEA argued that Paragraph 21.11 takes precedence over other hiring for, in this case, counselor.

The relief Mrs. S. seeks is simple: continued employment under the protection of Paragraph 21.11 of the *Professional Agreement.* GEA urges the district not to hire anyone to fill counselor vacancies until Mrs. S. is so placed.

The district responds that Mrs. S. knew two years ago that she was being placed in a position budgeted for with categorical or program money, so-called soft money. No promises were ever made to her that her job would be budgeted for in any future period with hard money. The district cites the *Professional Agreement,* Paragraph 21.9.1, that reads, ". . . regular contract teachers, and specially funded program teachers, . . . who are being released for reasons other than curtailment or discontinuance of funds" may request a formal hearing to review the proposed non-renewal notice. The district sees Mrs. S. as being terminated because of cuts in Chapter 1 funding. As to her allegation under Paragraph 21.11 that the positions of nurse and counselor are comparable, the district rejects that argument in its entirety. Three elementary school principals and the district's Staff Associate, Chapter I all testified that the two positions of nurse and counselor were not the same and that Mrs. S.

was not qualified as a counselor anyway. All four persons who so testified had themselves been counselors earlier in their careers, now supervised counselors, had supervised Mrs. S. directly or indirectly, and judged her not only not well qualified or best qualified but not qualified at all. On vigorous cross-examination by GEA and pointed questioning by the arbitrator, all four persons agreed that mere possession of a valid State Board Certificate as a counselor would mean a person was "qualified"—but the four *still would not hire Mrs. S. as a counselor, notwithstanding.* Testimony then was produced from these four witnesses that at least one of the three principals who testified and Mrs. S.'s direct supervisor felt her job performance as a nurse had become unsatisfactory in the last year or two and that there had recently been open talk of terminating her. Such action to terminate for cause had been dropped by the supervisor because the district intended not to renew Mrs. S.'s contract because of funding uncertainties, and no termination for performance would therefore be necessary. As Dr. Riches, deputy superintendent, expressed it, "The district was just trying to be nice to her."

GEA retorted that the district should have built its case by progressive discipline, due process, and discharge for cause and faced the issue squarely. GEA insisted Mrs. S. was not on trial, she had not been terminated for cause, and objected to testimony on her competence and performance as irrelevant and immaterial to the case at hand. No documents exist in Mrs. S.'s official files that refer to poor job performance.

The district does not believe Paragraph 21.11 applies at all in Mrs. S.'s instance because the two positions of nurse and counselor are simply not comparable. Funding restrictions and cuts have simply eliminated Mrs. S.'s position with the district. The district acknowledged that no discussion with Mrs. S. about her job performance and shortcomings ever took place.

Assignments

1. Discuss the ends versus means test for ethical behavior. For example, does a proper end ever justify improper means? Apply the question to this case. What conclusions do you reach?

2. This actual arbitration case lends itself to a simple simulation or game. Choose a role (the arbitrator, the school staff, the union representative) and act out the arbitration hearing. Afterward, discuss how you felt about the *ethics* of your role as the hearing proceeded. Did you sense conflict? Were you troubled by any of the assumed behaviors? What were your thoughts as the arbitrator concluded the hearing and rendered a decision? What are the ethical implications of the arbitrator's decision?

3. When a manager must fire an employee for cause, what are some recommended ethical behaviors? As a class (or as teams), draft a short policy statement to guide others in the future when they must confront a difficult course of action like this one. What are proper behaviors? Improper? What should be the ultimate ethical guide for managers?

CHAPTER 3

The Ethics of Censorship, Rule Making, and Discharge Procedures

What a dirty word censorship is, the county commissioner thought. He was not trying to censor anything or anybody. What upset him most was the implication in much of the press that he was a neo-Nazi embarked on a book-burning crusade. What he really wanted to do was get rid of the librarian who had caused all these problems. Where was her good sense? Why would she not cooperate in a reasonable request?

The commissioner was relatively new to elective office. Much of his career had been spent in the private sector, where employment at will was the law: He believed that a supervisor was free to hire and free to fire for any reasonable cause or for no cause at all. Likewise, workers were free to hire on, or quit, without restriction. Yes, the commissioner meditated, I know the courts and legislatures have eroded the traditional doctrine—you couldn't fire someone just because of sex, or race, or age, etc.[1] And, yes, many private firms have taken steps to protect the traditional employment at will doctrine from a series of court decisions on implied contracts.[2] But this case of the librarian was so complex—he had been elected to do a job and a board of citizens stood in his way. How had it all gotten so out of control? Government employment practices were certainly very different from the private sector.

The Case

A librarian[3] in a small county library system found herself in the middle of a book censorship fight with a coterie of elected officials, right-wing groups, religious zealots, a library board stacked against her, and law enforcement officials. This same librarian also found herself locked in combat over her career status in a county merit system. When discharged, she fought in U.S. District Court over her due process rights and again before a county merit council for a ruling on the merits of her discharge. She was on the front pages of all the daily newspapers in the state and on all the local television evening news broadcasts. She was featured in a popular Utah magazine and also in several national publications. This modest, middle-aged librarian found herself the center of controversy for several years. Her eventual reinstatement lead to an emasculation of Utah's county merit system statutes and a radical change in personnel procedures for Utah county governments. Ultimately, she settled to end litigation out of court for a substantial sum. The librarian is Jeanne Layton of Davis County, Utah. Her case teaches some interesting lessons to librarians and public administrators everywhere.

A popular local review of the early events in the Jeanne Layton case appeared in *Utah Holiday* for October 1979, "The Children's Hour" by Lynn Telford and Louise Kingsbury. In this article, which appeared before either of the merit council rulings or the U.S. District Court decisions cited in the present work, the authors wrote that Layton's case was "not just a clash between a politician and a librarian; this was a struggle for children's minds. How should they be taught to be responsible adults?" The censorship issue, however, became peripheral to much broader public policy issues, such as who governs? Who prevails? Who makes the rules?

The censorship issue is nevertheless essential to an understanding of what followed. In the fall of 1977, the parents of a teenage boy in Davis County read his library copy of Don Delillo's *Americana* (New York: Houghton Mifflin, 1971) and were shocked at the sexual detail in part of the book, which was required reading at the high school. The parents spoke to a Davis County library staff member, who told them to write their complaint to the library. Instead, the parents gave the book to a newly elected city council member who read the last chapter and agreed with the parents that the book shouldn't be in the library. The city council member turned the book over to the city attorney. The attorney also found the passages "obscene," and in a formal letter to the library requested that the book be taken off library shelves. Standard library policy required the Davis County librarian, Jeanne Layton, to appoint a committee of professional librarians to read and review *Americana*. A six-member committee reviewed the book and found it within library board criteria for adult fiction.

In March 1978 Layton informed the city attorney that the review committee recommended the book be retained by the library system. The city attorney advised the city councilmember of the review body's decision, and he dropped the matter after notifying the parents of the decision. In February 1979 a county commissioner, Morris Swapp, again raised the issue of the presence of *Americana* in the county's libraries. Swapp had been an elementary school principal for some twenty-five years before retiring in 1978. He had been a part-time city mayor for twelve years prior to his election to the three-member county commission. As a new county commissioner, he was made a member of the county library board in January 1979 and brought *Americana* up at his second board meeting in February. None of the participants to date (parents, city council members, or the city attorney) admit to telling Commissioner Swapp about what had already transpired, and Swapp has not indicated how he knew of the book. But as a library board member, Swapp had the right to raise the issue. Layton discussed the review of the book that had already been made, but agreed to review *Americana* again. This time Layton herself and five other librarians (none of whom were on the first review committee) read the book and found it "worthy of library support." The written report of the committee complied with all Davis County book selection policies. Commissioner Swapp was so notified in writing. According to *Utah Holiday,* Swapp was enraged.

In May, two Davis County library board seats were vacated when the terms of the incumbents expired, and the county commission appointed two new members—a close friend of Swapp's and the area representative of Citizen's for True Freedom (CFTF), a watchdog morality group strongly identified with conservative causes. CFTF reprinted portions of *Americana* and distributed them among its membership, denouncing book selection policies carried out by professionals (that is, librarians) rather than by the public. On August 13, 1979, Swapp and another county commissioner demanded Layton resign as librarian. She was handed a letter dated July 23, signed by Swapp and the two new library board members. The library board letter cited seven complaints, including one directly related to the *Americana* incident. The two county commissioners used the July 23 library board letter as justification for demanding Layton's resignation. She refused to resign.

It may be useful at this point to introduce a chronology of the events that followed:

August 9, 1979: Davis County Commission passes ordinance excluding Jeanne Layton from coverage under Utah's County Merit System Act.

August 13, 1979: Swapp delivers letter to Layton asking for her resignation.

August 21, 1979: Davis County library board formally ratifies letter.

September 18, 1979: Library board formally votes to dismiss Layton.

September 20, 1979: Layton appeals her dismissal to the Davis County Merit Council.

October 19, 1979: Merit council rules Layton was a merit employee and was therefore entitled to the protections of the Davis County Merit System Ordinance regarding her termination.

October 24, 1979: Layton files civil rights action against library board in U.S. District Court.

December 3, 1979: U.S. District Court Judge Bruce Jenkins rules that the merit council must determine whether Layton was discharged for cause and whether the library board complied with the merit system ordinance in her termination.

January 19, 1980: Davis County Merit Council rules Layton's dismissal was not "with cause" and orders her reinstatement with back pay.

May 1981: A lawsuit in the U.S. District Court against Swapp, Arbuckle, and Shumway (the other two library board members) for damages and legal fees was filed and ultimately settled out of court in 1983.

The Real Issues

The present concern is neither the literary merits of *Americana* nor the ethical issues surrounding censorship and control of pornography. The balance of this chapter focuses instead on due process, civil service (or merit system) protection of professional staff, and the findings of the district court and the Davis County Merit System Council. Surely all librarians ought to be able to place as much confidence in well-drawn personnel procedures as in traditional freedom of speech protections so frequently cited. If Jeanne Layton's discharge and subsequent reinstatement teach any lesson, it is that Layton was protected more by the merit system than by the First Amendment protections—administrators faced with judgment calls must look to the ethics of the laws they administer.[4]

On October 19, 1979, the Davis County Merit Council issued its ruling on Jeanne Layton's appeal from her September 18 dismissal. The three-member council was appointed under state law by the Davis County Commission. (Each of the more populous counties in Utah has a similar merit council.) The council's terms of office were staggered, it was a bipartisan lay body, and members could be removed by the county commission only for cause following a hearing. Members served six-year terms without compensation. The October 19 decision was as follows:

On Thursday, October 18, 1979, the Davis County Merit Council, with all members present, met to consider the appeal of JEANNE LAYTON from her dismissal as Davis County Librarian effective September 29, 1979.

A hearing was held on Thursday, October 11, 1979, at which time JEANNE LAYTON and the Davis County Library Board presented evidence on the issue of her termination.

The issue to be determined is: Whether or not MISS LAYTON was covered under Davis County Merit System at the time of her dismissal.

Jurisdiction

The initial question to be decided is whether or not the Merit Council has jurisdiction to decide the issue on appeal in light of the amendment to the Davis County Merit System Ordinance passed August 9, 1979, by the Davis County Commission, specifically specifying [*sic*] that the "Librarian of the County" is a major department head and, thus, exempt from the provisions of the Merit System.

Utah Code Annotated S17-33-16 (as amended) provides:

"(1) The following positions shall be exempt from the merit provision of this act:
   (e) The head of each major department charged directly by the governing body with the responsibility of assisting in the formulation and carrying out of matter of policy. *The council shall determine what is a major department and shall prepare regulations so as to limit the number of exemptions"* (emphasis added).

The amendment to the ordinance specifies which major departments are exempt from the Merit System rather than the Merit Council. Where a county ordinance is in direct conflict with state statute, the state statute must of necessity take precedence over the county ordinance. Therefore, the Merit Council holds that it has jurisdiction to decide the issue on appeal.

Issue on Appeal

Based upon the foregoing statute, the three elements necessary to exempt the position of County Librarian from the Merit System are:

(1) That the position is a major department head, and
(2) That the person so designated is charged directly by the governing body, and
(3) Assists in the formulation and carrying out of matters of policy.

The Council finds that, at the time MISS LAYTON was terminated as County Librarian, she was the head of a major department and assisted in the formulation and carrying out of matters of policy, thus complying with elements (1) and (3) for exemption. However, the evidence does not support a finding of compliance with element (2).

The "governing body" as defined in the state statute providing for a County Merit System is: ". . . *The Board of County Commissioners* of each of the several counties. . . . " Utah Code Ann. S77-33-2(1) (1953). (Emphasis added.)

MISS LAYTON was charged directly in policy matters by the Davis County Library Board, and, in fact, by statute, was its executive officer. Utah Code Ann. S37-3-8 (1953). As a consequence, at the time of her termination, she did not meet the second element for exemption from the Merit System in that she was not charged directly as to policy matters by the Davis County Commission.

> We therefore hold that she was under the Merit System at the time of her termination and, thus, is entitled to the protections of Article XIII of the Davis County Merit System Ordinance in connection with her separation.

The impact of this decision on the elected officials in Davis County was electric! By the summer of 1980, the Davis County commission had obviously conferred with other county commissions (through the Utah Association of Counties) and supported the drafting of a bill that would emasculate the existing merit systems in Utah's county governments. This bill was eventually modified following various Utah legislative hearings and other meetings. Even after these modifications, the majority of county librarians apparently opposed the bill (as did the Utah Association of Civil Service Commissioners and Merit Councils and sundry other groups). The bill successfully passed the 1981 Utah legislature, despite all efforts to kill it. The 1981 legislature was basically a younger body, more conservative and maverick than many observers had seen before. Strong editorial opposition to the bill arose in much of the press. For example, Utah's most prominent and powerful newspaper, the *Deseret News,* owned by the Mormon church, spoke against the new county merit bill in an editorial entitled "Don't Sap County Merit Plans." Nevertheless, the bill became law, effective July 1, 1981. County librarians are exempted from merit coverage under the new law. Although elected county officials will not have carte blanche in running their personnel systems (because of extensive modifications made in the original bill), skeptical observers are watching developments carefully.

But back to Jeanne Layton and the October 9, 1979, merit council decision. On October 24, 1979, Layton filed a civil rights action in U.S. District Court against the Davis County Library Board. On December 3, 1979, the court issued this statement:

> This is a Civil Rights action for damages and injunctive relief brought under 42 U.S.C. SS 1331 and 1343, and alleging violations of the First, Fifth and Fourteenth Amendments of the United States Constitution. Plaintiff was the long-time Davis County Librarian and served as such until her purported discharge by the defendants, the Davis County Library Board and its members, September 28, 1979.
>
> The major issue now before the Court is whether plaintiff was deprived of a property interest by defendants without procedural due process.
>
> Some preliminary matters first need to be resolved. Defendants originally raised an issue as to service of process; they now concede and consent to the personal jurisdiction of this Court. Defendants contested the subject matter jurisdiction of the Court on the ground that the Library Board is not a "person" within the meaning of 42 U.S.C. SS 1983. *Monell v. New York City Department of Social Services,* 436 U.S. 658 (1978) teaches otherwise and the Court finds that the Library Board is a "person" for purposes of 42 U.S.C. SS 1983. Defenses raised by the individual defendants concerning their alleged immunity from suit are unavailable to them in an injunctive matter of this kind. At this stage of the proceeding we are not concerned with the First Amendment issue of the availability of books of one kind or another.
>
> The property interest claimed by plaintiff is an interest in continued employment. The scope of this interest is determined by state law; namely the law governing whether she is or is not a merit employee, or is otherwise a tenured employee. See, *Utah Code Annotated SS 17-33-1 et seq.* and the Davis County Merit System Ordinance,

copies of which have been filed with the Court. A merit system employee has a statutorily protected interest in continued employment; may not be discharged from employment except for "cause," and is granted certain procedural rights both before and after discharge. An employee "exempt" from merit status is less favored.

Both before and after plaintiff's purported discharge, defendants considered her to be exempt from merit status, not entitled to the procedural protection of a merit employee, and subject to discharge at the discretion of the Library Board. However, plaintiff contended otherwise and filed a timely appeal of the purported discharge to the Davis County Merit Council. The appeal asserted that plaintiff was covered by the merit system, that she was denied pre-termination procedural protections guaranteed to merit employees under Article XIII of the Davis County Merit System Ordinance, that she was not discharged for "cause" within the meaning of that ordinance, and that she was entitled to reinstatement and back pay. Alternatively, plaintiff argued before the Merit Council that if the position of Librarian was not covered by the merit system, she had been promoted to that position from a covered position and was entitled to return to her former position pursuant to Article XII, Section A (6) of the ordinance.

Plaintiff's contentions were considered, in part, by the Davis County merit Council on October 11, 1979. Transcripts of that hearing have been filed with this Court. It appears that the *only issue* fully considered by the Merit Council at that hearing was whether it had jurisdiction to hear the appeal, i.e., whether plaintiff was or was not a merit employee. Despite the fact that the Davis County Commission, for reasons known only to its membership, passed an ordinance on August 9, 1979, purporting to "exempt" the position of County Librarian from merit status, the Merit Council correctly determined that under *Utah Code Annotated* SS 17-33-16 (1) (e), only the Council could confer exempt status and that the County Commission could not do so. Indeed, under that same statute, even the Merit Council could exempt only major departments heads "charged directly by the governing body" with assisting in policy formulation and implementation.

By written decision dated October 19, 1979, a copy of which was filed with the Court, the Merit Council determined that Plaintiff *was* a merit system employee entitled to the pre-termination protections of Article XIII of the Davis County Merit System Ordinance. However, at least on the face of its written decision, the Council did not determine whether those pre-termination protections had been provided to plaintiff by the Library Board, and did not determine whether adequate "cause" existed for plaintiff's dismissal by the Library Board.

Plaintiff places great emphasis on defendants' alleged failure to follow her interpretation of the pre-discharge procedures. Defendants urge substantial compliance with the requirements in Article XIII for, "[n]otification in writing by the department head" (Section C.1.a.(1)). The factual record reveals that a letter was sent to plaintiff on July 23, 1979, by or on behalf of a majority of the Library Board, listing seven "objections"; that plaintiff responded to that letter with a letter of her own; and that at the Library Board meeting of September 18, 1979, which resulted in plaintiff's discharge, both plaintiff and her attorney were allowed to offer statements, although no evidence was taken and the chairman of the Board stated that the meeting was not a "hearing."

Plaintiff in substance argues that she is entitled to formal procedures, including an evidentiary hearing, prior to discharge. Article XIII does not specify whether an evidentiary hearing must be held prior to discharge, and, standing alone, it does not adequately protect plaintiff's constitutional rights.

But, Article XIII cannot be considered "standing alone" because *it is but step one in a two-step process.* When considered in conjunction with step two, the post-termination appeal under Article IX, step one may well be sufficient protection of a recognized interest in continued employment at that initial state.

Step one seems to contemplate a relatively informal procedure which may well vary from department to department. It does have the virtue of requiring the employer—the Library Board—to put its dissatisfactions in writing. It does provide that an employee be given a chance to respond—and that the employee's grievances be "heard" by the employer, and, at that stage, may well require nothing more.

Step two, the appellate process, provides the check and the balance against precipitous, biased, unreasoned, ill-motivated, vindictive or myopic action on the part of the employer. It provides for review by a neutral body, the Merit Council, after a full-blown evidentiary hearing, to make sure that the reasons given by the employer for termination are good, legal reasons—that there is "just cause" for termination within the meaning of the ordinance—and to make sure that step one has been fully complied with. Due process is a variable concept. It depends generally on the nature of the competing interests involved. As long as meaningful relief through formal procedures is available in a *timely fashion* after government action, relatively informal procedural protections are often sufficient prior to government action. *See Mathews v. Eldredge,* 424 U.S. 319 (1976).

Implicit in the concept of "due process" are two ideas:

First, government, here Davis County government, must follow its own rules.

Second, it must do so within a reasonable time.

Step one, the pre-termination ordinance, and step two, the post-termination ordinance, obviously contemplate that orderly procedures be followed with reasonable dispatch.

This has not occurred in this instance because the Merit Council has done but half its work. I don't say that in criticism. I say it by way of observation.

The Council having made its determination that plaintiff is a covered employee, it must then, in that same proceeding, determine whether the pre-termination procedures mandated by Article XIII, Section C of the Davis County Merit System Ordinance were followed by the Library Board. It follows, if these procedures were not complied with, that plaintiff is entitled to reinstatement plus back pay from the effective date of her discharge. The discharge would be procedurally defective—and null and void. If the Merit Council determines that the required pre-termination procedures were followed, plaintiff, having filed a timely appeal, is entitled by the post-termination appellate process to have the Council determine in that same proceeding after a full evidentiary hearing whether or not she was discharged for "cause," all as set forth in Article IX of the ordinance.

If she has not been discharged for "cause" she would be entitled to reinstatement plus back pay from effective date of discharge, because absent "cause" the discharge would be legally insufficient and null and void.

It is important for the Merit Council to complete its work and to make its determinations as part of the proceeding which it is charged with overseeing. It is important to the plaintiff because she stands jobless through what may well be inappropriate action on the part of her employer. She needs relief now, not after the jurisdictional issue wends its way through the legal labyrinth to the state supreme court. Even if at the end she triumphs, such a "victory" may be hollow indeed.

It is important to the plaintiff because a due process factual inquiry may well end on the administrative level. It is important to the public and to the employer that the employer—the Library Board—be required to present its reasons for taking the action it has taken and have those reasons initially tested for truthfulness and for legal adequacy by the agency charged with the responsibility for doing that very thing—the Merit System Council. It is important for the public to know that the Merit Council is fulfilling its complete function in protecting experienced employees from arbitrary employer action and thus preserving the investment government has in the expertise and knowledge of such employees. It is also important to the public that where "cause" exists the action of the employer be given the imprimatur of an objective and neutral eye.

It is of course vitally important for this and for any other court to have before it a full and complete administrative record in a status ripe for determination.

In summary, the district court ruled that the Davis County Merit Council must first determine whether Layton was properly discharged for cause and whether the library board properly followed merit system procedures in terminating her services. Public administrators everywhere would do well to ponder U.S. District Court Judge Bruce Jenkins's words in the above quotations from his order (Civil No. NC 79-0177). That decision is pregnant with meaning for the protection of public personnel who may be "due processed" as Jeanne Layton was.

On January 10, 1980, the Davis County Merit Council reinstated Layton and awarded her all back pay and benefits. The council ruled that the library board acted without proper cause. The council said in part,

Under Article XIII, Section G, 1(a), the Library Board *must* before it can terminate Appellant: (a) Notify Appellant in writing of the specific reasons for the discharge, and (b) grant Appellant an opportunity to reply to said written charges, also in writing, and have the board consider the same, and (c) grant Appellant the opportunity to be heard by the Board.

In the instant matter, the Council concludes that the Library Board, in substance, though certainly not in form, substantially complied with "notice," "reply" and "hearing" provisions of Section G, Article XIII of the Ordinance sufficient to give the Council jurisdiction to hear the appeal. However, in the view of the Council, such compliance was barely minimal and indeed, leaves much to be desired regarding form.

A more appropriate format would have been for the Library Board to:

a. Have had the charge approved by the Board prior to its delivery to Appellant thus eliminating the need for subsequent Board ratification;
b. For the charge to have been on Library Board stationery signed by its chairman;
c. For the charge to have specifically set forth the right of written reply and a date and time at which Appellant could be heard; and
d. The charges could be more artfully drawn as to the specifics and alleged misconduct justifying termination.

The Council does not view the third element of the pre-termination procedures, i.e., the "right to be heard" as requiring a full-blown evidentiary hearing. On the contrary, such a hearing is provided under Article IX of the ordinance concerning appeals. However, the "right to be heard" does contemplate that the administrative officer conducting the informal pre-termination hearing be free from any arbitrary or biased pre-disposition as to termination of the employee.

The book *Americana,* which seems to be the center of this charge, was reviewed twice by the Library Reviewing Committee concerning the propriety of its being on the shelves of the County Library pursuant to two separate patron's complaints. Each time, the review was done in accord with existing and written Library reviewing policy, and indeed, after completion of the second review, the Library Board specifically ratified the reviewing procedures as being in accord with said policy. While the Council makes *no judgment* as to the merit of the book *Americana,* it does conclude that Appellant's actions associated therewith were not improper nor cause for termination. If, indeed, the book should not be on the library shelves, then it is for the Library Board to alter the policy of both selection and review of books so that books such as *Americana* are excluded.

Following Layton's reinstatement things quieted down, and while they may never return to normal, Layton is still a librarian (1989). The Davis County Library Board sued to overturn the merit council's decision, but on October 17, 1980, the U.S. District Court affirmed the merit council's authority to rule Layton merit covered and to order her reinstatement. Layton then sued for damages for violation of her civil rights. Her lawsuit against the three library board members was settled out of court in 1983 when the county paid Layton's legal costs and damages. Layton has shunned publicity in recent years.

This case teaches four critical lessons:

1. A well-drafted personnel statute or ordinance is essential for the protection of career professionals against witch hunts, extremists, incompetents, and crusaders;
2. Due process protections afforded by the Constitution are not enough—local governments must themselves follow the procedures for notice, defense, and appeal;
3. While the First Amendment may well protect librarians against censorship and book burners, the merit system is what kept Jeanne Layton's job; and
4. Administrators must pay special attention to ethical concerns in their administration of the laws.

Whether or not the due processing of Layton was really a struggle for children's minds, it was clearly a vivid demonstration of how career professionals can be protected from arbitrary dismissal and extremist pressures. Utah is certainly not unique in these matters. All states and all librarians can profit from this case and its outcomes. As Jeanne Layton told the author on May 8, 1981, "I'd advise all [public administrators] to pay particular attention to their personnel policies and procedures."

Assignments

1. As a class, or as teams, discuss and seek to resolve the issue—should Jeanne Layton's firing have been upheld? Or should she have been reinstated? What are the ethical implications of each position?

2. As a class, or as teams, discuss and seek to resolve the ethics of this key issue—*what saved Layton's job?* The Bill of Rights? The courts? A well-drafted merit system statute? An inept prosecution? The press? Administrative concern for public relations? What does this case suggest about ethics in today's public personnel administration?

3. Discuss what will happen to the next librarian Layton. What will protect her or him? Suppose Layton were now being discharged under the present existing system—what differences would it have made to her defense? To the prosecution? To the eventual outcome?

4. What model statute(s) or ordinance(s) do you recommend for local governments to best protect employee rights in such cases? Management rights? The broader public interests? Construct such a policy and subject it to debate, discussion, and cross-examination, especially in light of the ethical issues this case raises.

Notes

1. An excellent legal discussion of this issue can be found in L. Z. Lorber, et al., *Fear of Firing: A Legal and Personnel Analysis of Employment at Will* (Alexandria, VA: The ASPA Foundation, 1984).

2. The BYU Skaggs Institute of Retail Management at Brigham Young University provided funding to the author to conduct research on national firms and their responses to such new restrictions on their right to terminate employees at will. Administrative ethics becomes an issue here as corporate responses to the new legal environment are analyzed (see various responses below). The author wrote to some one hundred smaller and major corporations across the United States, and some seventy-four usable responses were received.* In addition, the author visited and conducted in-depth interviews with personnel officers of more than a dozen major businesses. As would be expected, most companies have responded to new legal developments quickly and with determination to protect traditional management rights.

One common reaction, especially among the larger retailers, was to revise their employee handbooks to include clarifying language like this:

> This handbook is intended to provide company employees with a general understanding of the personnel policies at _____ . The personnel policies in this handbook supersede and replace all prior published or unpublished policies. The information in this handbook should be helpful in familiarizing employees with the company. The handbook, however, cannot anticipate every situation or answer every question about employment. *Neither this handbook nor any provision in this handbook constitutes a contract of employment or any other type of contract.* The company must demonstrate flexibility in the administration of policies and procedures, and reserves the right to change or revise policies and procedures without notice whenever such action is deemed necessary by the company.

*The profile of survey respondents: 22% (16) had 1–100 employees; 16% (12) had 101–1,000 employees; 11% (8) had 1,001–5,000 employees; 19% (14) had 5,001–10,000 employees; and 32% (24) had over 10,000 employees.

Indeed, one major junior department store added this additional language to its employee manual:

> Employees are classified at the time of their employment as Permanent, Part Time, or Temporary:
>   Permanent Employees: *The word Permanent used as an employee classification, is a title only and has no reference to any measurement of time as commonly defined.*

A third firm, with over 5,000 employees, has just revised its employee handbook with the attached disclaimer:

> The policies described in this booklet are not conditions of employment, and the language is not intended to create a contract between _____ and its employees.

A last example of such policy changes in corporate employee handbooks comes from a firm with over 10,000 employees. Note the careful wording of this company employee handbook:

> I have received orientation to the policies, procedures, and regulations of _____ . As a part of that orientation, I received a copy of the company employee handbook, which includes the standards of conduct, principles of business conduct, equal opportunity employment policy, and the company's policy regarding solicitation and distribution.
>   The provisions of this employee handbook may be changed at any time. These provisions do not constitute a contract of employment, nor are they covenants. They are guidelines only and may be changed when, in the judgment of the company, circumstances so require.
>   Every effort has been made to measure that the information contained in this booklet is consistent with that contained in our written policies and procedures. If there is any difference, the written policies and procedures will govern.
>   I fully agree to comply with these policies, procedures, and regulations.

Firms also reported numerous other changes besides just disclaimers or statements in employee handbooks. One of the largest and most successful department store chains in the world has added the following applicant signature paragraph to its employment application blank:

> I certify that the information contained in this application is correct to the best of my knowledge and understand that any misstatement or omission of information is grounds for dismissal in accordance with _____ policy. I authorize the references listed above to give you any and all information concerning my previous employment and any pertinent information they may have, personal or otherwise, and release all parties from all liability for any damage that may result from furnishing same to you. In consideration of my employment, I agree to conform to the rules and regulations of _____ , and my employment and compensation can be terminated with or without cause, and with or without notice, at any time, at the option of either the company or myself. I understand that no unit manager or representative of _____ other than the president or vice-president of the company, has any authority to enter into any agreement for employment for any specified period of time, or to make

any agreement contrary to the foregoing. In some states, the law requires that
_____ have my written permission before obtaining
consumer reports on me, and I hereby authorize_____
to obtain such reports.

Applicant's Signature _____ .

Date _____ 19 _____ .

Another major firm with well over ten thousand employees requires each applicant/employee to sign the following:

> I agree that if employment is offered to and accepted by me, it is mutually understood
> and agreed that any employment is not confined to a fixed term and may be ended
> by either party without prior notice, unless otherwise affected by written company
> procedures.

A majority of the respondents to the survey noted that corporations are making numerous other changes and adjustments to preserve their right to terminate at will and to avoid expensive litigation. These changes may be summarized as follows:

• Recruitment ads, literature, and brochures have been reviewed to delete or disclaim contractual employment.

• Interviewers have been trained and instructed to be extremely cautious in pre-employment interviews and hiring interviews and not to make verbal promises or commitments about "career," "lifetime employment," "continuous employment," and so forth. One firm with 5,001 to 10,000 workers told the author in an interview, "All our supervisors who do the hiring are trained and retrained in this all the time—continued employment is based only upon satisfactory performance and at the sole discretion of the company, and supervisors say this to new recruits, reinforce it in annual performance reviews, and state it in all disciplinary actions. We may be too cautious . . ."

• Personnel manuals (written policies and procedures) have been carefully reviewed, section by section and topic by topic, to eliminate implied contracts or actual binding language.

• Employee evaluation forms have been reviewed (and revised, where any "contract" language is implied or actually present), supervisors have been carefully trained in what to say (and what *not* to say), and so on.

In summary, most firms are very sensitive to the legal and fiscal implications of the "termination at will" doctrine. More than two-thirds of even the smallest firms (below 100 employees) have made some or most of these adjustments, and virtually *every* large firm has at least rewritten its employee handbook or revised its employment application form.

But some companies feel there is no need to adjust. An owner of a small women's business wrote, "Have not had any problems to date." Another owner of a food business (three stores) wrote, "Our company is a family business, and (we) are very protective of our employees. We believe in lifetime employment and strongly believe and practice participatory management." The owner objected strenuously to the whole idea behind the survey and felt it was a sad commentary on our times.

Other respondents lamented that the "courts and legislatures have brought us to such a point" where employers have to guard so carefully against litigation.

Nevertheless, nearly all companies have made the necessary changes and adjustments (the larger businesses have been much more thorough than smaller ones) and are routinely implementing these new policies by training and periodic reviews. About 75 percent have limited changes (to date) just to the application blank and to the procedures manual or handbook, however.

Not one company reported any negative feedback from applicants, employees, customers, or stockholders, or any difficulty in recruitment or retention of workers by wording on application blanks, handbooks, and so forth. Most attributed such success (to date) to careful advance planning, thorough training of recruiters and managers, and continued personnel office follow-up to ensure company-wide compliance. Many firms pay great attention to *not* offending applicants or employees as the doctrine is explained by stressing what a good place to work the firm is, how competitive wages and benefits are, etc.

While some who read this will mourn the death of "firing-at-will," they must also be prepared to face the consequences of the new rules in the employee rights arena.

3. A shorter version of this article appeared earlier as Timmins, "The Due Processing of Librarian Layton," *Review of Public Personnel Administration* 3 (Fall 1982): 75–80.

4. Kenneth D. Walters, dean of the School of Business, California Polytechnic State University, wrote: "Managers were seemingly quite oblivious to ethical concerns and even seemed to be poorly schooled in public relations." See N. Dale Wright, ed., "Ethics and Responsibility," *Papers on the Ethics of Administration* (Provo, UT: Brigham Young University, 1988), p. 123.

CHAPTER 4

The Ethical Issues
Behind Comparable Worth

Sexism was the charge leveled by the city's entire staff of secretaries and clerical workers in a class action suit. During a position reclassification study being performed by the city, a series of job factors had been used to analyze classes of city positions against the larger labor market. The intention was to match benchmark jobs in the city against similar jobs in the various labor markets the city recruited from—local markets for clerical jobs, national markets for administrative jobs, for example.

In addition, use of these common job factors permitted "internal alignment"; that is, fairly compensating positions that weren't—or couldn't be easily—matched with jobs in the outside market. For instance, a job as a traffic light engineer might not exist outside municipal government.

The women employees in clerical positions soon realized that an analysis of many of these job factors (complexity, working conditions, knowledge, and training, for example) indicated that their particular jobs were worth much higher compensation levels than the city's present pay plan recognized. Indeed, many of the most highly skilled female clerical workers (executive secretaries, for one example) *should* have been paid much more than many blue-collar workers, who were exclusively men. When the city's top management was confronted with this obvious fact (obvious to the women at least), it was carefully and patiently explained away as the way the free-market system operated—supply and demand, wage curves, availability of labor, and so on. One of the women, Trudie, was not satisfied with this explanation. Her research led her to read extensively about comparable worth. The many ethical issues this research raised in her mind and the minds of her colleagues led to the lawsuit.

The Importance of Comparable Worth

Comparable worth has become a key issue in the late 1980s. Many states have initiated comparable worth statutes (at least covering public employees), and several national labor unions have openly endorsed the concept. A number of women's groups have called for national comparable worth legislation, and several U.S. Supreme Court decisions have recently dealt with this critical policy issue. In the state of Washington, female (and some male) public employees were awarded over $500 million in corrective salaries and wages in a negotiated settlement.

The Reagan administration condemned the concept of comparable worth. A few U.S. District Courts have rejected the idea. Most management groups are opposed to it.

Understandably, the subject has become a popular topic for program speakers, conference panels, journal articles, and consultants.

Proponents of comparable worth argue that all jobs in organizations should be compared one to another, using a sex-blind evaluative system. When jobs are worth the same to an organization, the jobs should be paid the same.

This concept should not be confused with the concept of equal pay for equal work. That issue was settled in 1963 by Congress (and subsequently the courts) when it mandated that a woman who does the *same job* as a man should receive the *same pay.*

Comparable worth goes far beyond equal pay for equal work. Proponents argue that our culture (nearly all cultures, really) financially reward male-dominated positions more generously than female-dominated positions, and this inequity is based on the labor market. Salaries of "men's jobs" and "women's jobs" are set in the open, competitive market as determined by salary surveys and other methods. Thus, even if the jobs traditionally held by females are worth more to an organization than the jobs traditionally held by males, male-dominated jobs are paid more. To proponents of comparable worth, the market perpetuates historical biases, particularly sex-based discrimination.

To eliminate this market bias, proponents of comparable worth argue that organizations should design sex-neutral evaluation systems that compare jobs for their intrinsic worth to the organization on a systematic, point-by-point comparative basis, ignoring the market.

Opponents argue that wages and salaries are properly set by the market system. They say it is sheer lunacy to tinker with something as basic to our economic order as letting wages and salaries be set by the free market—Adam Smith's famous "invisible hand" leading people to make countless individual choices based on self-interest that result eventually in the greatest good for the greatest number.

Opponents of comparable worth don't deny that a sex-neutral system could be designed (indeed, opponents argue that many such systems now exist), but they believe organizations must base wage and salary decisions on the free market. Any other system, no matter how well-intentioned, they say, will cause economic disaster and become a cure far worse than the disease. Opponents of comparable worth argue that the real solution is upward mobility for women, entry of females into non-traditional jobs, and opening all jobs in all organizations to women.

A Sex-Neutral System in Practice

What would a sex-neutral system look like and how would it be used to evaluate jobs? The balance of text in this chapter summarizes such a system. It compares a traditionally male-dominated position with a traditionally female-dominated position. The forms are presented to illustrate what to many is an arcane process and procedure.

The rating forms are used to determine what each job is worth based on a point system. This point system shows unequivocal sex-based bias. (Readers are reminded that salaries for such jobs are normally set based on free-market standards.)

In the forms, two selected jobs are compared using six factors—complexity, knowledge and training, contacts, supervision, working conditions, consequence of error—and twenty-one subfactors. A range of points and weights is assigned, and

Rating Form*

Dept.: City Police Department   Description: Secretary 2—Police

Factor		Points	Weights[a]		
I) Complexity	A	60 × 2	120		
	B	50 × 2	100		
	C	30 × 2	60		
	D		0		
				Sub-score	280
II) Knowledge and	A	20 × 3	60		
Training	B	40 × 3	120		
	C		30		
				Sub-score	210
III) Contacts	A		60		
	B		20		
				Sub-score	80
IV) Supervision	A		30		
	B		40		
	C		0		
	D		0		
				Sub-score	70 ÷ 2 = 35
V) Working	A		0		
Conditions	B		0		
	C		40		
	D		40		
	E		0		
				Sub-score	80 ÷ 5 = 16
VI) Consequences	A		0		
of Error	B		0		
	C		60		
				Sub-score	60 ÷ 3 = 20
				Total Points	641

Grade ___11___

---

[a]Adjust weights as desired by company/agency. The above are typical weights.

*The insttrument (including two Rating Forms, Factor VI—Consequences of Error, and two Position Descriptions) excerpted on the following pages is a registered copyright of TCI, Inc., and must not be used without the express written permission of the author.

Rating Form*

Dept.: City Sanitation   Description: Solid Waste Collector Driver

Factor	Points	Weights[a]		
I) Complexity	A $\underline{40} \times 2$	80		
	B $\underline{20} \times 2$	40		
	C $\underline{20} \times 2$	40		
	D	0		
			Sub-score	160
II) Knowledge and	A $\underline{30} \times 3$	90		
Training	B $\underline{30} \times 3$	90		
	C	20		
			Sub-score	200
III) Contacts	A	60		
	B	20		
			Sub-score	80
IV) Supervision	A	20		
	B	20		
	C	20		
	D	20		
			Sub-score	$80 \div 2 = \underline{40}$
V) Working	A	80		
Conditions	B	100		
	C	20		
	D	20		
	E	60		
			Sub-score	$\underline{280} \div 5 = \underline{56}$
VI) Consequences	A	40		
of Error	B	60		
	C	40		
			Sub-score	$140 \div 3 = \underline{47}$
			Total Points	583

Grade $\underline{\quad 10 \quad}$

---

[a]Adjust weights as desired by company/agency. The above are typical weights.

Factor VI—Consequences of Error

This factor measures the degree to which loss to either property, persons, funds, organizational efficiency, or public image may be affected by performance on the job. It is measured in terms of the results of error, whether through inaccuracy, inattention, lack of dependability, inadequate social skill, poor decisions, or improper supervision of others. The severity of loss is thus based on the consequences *which will probably occur when the employee fails to exercise normal skill, prudence and care.* Consider the loss on an annual basis. This is not to measure the probability of the error, but the probable result if there is an error. Consider especially the type of supervision given to employee. If employee is closely or generally supervised, the likelihood of an error being caught is greater.

A. Material Loss—Describes loss of funds, time, material and equipment which may be lost due to error.

0	20	40	60	80	100
none	loss of tools or small amount of funds—to $1,000	loss of equipment or moderate amount of funds—$1,000 to $50,000	considerable loss of equipment or of funds—$50,000 to $500,000	great loss of funds— $500,000 to $1,000,000	extensive loss of funds—over 1 million dollars

B. Injury or loss of life due to error (to consumer of services, the employee or co-workers).

0	20	40	60	80	100
none	minor injury	time loss injury 1 day to 1 month	time loss injury over 1 month	permanent injury	death

C. Organizational Efficiency or Public Image—Measures the effect of error on the efficiency of operation of the company/agency or has an adverse effect on the image of the company/agency on the public.

0	20	40	60	80	100
little or none	effects felt only within the division (or equivalent)	effects felt in several divisions or in a few public places	affects the whole department or large numbers of the public	affects the whole company/agency organization or a majority of the public	public outrage—affects the entire organization. The error is of such magnitude that the result is public outrage (seen by negative media reports, demonstrations, etc.)

the resulting scores, or ratings, permit the comparable worth of two diverse jobs to be systematically compared.

In the two examples provided here, actual (market-based) salaries are compared with the intrinsic worth of the jobs to the organization based on actual job descriptions. Readers can draw their own conclusions based on their own views of the free-market system, sex discrimination, and equity.

Factor VI, Consequence of Error, is used to illustrate the procedure. Factor VI has three subfactors: A. Material loss, B. Injury or loss of life . . ., and C. Organizational efficiency or public image.

Each subfactor—A, B, and C—is assigned a range of points from 0 to 100. An experienced rater would review the specific job being evaluated (pointed) and assign points for each subfactor, using a rating form similar to the ones on pages 32 and 33. In making these judgments, the rater would rely on some or all of the following information:

- An "audit" or actual observation of incumbents working in the position (performed by a skilled observer)
- An up-to-date position description (reviewed for content and accuracy by several levels of management)
- Job analysis questionnaires completed by incumbents and supervisors to supplement observation and position descriptions.
- Up-to-date organization charts (to properly relate a specific position to others)
- Interviews with supervisors and others to verify, clarify, and assess details of job tasks, skills, and abilities needed; length of training required; and so forth
- Research of available literature about the position (such as the *Dictionary of Occupational Titles*)
- Comparison of specific jobs with one employer with similar or like jobs in other jurisdictions

The rater then enters on the rating form, factor by factor, the points determined to be accurate for the specific job. Note that weights have been assigned to the various factors. In the case of Factor VI, Consequences of Error, the assigned points are divided by three; in Factor II, Knowledge and Training, the points are multiplied by three. These weights are based on extensive field research, job analysis with many employers, and value choices of a particular jurisdiction.

The total points for a particular position are easily converted to a salary (or pay) grade by means of a grade conversion table. For example:

Pay grade 1   85–160 points
Pay grade 2   165–210 points
Pay grade 3   215–260 points
Pay grade 4   265–310 points
Pay grade 5   315–360 points
Pay grade 6   365–410 points
Pay grade 7   415–460 points
Pay grade 8   465–510 points
Pay grade 9   515–560 points
Pay grade 10   565–610 points

Pay grade 11   615–660 points
Pay grade 12   665–710 points
Pay grade 13   715–760 points

To illustrate the comparable worth issue, two specific public sector positions are "pointed" so that readers can see how the process works. Actual position descriptions, rating forms, and actual salary comparisons are shown.

The examples are two municipal jobs: a secretary (traditionally a female-dominated position) and a solid waste collection driver (always male in this jurisdiction). In this city, the secretary is a grade 11 ($942–$1,200 monthly) and the driver is a grade 13 ($1,040–$1,323 monthly).

Position Description

Secretary 2—Police Department

Duties: Types and may edit correspondence, reports, forms, and other documents; makes copies; operates and may maintain various office machines; maintains appointment schedules; receives calls and greets the public; explains procedures and gives information; takes and relays messages; maintains work unit filing and records systems, and ensures recorded information on assigned programs is available on request; prioritizes individual daily workload; meets deadlines; may supervise and train others; takes shorthand from oral dictation; handles confidential information; performs other related work as required.

Minimum requirements: High school education or its equivalent and one year experience in typing and general office work, or one year post secondary secretarial training and six months of like experience, or two years post secondary secretarial training. Typing at 60 wpm net, spelling at grade 3, and shorthand at 70 wpm.

Applicant should have knowledge of basic English composition, spelling, and grammar; an ability to understand and follow oral and written instructions; an ability to type accurately and take and transcribe shorthand notes; an ability to work with speed and accuracy when dealing with the public.

Testing: All applicants must take the skills test offered through Job Service. All applicants must be filed with a test verification card from Job Service, or the application will be screened out.

Typing   60 wpm net
Spelling   Grade 3
Shorthand   70 wpm

Salary: $942.00–$1,200.00 monthly (grade 11)

Screening: Based on job-related experience and meeting the minimum requirements.

Applications: All applications must be filed with the City Office of Personnel Services before 5.00 p.m. on the closing date.

Note: Final applicants will be required to satisfactorily pass a police background check.

Position Description

Solid Waste Collection Driver

Duties: Operates a side- or back-loading pack truck or dump truck with trailers in a safe manner on an assigned solid waste pickup route; operates loading and unloading mechanisms and ramming equipment; maintains the route schedule and records and ensures that all pickups on the route are made; assists other drivers and crews on pickups; learns assigned routes; discusses service complaints with the public; is responsible for all work performed on an assigned route; trains and supervises subordinate workers; reports problems, damage to or needed repair of containers; performs all the work of a laborer as needed; may operate a brush truck; may maintain and repair the brush truck, chippers, power and hand tools; maintains records of work performed. Performs other related work as required.

Minimum requirements: One year experience at a level of work equivalent to a Solid Waste Back-up Driver. (Solid Waste Back-up Driver includes driving collection vehicle on a relief basis and six months experience as a laborer or equivalent.)

Applicant should have a knowledge of methods and techniques of waste collection; an ability to understand and follow oral and written instructions; an ability to work with speed and accuracy in a courteous manner when dealing with the public; and an ability to supervise others and maintain equitable working relationships.

Note: This position requires physical strength and agility enough to perform the work; this work requires exposure to adverse weather conditions, hazardous conditions, and odors. This work requires the employee to work in and around heavy traffic.

License: Valid lawful chauffeur's license is required upon appointment.

Salary: $1,040.00–$1,323.00 monthly (grade 13).

Screening: Based on job-related experience and meeting the minimum requirements.

Applications: All applications must be filed with the City Office of Personnel Services before 5:00 p.m. on the closing date.

A point-by-point comparison shows the female-dominated position to be correctly classified as grade 11 (641 points). However, the male-dominated job is significantly overpaid, since it points out at a grade 10 (583 points), not a grade 13.

Serious sex-based discrimination exists, according to comparable worth proponents. Opponents would argue, of course, that the labor market dictates lower salaries for secretaries than for solid waste collection drivers. It would be interesting to see how the U.S. Supreme Court would resolve this fundamental conflict in values.

Assignments

1. Discuss the ethical issues surrounding "equal pay for equal work," "comparable worth," and "sex-based job discrimination." (Any number of recent U.S. Supreme Court cases are helpful background; many textbooks on compensation and benefits will provide the raw materials.)

· 2. What is wrong about comparable worth? What is right about it? How can employers, public and private, best resolve the complex pay equity issues?

3. Using the simple (admittedly incomplete) example in this chapter as a guide, select a male-dominated position and a female-dominated position with a local government, where current pay is about the same, and compare them using factors similar to those illustrated. What are the results? What conclusions should you reach? What next steps should be taken, if any? Are there other ethical issues raised by the results of this exercise?

CHAPTER 5

The Right to Strike by Public Employees

An Ethical Dilemma

"Strike!" Marilyn shouted out with scores of other union voices. She'd worked for decades as a nurse's aide in the county's 300-bed nursing home. After all these years she still earned less than seven dollars an hour. She could see the faces of the hundreds of elderly people she'd bathed, shaved, cleaned, cheered up, read letters to, given back rubs to, and held when they cried in their loneliness or suffering. She loved her work. It was very satisfying. She actually cared about the patients who came and went. She had a scrapbook full of notes and letters from grateful patients and their families, as well as several citations from a series of administrators for outstanding performance, courtesy, and skill.

Still, the county did not treat its career employees well. Pay was low. Benefits were token (her retirement "plan" was mostly Social Security). Working conditions were terrible. Marilyn was assigned more and more "beds" each year (a joke, she thought; beds didn't need back rubs or help finding the bathroom), and she was working longer shifts and more evenings because the county was in a period of "economizing." Fewer aides were caring for more people over longer shifts than at any time since she'd started as an aide just after her divorce so long ago. She had supported herself, even sent "their" son (*my* son, she bitterly recalled, since support checks had stopped a year or two after her ex moved out of the state) through college, and seen him happily married. But these had been lean, tough years. She was grateful she loved her work. That made it all doubly worthwhile.

Recently a service employees union had organized most of the county's nursing home workers. After months of collective bargaining, the county and the union were at a stalemate. Tonight was the strike vote meeting. Normally, Marilyn was a peaceable woman, but after hearing the speeches and sensing the angry mood of her co-workers, Marilyn almost surprised herself by how loudly she yelled "Strike." So the strike was on. Was it legal? No one really cared. This was a matter of justice, fairness, and equality. As they were leaving the union meeting later that evening, a friend asked Marilyn, "Do public employees have the right to strike?" (In Marilyn's state as in most states, such a strike is illegal by state statute; but such laws rarely deter strikers.)

A Right to Strike?

Strikes by public employees have become commonplace in the last few years despite almost universal objection to the disruption of public services—recall strikes in Pennsylvania, Illinois, California, New York, and other states and cities.

The right of public employees to strike has long been a topic of debate, and it has become more significant in the last few years because public employees at federal, state, and local levels have organized in unprecedented numbers. Furthermore, state and local public workers have been granted the right by state statutes to collective bargaining with public management in some thirty-five or more states. No federal law applies to state and local government labor relations. It is estimated that more than half of all public employees in the United States now belong to public employee unions or associations. Public workers and public unions are increasingly vocal, increasingly militant, and increasingly successful at the bargaining table.

The right of state and local public workers to strike is advocated by those who say no other effective means currently exist to deal with labor relations problems. The traditional civil service systems or merit systems are no longer seen in a favorable light by these advocates. They also argue that anti-strike legislation has not prevented strikes in the past and may actually have caused disputes and work stoppages. Thus, their argument goes, laws should be concerned not with prohibitions but with effective ways to resolve differences that arise out of "good faith" collective bargaining. Prohibitions, especially strike prohibitions, proponents state, are hard to enforce and often complicate labor-management relations for public employees.

Proponents also state that the belief that all strikes by every type of public worker are illegal is antiquated. They argue that the essential services argument (namely, that all public employment functions are essential to the proper functioning of the state) is no longer applicable. Workers in the private sector performing the same or similar tasks and supplying the same services as workers in the public sector (for example, nurses, bus drivers, teachers, public works contractors) are permitted to strike, while those in the public sector are not. Solely because of their public sector employment status, they are denied many of the rights enjoyed by their counterparts in the private sector. Because of these conditions, proponents claim that only work stoppages presenting a clear and present danger to the public health or safety should be prohibited—regardless of the status of the worker.

Proponents of the right to strike by state and local government employees also claim that "good faith" bargaining in the public sector can be ensured only if the unilateral power of the public employer in setting salaries and working conditions is equalized by granting to public employees, subject to reasonable conditions, the right to strike—the same ultimate weapon available to workers in the private sector.

Opponents of the right of public workers to strike claim that such strikes disrupt essential services, that unions with the ability to call a strike would diminish or eliminate civil service or merit systems, and that the power exercised by these public unions might result in a disproportionate share of public funds going to militant public employees—the dispersal of funds being a policy decision that ought to be made by elected officials in the normal political way without the coercion that might result from organized activity by public employees.

The traditional doctrine of sovereign immunity, which holds that the state cannot be forced to do what it does not agree to do, denies the right to strike to public employees. A strike claim against the state is considered to be a derogation of the state's ultimate authority and responsibility to govern and may actually threaten the ability of government to ensure the survival of the political process.

Opponents of the right to strike by state and local government employees often cite the protections against discharge allegedly enjoyed by public employees under civil service or merit systems and the other protections tenured public workers enjoy. Opponents also argue that because government is essentially a monopoly, a strike of state or local government employees leaves the public without alternatives—especially for critical services such as law enforcement and fire protection.

Seven States

Nearly all states proscribe strikes by public employees, but seven states have granted a limited right to strike to some public employees.

Alaska passed legislation that identifies *classes* of public employees who may or may not be permitted to strike. Under the Alaska statute, public employees perform services in one of three classes: (1) those services that may not be given up for even the shortest period of time; (2) those services that may be interrupted for a limited, but not an indefinite, period of time; and (3) those services in which work stoppages may be sustained for extended periods without serious effects on the public.

The first class is composed of police and fire protection employees; jail, prison, and other correctional institution employees; and hospital employees. Employees in this class are forbidden to strike. If a public employer (or the state labor relations agency) can show that employees in this class are engaging or about to engage in a strike, the court in the relevant judicial district can issue an injunction, a restraining order, or other appropriate order. The Alaska statute also provides that if a deadlock occurs in collective bargaining between the public employer and employees in this class, and mediation had been tried without resolving the deadlock, the parties shall submit their dispute to arbitration.

The second class consists of public utility, snow removal, sanitation, and public school and other educational institution employees. These employees can strike for a limited time, after mediation and subject to a majority vote of the employees. The length of the strike is determined by the interests of the health, safety, or welfare of the public. The public employer or the labor relations agency may apply to the superior court in the judicial district in which the strike is occurring for an order enjoining the strike. A strike may not be enjoined unless it can be shown that it has begun to threaten the health, safety, or welfare of the public. A court, in deciding whether or not to enjoin the strike, must consider the total equities in the particular class of employee. "Total equities" includes not only the impact of a strike on the public but also the extent to which employee organizations and public employers have met their statutory obligations. If an impasse still exists after the issuance of an injunction, the parties must submit their dispute for arbitration.

All other public employees in Alaska not included in the first two classes may engage in a strike if a majority of the employees in a collective bargaining unit vote by secret ballot to do so.

Critics of the Alaska statute argue that district courts are not necessarily the best forums for the resolution of labor-mangement impasses. Judges and lawyers may not necessarily be any better able to resolve conflicts than are others skilled in impasse-resolution techniques. Indeed, the courtroom may only submerge the real sources of conflict because of the litigation-oriented setting and judicial atmosphere.

Borrowing from the private sector's idea that a cooling-off period can be useful in labor disputes, Hawaii provides by statute that a sequence or series of timed actions be exhausted before a strike. Minnesota penalizes violations of its limited right to strike by public employees by stating:

> Notwithstanding any other provision of law, any public employee who violates the provisions of this section may have his appointment or employment terminated by the employer effective the date the violation first occurs. Such termination shall be effective upon written notice served upon the employee. Service may be made by certified mail.

Such penalties are rarely enforced in the public sector, however. In fact, once the strike ends one of the first agreements usually signed by both parties to the dispute is that no penalties will be enforced or required.

Other states legally permitting the right to strike by public employees are Montana, Oregon, Pennsylvania, and Vermont. Montana's legislature did not deal with the right to strike in the enabling statute passed several years ago, but did include the following statement:

> Employees' right to join or form labor organizations and engage in collective bargaining activities. (1) Public employees shall have, and shall be protected in the exercise of, the right of self-organization, to form, join or assist any labor organization, to bargain collectively through representatives of their own choosing on questions of wages, hours, fringe benefits, and other conditions of employment and to engage in other concerted activities for the purpose of collective bargaining or other mutual aid or protection, free from interference, restraint or coercion.

The Montana Supreme Court in 1976 ruled that "other concerted activities" included the unlimited right to strike.

More Not Less

Laws have not and will not prevent strikes, and state and local government employees are striking more, not less. Can the demands of public employees be reconciled with the public's expectation of uninterrupted public services? A number of ideas have been proposed, although they have not been tested enough to tell us if they will really work.

Sam Zagoria, director of the Labor-Management Relations Service (sponsored by the National League of Cities, the U.S. Conference of Mayors, and the National Association of Counties), has succinctly summarized some of these ideas:

> Productivity, once a dirty word, is receiving increasing attention as both labor and management recognize the need to prove their good works to the constituency. Some innovative efforts in productivity bargaining have failed to achieve permanency, but there is a growing togetherness among individual workers, labor unions and management, in trying to find ways to get the job done better and cheaper, without bargaining out the gains.

> The strike—the *sine qua non* of most union leaders—is proving to be not as effective a weapon as it was for the private sector unions, or even as it used to be for the public sector unions. An alternative, compulsory arbitration, once unknown, is now better understood by public management and is therefore roundly opposed. Elected officials, understandably, believe they should retain the right to say "yes" or "no" to union proposals. Arbitration removes this right of control from the parties and turns it over to the outside professional. My guess is there will be more "goldfish bargaining."[1]

Public employees will continue to demand that their needs be provided for. Voters, on the other hand, may begin to resist the tax increases needed to finance salary increases and fringe benefits packages for public workers, given the state of the economy. Public officials in the legislative and executive branches of state and local governments will need to find new techniques and approaches for resolving public employee-employer conflicts.

A host of efforts is now underway in the public sector to try to bring public management and public workers together, but not necessarily at the bargaining table. The National Center on Productivity and the Quality of Working Life has reported on many of these experiments. A number of them seem to hold great promise.

Individual state legislatures need to grapple with the issues and stimulate research and experimentation in public sector labor relations by our nation's colleges and universities. Individual citizens need to apply their creativity in suggesting new solutions and better ideas. Ultimately, however, it is the general public that must make its feelings known and ratify new developments.

Assignments

1. As a class (or as teams) research and debate the statement, "Resolved, public employees should (or, should not) have the right to strike." Be sure all the ethical ramifications are explored.

2. Select one or two of the contrasting state statutes referred to in the chapter and compare these laws in detail—with careful analysis of definitions, time periods, and alternatives.

3. Assuming public employees should *not* have the right to strike, what is the most ethical alternative? Why? Discuss or analyze your proposal(s) in some detail— from the public's point of view, the employees', and from management's.

4. As a class (or as teams), where possible and without risk or any hazard, arrange to visit strikers on a picket line or workers who are actually involved in a strike. Later, share with other class members the feelings of strikers, pick up strike literature and pass it around, gather some press releases, and discuss the drama of the strike and ethical issues involved.

Notes

1. "Attitudes Harden in Governmental Labor Relations," American Society for Public Administration: *News and Views* (December 1976): 22.

CHAPTER 6

Ethical Issues of Employee Fitness Programs

Marianne scowled at the thought that she was overweight. What possible business did the city have in telling her she had to enroll in a weight reduction program? This was taking health-care cost containment a bit too far, she felt. Since when does someone's obesity have anything to do with job performance in a job like hers? She checked restaurants for compliance with regulations governing the handling of food, for heaven's sakes. She was not a police officer or a fire fighter or a tree trimmer. Could the city really force her to enter a weight reduction program and lose pounds?

An increasing number of employers, both public and private, are providing physical fitness programs for their employees. This chapter describes such programs, estimates their number in the public sector, and evaluates their success.

In 1894 John H. Patterson, founder of the National Cash Register Company (N.C.R.), appointed for his firm a health and hygiene trainer named Palmer, who initiated an unusual corporate physical fitness program:

> He prescribed early morning exercises for all executives and immediately all of the executives were required to be at the factory at five o'clock in the morning, to go through calisthenics, take a bath, and be rubbed down. They were given breakfast at the factory. A little later Palmer decided that all of these men should ride horseback in the morning. Mr. Patterson bought a great string of saddle horses, and for a long time any one who happened to be wandering about Dayton at dawn could see a cavalcade of N.C.R. executives, led by Mr. Patterson and Palmer, riding through hills and dales. Probably nothing like this ever happened before in an American business institution. Those of the executives who did not know how to ride and would not learn how to ride ceased forthwith to be executives. It was laid down as the maxim that no one who could not manage a horse could be expected to manage men.
>
> The whole adventure has its funny side, but actually it was a mighty good thing for these men, shut up all day as they had been to get out into the open. The N.C.R. people who date from this period are about as healthy as a lot of individuals today as can anywhere be found.[1]

The N.C.R. experience is no longer singular. Corporate fitness programs are relatively widespread now—more than four hundred major corporations now provide extensive exercise facilities, including large gymnasiums (for example, Xerox in Webster, New York; Phillips Petroleum in Bartlesville, Oklahoma; and Gates Rubber in Denver). Such corporate exercise programs vary. Some companies offer simple in-house exercise facilities, while others provide full-fledged cardiovascular fitness centers (for example, McGraw-Hill and Exxon Corporation in New York and Times-

Mirror in Los Angeles). Some corporations have sponsored extensive competitive sports programs.[2]

Kimberly-Clark Corporation spent several million dollars building health and physical fitness facilities in Neenah, Wisconsin, near the corporate headquarters. The complex is staffed by fifteen full-time personnel who "help employees maintain or improve their health instead of providing medical assistance only after they become ill." The program for the 2,100 employees was voluntary, but some 60 percent of eligible workers signed up.[3]

Premature death is computed to cost American industry $25 billion annually and 132 million lost workdays. Companies are spending large sums of money to cut employee costs by sponsoring medically approved and directed cardiovascular fitness programs. For instance, employee health plans cost General Motors $825 million a year. Even small improvements in employee health can effect large savings for the company.[4] Steven Levisohn described some significant benefits after only the first year of a program at the National Fire Protection Association in Boston, Massachusetts.[5]

Basic procedural steps for companies interested in developing corporate physical fitness programs have been recommended by Robert Kreitner:

1. Stimulate top management's interests in and, later, a firm commitment to employee physical fitness.
2. Survey employee feelings concerning proposed facilities and programs.
3. Collect relevant information and data from government and industrial sources.
4. Proceed with the definition of program policy and objectives.
5. Provide the essential facilities and equipment while retaining the option of later expansion if warranted. (Leasing or sharing of public or private facilities must not be overlooked as alternatives to construction.)
6. Adequately staff the program with qualified experts. (Some may choose to carry out this step prior to or concurrent with the preceding step to ensure the compatibility of facilities and programs.)
7. Provide an appealing variety of programs and employ motivational aids as necessary.
8. Maintain a cycle of diagnostic-remediation evaluation with appropriate stress testing facilities, staff, and programs.
9. Integrate the physical fitness and coronary heart disease prevention programs into daily organizational activity through promotional and educational strategies.
10. Periodically evaluate and revise programs as necessary.[6]

Public employees are not less prone to heart attacks, strokes, and other forms of coronary heart disease than their private sector counterparts, nor is the cost of premature death and loss of workdays less significant in the public sector. Unfortunately, government has moved more slowly than business and industry in providing for employee fitness. But some positive gains are readily apparent.

How common are such employee physical fitness programs in the public sector? What general characteristics are there among existing programs? Can recommendations be made?

A questionnaire was mailed to a random sample of seventy-five public agencies selected from the IPMA (International Personnel Management Association) *1980*

Directory of Membership. Fifty-three responses were received (a return rate of over 70 percent) from cities, counties, and school districts. Jurisdictions averaged 3,700 employees with a high of 77,000 workers and low of 80. Of the random sample, eleven (or 21 percent) have some form of physical fitness program. Additionally, at least three other public agencies that responded to the survey are presently considering adoption of such efforts. The balance of the survey, thirty-six agencies (or some 72 percent), reports no such fitness programs.

The eleven systems reporting employee fitness programs tended to be the larger systems. While these eleven ranged from 77,000 employees to as few as 83, seven had more than 1,500 workers (and averaged over 22,000 because of sample skewing; the mode was slightly greater than 2,700). Five respondents were local governments in the Southeast (Georgia, North Carolina, South Carolina, and two in Florida); three were local jurisdictions from the Midwest (Minnesota, Nebraska, Iowa); one was from the Mountain states (Utah); and two were from the West (California, Hawaii). While responses were received from all sections of the country, of course, the eleven with employee fitness programs were more concentrated geographically. No particular importance is hypothesized for this clustering, however.

Fitness Program Examples

The four contrasting fitness programs summarized here are taken as representative of the eleven survey respondents that provide programs.

Typical of the small jurisdiction with a restricted employee physical fitness program was the city of Rock Hill, South Carolina. Rock Hill had 600 employees. In 1979 the city initiated a voluntary fitness program that was conducted after normal working hours. No pay or benefit incentives were linked to participation in the physical fitness program. Fewer than 10 percent of the employees participated. Participation was typically in weight lifting, softball, tennis, bowling, and jogging. Employees averaged a half-hour to one hour a day in such fitness activities, with participation by some executives, middle managers, first-line supervisors, and nonsupervisory professional employees. The city provided a facility with weight-lifting equipment, but did not provide any other facilities and did not subsidize membership in a spa, YWCA/YMCA, or health club. Very little or no difference in efficiency was noticed in the small number who participated in fitness activities (although few records were kept).

Macon, Georgia, with 1,500 workers, conducted a vigorous physical fitness program for its fire fighters (starting in 1977) and police officers (starting in 1979). The city provided an exercise facility, exercise clothing, and shoes. Macon provided worker compensation and other leave privileges for those injured while working out. Over 86 percent of police and fire personnel participated in Macon's mandatory program (the practice is mandated by ordinance). Personnel spent from thirty to sixty minutes a day in jogging, soccer, basketball, weight lifting, and other exercise routines before, during, or after normal working hours—indeed, public safety personnel were encouraged to work out while on duty. While no pay or benefits were linked to participation in the physical fitness program, continued employment was conditional

upon such regular workouts. Macon's director of personnel reported that a very significant difference had been noted among participating fire fighters (fewer on-the-job
injuries, less fatigue at fires, less sickness, faster response time, for example) but
added it was too soon to tell about police officers because of the newness of that
part of the city's program.

The city and county of Honolulu (8,000 employees) had provided several exercise facilities (with gym equipment) for executives, middle managers, and first-line
supervisors for many years. Participation was mandatory among police and fire department managers and supervisors and voluntary for supervisors and managers in the
other city-county departments. An estimated half or fewer of all such personnel took
part in fitness activities—usually jogging, volleyball, basketball and tennis—for periods
of sixteen to thirty minutes daily and mostly during regular working hours. No pay
or benefits were linked to participation (other than the mandatory participation by
police and fire department supervisors and managers), but the city-county had exercise physiologists plan programs based on individual physical profiles in at least some
cases. A very significant improvement in efficiency was claimed for those who participated in such efforts.

The largest system responding to the survey was Los Angeles County, with a
total of 77,000 employees. The county initiated its program in 1971 for executive-
level administrators, middle managers, and all members of the fire and sheriff's
departments. Fitness program participation was mandatory for fire and sheriff's department personnel and voluntary for executives and other managers, but no pay or other
benefit incentives were linked to participation in the physical fitness program. The
county estimated that although approximately 10,000 personnel participated in the
program, participation was less than 10 percent among personnel for whom the program was not mandatory. The county furnished stationary bicycles, wall pulley weights,
and Universal Gyms in some locations, but it provided no sponsorship of health club,
spa, or YMCA/YWCA memberships. The most frequent activities were jogging, calis-
thenics, weights, and some ball sports, with participants spending perhaps fifteen
to thirty minutes daily. Fire department personnel participated during regular working hours, sheriff's department personnel and other executives and managers participated before and after normal working hours. The county felt it was difficult to
assess differences in performance and efficiency for those who participated except
that "performance on periodic medical examination shows physical working capacity improved" in participants.

The Los Angeles County Sheriff's Department requires an agility test as part
of an annual fitness requirement and suggests the following exercises to assist county
employees in meeting those physical fitness needs:

Cardiovascular

Activities that will involve the heart, blood vessels, and lungs are the most important
type of physical fitness activities to improve and maintain good health. The target
heart rate to achieve minimum cardiovascular health benefits is approximately 140
beats per minute. One's heart rate should be self-monitored, which can be done by
counting the pulse for ten seconds and multiplying by six to get the rate for the minute.

A heart rate of 140 beats per minute is a desirable *intensity* to achieve a training effect. The *duration* of this work level should be continued for twenty to thirty minutes. The *frequency* should be at least three times per week.

The cardiovascular-type activities should be performed in a designated area, either at the station to which the deputy is assigned, by using a stationary bicycle, handball or racquetball court, or jogging track around the station. Other specifically designated areas close to the station may be utilized, such as local greenbelts, school tracks, or playing facilities. In addition, the Academy at Eastern Avenue or the Agility Testing Station at the county jail may be used for exercising and practice.

Muscular Strength

The use of the Universal Gym at each of the stations should be able to meet the needs of muscle development for those requiring a maintenance program as well as specific improvement needs. The Universal Gym exercise charts and film may be used to involve the major muscle groups for a general conditioning program. When poor performance on the agility test requires special training and conditioning, an exercise physiology technician will work with the deputy to suggest and supervise specific training procedures. These will be designed to improve performance and, if properly carried out, enable the deputy to pass the test. Deputies who desire to exercise in preparation for taking the agility test will find the following exercises helpful. They have been grouped by the different agility tests. The exercises are illustrated in the Universal Gym Exercise poster, which should be posted on the wall wherever the Universal Gyms are located. In general, the exercises should be performed in two or three sets of six to eight repetitions, three times per week. The amount of weight selected will, of course, be relative to the size of the person and his or her past history of using weight resistance in an exercise program to improve performance. It is somewhat of a trial-and-error procedure to establish the correct amount of weight that one actually uses. In view of this, it is always better to try the lighter weight until one feels a gradual increase is possible.

Flexibility

Many athletes will attest to the fact that when they are in good physical condition and maintain their flexibility they have fewer injuries. Athletic trainers utilize this concept in the teams they work with.

In maintaining maximal range of motion through regular stretching exercises, it is possible to prevent sudden extensive movements from overstretching the muscles and connective tissues, thereby causing an injury. Back problems are the second most expensive worker's compensation type of injury for county safety employees.

Specific stretching exercises are suggested in the handout materials given during Phase II of the medical examination. Additional stretching exercises will be developed as the need arises in assisting deputies to pass the battery of agility tests.

A series of exercises may be used to assist in muscular development for deputies needing to improve their ability in the respective agility tests.

In summary, the Los Angeles County Sheriff's Department covers these exercises and related fitness programs in briefing sessions and in-service training, using training films, visuals, handouts, and an exercise chart showing some twenty-one exercises. The department uses materials developed by the Los Angeles County Cardiopulmonary Laboratory of the Occupational Health Service.

Examples of the public agencies responding to the survey that are now developing an interest in employee fitness programs are Pinellas County, Florida, which "recently joined in the formation of an employers' group called the Bay Area Employers' Group on Health, which will pursue employee fitness as one major area of concern in decreasing employer health costs, while simultaneously improving employee well-being and effectiveness," and the U.S. Department of Commerce (38,000 employees) which plans to open a physical fitness facility for departmental employees.

Summary

The private sector has demonstrated for many years that employee physical fitness programs pay off in reduced health-care costs, reduced sick leave and disability leave, and improved morale and productivity.[7] The IPMA survey shows that nearly 25 percent of the public agencies that responded are now engaged in some sort of fitness program(s) or are planning to initiate some such effort.

Typically, such public agencies are larger employers—that is, with 2,700 or more employees. Usually such fitness programs are mandatory for public safety personnel and optional for others. Most such programs are modest in scope, short-term (half an hour or less each day), offer no incentives for participation (other than job retention for public safety employees), and are most commonly carried out before or after regular working hours. Public agencies that have provided gym equipment or facilities tend to be very large employers.

Finally, little serious research is presently being carried out to document the benefits of such employee physical fitness programs. This suggests a rich opportunity for funding of several research projects and further exploration by students and researchers. What is needed now is to apply what the private sector can teach about employee fitness to experimentation and innovation in the public sector. We have nothing to lose but our waistlines and flab, and an opportunity to make public workers live better and work better.

About three-fourths or more of public agencies (according to our survey) have yet to become involved in better ensuring their employees' health and well-being.

Assignments

1. As a class (or as teams) discuss the ethical issues surrounding employee fitness programs. What "rights" should workers have? What "rights" do employers have? What is the best way to resolve such conflicts? What ethical issues should prevail?

2. Identify an employee physical fitness program in your community. Invite guests (perhaps a director, a participant, an insurance underwriter) in for structured interviews. Explore ethical issues from many perspectives. Decide what ethical guidelines and policies *should* govern such programs in the future.

3. Apply your discussion from assignment 1 to the paramilitary employees of a city (police or fire fighters). Should there be a higher physical fitness standard applied to these physically demanding occupations than to other city jobs?

4. As a class (or as teams) discuss the ethical issues surrounding hiring the handicapped (mental, physical, emotional)—for instance, hiring workers who are visually impaired or in wheelchairs or retarded. What are some of the ethical considerations here? Should the same fitness standard(s) apply?

Notes

1. Samuel Crowther, *John H. Patterson: Pioneer in Industrial Welfare* (New York: Doubleday, Page & Company, 1923), p. 221.

2. "The Healthy Trend Toward Corporate Exercise Programs," *Business Week* (3 April 1978): 91.

3. "Kimberly-Clark is Spending Millions to Insure Employees' Health, Well-Being," *Paper Trade Journal* (15 December 1977): 40; and "The New Business Boom—Fitness," *Nation's Business* (February 1978): 68–70, 73.

4. "Keeping Managers in Good Heart," *International Management* (January 1979): 40.

5. Steven R. Levisohn, "One Man's Guide to Corporate Fitness," *Harvard Medical Alumni Bulletin* (Fall 1979): 23–26.

6. Robert Kreitner, "Employee Physical Fitness: Protecting an Investment in Human Resources," *Personnel Journal* (July 1976): 340–344. Kreitner's article cites more than twenty-five excellent references and sources of information.

7. For example, see William M. Timmins and Brent J. Middleton, "Utah Power and Light Company," *Corporate Fitness and Recreation* 5 (April/May 1986): 17.

PART II

Ethics and Politics

The three cases in this section introduce political policy issues with ethical overtones. One case raises issues of organized groups (in this case, public employee unions) interfering with the majority's will, the outcome of a home rule election campaign. How ethical were elected officials? Union officials? County employees? The media? Another case touches on the ethics of candidates for a U.S. Senate seat and last-minute charges of a smear. What is the best way to handle "dirty tricks" and unfair campaign practices? The third case will hit home to nearly everyone who has ever worked in public service because it deals with the inevitable conflicts that arise between career public workers and political appointees. Each has an agenda, each has priorities, each pits its position against the power of the other. What are the ethical ways of reducing such conflicts? How best to work together to achieve the most rewarding outcome for the greatest number?

CHAPTER 7

Interference with Free Local Elections

"Unions!" spat the young public administrator. This election was a textbook example of how someone from outside—in this case, public employee unions—could so interfere with a free election as to alter the anticipated outcome completely. Scare tactics, misinformation, and organized teams of union toadies had ruined everything! All the years of efforts to provide for home rule were now down the drain. It was frightening how effective the unions had been. Effective—but unfair! Unethical! This kind of thing should not be tolerated in a free society, he thought.

Professor Frank H. Jonas, in his book *Political Dynamiting* (Salt Lake City: University of Utah Press, 1970), has defined political dynamiting as ". . . sudden strategically timed publication of carefully researched, damaging, difficult to answer charges based upon selected excerpts from the truth." He cited examples of political dynamiting in congressional campaigns in California, Arizona, Montana, and Utah. This chapter examines political dynamiting at the local level by organized public employees and shows the ethical issues very clearly as a vocal minority steamrolls a quiet majority. The rapid rise of membership in public employee unions, especially in local government, has been termed a "revolution" in public affairs. In *Public Workers and Public Unions* (Prentice-Hall, 1972) Sam Zagoria observed that "Public workers . . . are edging into the government and policy-planning and policy-making machinery. Some are quite plain about the ultimate objective—sharing of power."

Public worker unions in this case used political dynamiting to defeat an effort at incorporation by citizens in a large neighborhood on the west side of unincorporated Salt Lake County, Utah. (The author, a faculty member at Brigham Young University, served as consultant to the public worker unions opposed to the effort.)

In 1978, Salt Lake County had an estimated population of 560,000. The valley had ten incorporated municipalities ranging in size from Alta (250 persons) to Salt Lake City (about 175,000). About 277,000 persons lived in the unincorporated county. (Population and socioeconomic data used in this study were provided in 1978 by the Salt Lake County Planning Department and the Salt Lake County Auditor.)

The Salt Lake Valley is roughly bisected into an east side and a west side by State Street, with the Utah state capitol anchoring the north end of State Street and the Utah State Prison the south end, about twenty miles away.

The east side is generally more affluent; the west side has recently been the site of rapid growth in moderate- and low-cost housing. In 1978 about three persons lived east of State Street for every one on the west side.

The west side has a clearer sense of identity and community than can be found east of State Street. Most of the cities on the west side are relatively new (for example, West Jordan, 1945; South Jordan, 1935; Riverton, 1948). The area has strong community pride, often focused on its high schools. Interschool rivalry is strong, and west-side schools have notable records of athletic success.

West-siders, however, have historically felt shortchanged by county government. They have complained for a generation or more that the east side has been favored in terms of roads and bridges, parks and recreation, law enforcement and fire protection, and planning and zoning.

The west side's inferior political clout was apparent in one visible 1978 index: As of that year, only five county commissioners had ever been west-siders. (The county government was composed of a three-person commission and eight other elected officials.) In fact, the west side had not elected a county commissioner for ten years, although west-siders had served on several county boards or commissions. For example, in 1978 two of the six Salt Lake County planning commissioners were west-siders.

Former county commissioner Marvin Jenson reflected in February 1978 that

> the west side could elect one or more county commissioners—and other elected officials at the county level—virtually anytime they wanted. All it takes is stepping forward and becoming a candidate. Yet, few west-siders have been willing to even consider it. Why? The chief reason is money—or the lack of it. It costs a lot of money to run for public office, particularly the Commission. And west-siders typically don't have that kind of money. A Commission candidate needs maybe thirty or fifty thousand dollars to run a campaign. The political parties never have that much money to offer a candidate. . . . The salary is not high enough to compensate for the cost of campaigning [Commissioners were paid $31,000 a year as of 1978].

Incorporation Is Proposed

Early in 1977, the Granger–Hunter Community Council, an ad hoc body composed chiefly of local businessmen and community leaders, requested the University of Utah to conduct an analysis on the feasibility of incorporating the Granger–Hunter area on Salt Lake Valley's west side.

The 34-member Granger–Hunter Community Council, organized as a nonprofit corporation, was drawn from such groups as the Kiwanis, Rotary, Granger Lions, Hunter Lions, Eagles, Veterans of Foreign Wars, and the West Valley Chamber of Commerce, and also included several members at large. Two women were on the council, and members of both leading national political parties. Most of the surnames were those of well-established west-side families. Randy K. Baker was named as the administrator for the council. (He had been a graduate student of the author's from 1975 to 1977, and personal communications were maintained during the incorporation controversy, even though the two were on opposite sides.)

The proposed city would have had approximately nineteen square miles and a population of between 50,000 and 60,000. (Its boundaries are shown in Exhibit 7-1.) The University of Utah analysis was published in May 1977 as the *Granger–Hunter Area Incorporation Study* (Salt Lake City: University of Utah, Bureau of Community

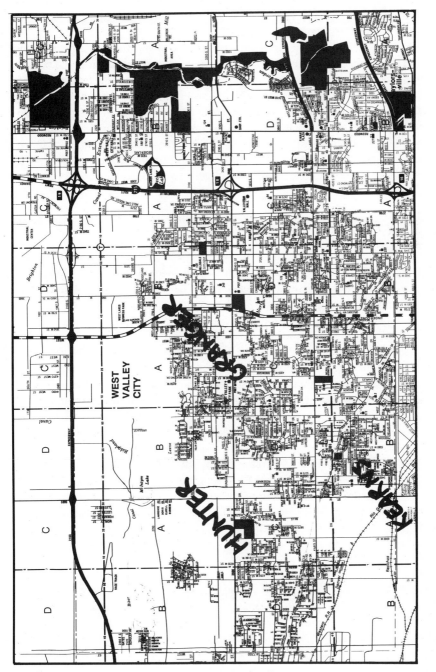

Exhibit 7-1   The Granger–Hunter area. Courtesy of the West Valley Area Chamber of Commerce and © Champion® Map Corporation, Daytona Beach, Florida.

Development, 1977). Its purpose was "to identify the potential advantages and disadvantages of Granger–Hunter incorporation as a city, and exploring [sic] the ramifications of Granger–Hunter remaining a part of the unincorporated area of Salt Lake County." Copies of the *Study* were scarce long before the formal campaign for incorporation began, and supplies were exhausted by early January of 1978.

The *Study* concluded that Granger–Hunter had an adequate tax base and could "afford" to incorporate. Revenue sources were estimated, and several proposed budgets (at different service levels) were presented. The *Study* emphasized repeatedly that the economics of the proposed city depended heavily on a supportive response by Salt Lake County—for instance, if the county negotiated favorable inter-local contracts, the new city would be able to manage comfortably on a modest, additional property tax levy. The *Study* was reported to the Granger–Hunter Community Council, which received it enthusiastically. Plans for incorporation were promptly set in motion by the members of the community council, particularly by a few prominent businessmen.

Incorporation Versus Other Proposals

The Granger–Hunter Incorporation Study was only one of several possible changes in Salt Lake Valley that were in the air at that time. A more fundamental proposal was a so-called wall-to-wall cities plan that the Salt Lake County Council of Governments had begun studying early in 1977. It called for either annexing all unincorporated county land into already existing cities or incorporating new cities. Even more sweeping was a 1977 proposal for which the League of Women Voters of Salt Lake was circulating a petition. It called for a charter for a unified (that is, consolidated) Salt Lake City and County government. Some of the leading citizens outside Granger–Hunter who supported these two reorganization plans were opposed to, or had reservations about, early action on the small, local incorporation or annexation requests that were gathering momentum by late 1977. Granger–Hunter was one of only two incorporation votes permitted by the county commission in the first half of 1978. The other concerned a small local government unit unrelated to Granger–Hunter. Both elections were to take place on the same date, February 7, 1978. This chapter focuses on the Granger–Hunter campaign, but the reader should bear in mind that the overall future of local governments was a subject of study, discussion, and even support-mobilization all over the county while the Granger–Hunter campaign was going on.

Proponents Are Heartened

The drive for incorporation in Granger–Hunter had moved rapidly after the May 1977 *Study* had been released. The *Study* said that the proposed new city could probably operate on a budget of $3.66 million and with an increased mill levy (beyond taxes already being paid to Salt Lake County) of some 10 mills. (A mill is a fractional percent of an assessed valuation of real property.) The findings of the *Study* (but not its hedging and cautionary statements) were widely disseminated throughout the Granger–Hunter area.

As noted, in May the Granger–Hunter Community Council hired Randy Baker as administrator. Baker had been an employee of the University of Utah and had written parts of the *Study*. Baker got the council to file papers as a nonprofit corporation; began research into incorporation procedures; investigated revenue sources (for example, federal grants) to finance the transition period until municipal revenues began to be collected; and started a small public information campaign to boost incorporation. Baker and the council were ebullient when a telephone poll taken in early December 1977 showed that as many as 82 percent of Granger–Hunter residents overwhelmingly favored city status. The polling instrument was constructed mostly by Baker; the sample was selected by him and high school social studies students from the area; and the survey was carried out by the students. One thousand residents were telephoned. The survey showed overwhelming support for incorporation, and the more informed about incorporation residents were, the more they appeared to support it. The results of the poll were widely reported on television, radio, and in the newspapers.

Three things appeared to ensure success to the proponents of incorporation: the nonprofit corporation charter granted to the community council under state law; Baker's energetic and enthusiastic leadership of the incorporation movement; and the overwhelmingly favorable public response suggested by the telephone survey.

After the Salt Lake County Commission scheduled the incorporation election for February 7, 1978, candidates for mayor and council began to file for office. Their campaign literature was circulated throughout the area. Many meetings were held with civic groups and clubs to provide information on the proposed new city. A series of news releases in local suburban papers carried campaign statements by candidates for the new city offices and stories on the new charter. Baker talked openly of the possibility of becoming the first city manager of the new municipality, which would have been Utah's fourth largest city. The mood of proponents during December and early January was euphoric in interviews conducted by the author and in news stories in the *Deseret News* from December 29, 1977, to January 27, 1978.

The Deputy Sheriff's Plan

Almost entirely unknown to proponents of incorporation, however, a political dynamiting campaign against incorporation was formally ratified and underway by January 3, 1978.

In late November 1977, about a dozen representatives of the Salt Lake County Sheriff's Mutual Aid Association and the International Brotherhood of Police Officers, Local 471, invited the author to meet with them in downtown Salt Lake City. At this session, the members informed Timmins that they wanted to retain a consultant to conduct research, draft position papers, and prepare campaign strategies to oppose Granger–Hunter incorporation. These union spokespeople represented approximately 300 Salt Lake County deputy sheriffs. The union had gradually built up a substantial war chest of voluntary donations from union members. Later meetings of the group were attended by representatives of several hundred local members of the International Association of Fire Fighters and some members of the Utah Public Employees' Association.

Salt Lake County personnel records showed that more than 400 county employees lived in the Granger–Hunter area in 1978. A total of perhaps 1,000 state and county employees resided in the area of the proposed incorporation. A conservative estimate was that 1,500 to 2,000 eligible voters in the Granger–Hunter area were either public employees or in the family of a public employee who would be directly affected by incorporation.

The union opposition to incorporation was based on four major premises that had been arrived at by the union leaders after many months of internal debate and study during 1977. The union positions were as follows:

1. Salt Lake County was threatened by a domino effect if Granger–Hunter incorporated; that is, if Granger–Hunter succeeded, then Taylorsville, Bluffdale, Magna, Union, and so forth, would be next. Granger–Hunter's incorporation would "hurt" the county (loss of tax base, etc.), but a domino effect would be catastrophic.

2. Granger–Hunter was a test case. If the county (union members perceived themselves as "the County" in a very real and direct way) did not make a stand in Granger–Hunter, it was the beginning of the end for county government. All that would be left would be a rump county government—no tax base, no services, no employees.

3. County sheriff's officers and fire fighters believed the proposed new city could not possibly match the level or quality of government services being provided at present by the county, especially the levels of law enforcement and fire protection. Union members felt that the county sheriff and fire departments had arrived at a level of professionalism that a new city simply couldn't provide, at least not for years. Union members (especially those who were Granger–Hunter area residents) frequently expressed concern over possible deterioration of services and the dire consequences to taxpayers in the proposed new city.

4. Never openly discussed, and always denied vigorously if anyone raised the issue as the real motive for union opposition, was the premise that substantial numbers of career employees (particularly sheriffs and fire fighters) could lose their jobs if incorporation succeeded. Reality was that thirty to sixty county employees would be superfluous following incorporation. Union members repeatedly denied that loss of jobs was their real motivation. Never stated in the media, but on the minds of union members, was also a concern over loss of long-range promotional and career ladder opportunities if Granger–Hunter incorporated. Normal attrition might accommodate some superfluous personnel. But permanent loss of services and manpower (especially if a domino effect took place) would cripple many careers—a salient argument to union members with ten, twenty, or even thirty years of service, whether in the fire or sheriff's departments.

The spokesman for the union group, holding the rank of captain (and himself a former candidate for elected sheriff), stated to Timmins at the initial meeting that the group representing union members had interviewed a number of university faculty members and area consultants and had invited Timmins to the meeting to offer him a contract, which was eventually negotiated and signed December 2.

The University of Utah, through its Bureau of Community Development, had scheduled a day-long gathering December 15, 1977, to provide a forum for proponents of the various plans for local self-government being proposed for Salt Lake County to present their positions. The unions wanted to take a strong position opposing some of the options. Timmins visited the director of the bureau on December 2 and learned that the bureau would offer one or more groups an opportunity to react to the proponents of the various proposals. Timmins was shortly thereafter advised by the bureau that he would serve as a reactor in the afternoon session of the conference, representing the point of view of the public employee groups. The union members met with Timmins on several dates prior to the December 15 conference to explore positions.

The conference drew a large crowd and excited far more controversy than the organizers had apparently intended. Timmins called for a moratorium on all proposals until a valleywide consensus on new directions could be reached. He called the proposed incorporation premature. The conference was widely reported in the media.

One result of the conference was that Baker and Bill Barton, a candidate for the Granger–Hunter City Council and one of the earlier proponents of incorporation, met with Timmins to ask why the public employees were so hostile to incorporation. After this first meeting with incorporation proponents, Timmins tried for a few days to bring the Granger–Hunter Community Council and the union representatives together. He urged that inter-local contracting be explored and that the community council develop tentative pay schedules and career programs for the new city in consultation with concerned county employees. However, the public employee unions were not at all interested in a reconciliation with proponents of incorporation.

Opposition on Two Fronts

All three county commissioners opposed the Granger–Hunter incorporation. Their opposition was based on a projected "loss" of some 50,000 persons, or 14 percent of the county's estimated 1978 population. Further, over $84 million of assessed property valuation (or tax base) would be lost to the county along with over $1.6 million in sales tax revenue. The $84 million figure was unreasonably low. The Utah State Tax Commission and Salt Lake County Assessor finished a reappraisal in 1978 of all Salt Lake County properties. County properties were being assessed at about 12 percent of real or fair market values prior to the reappraisal. State law required appraisal at 20 percent of the fair market value. The author estimates that the real value of properties in the Granger–Hunter area in 1978 was thus closer to $1 billion and that this figure may also be too low.[1] These losses would be significant enough to cripple Salt Lake County's financial base.

In addition to the commissioners, virtually all Salt Lake County elected officials and department heads were opposed to incorporation. In private sessions most of them were vigorous, outspoken opponents of Granger–Hunter incorporation. In public, most of them—especially the commissioners—took a neutral or moderate position. This waffling both baffled and irritated the sheriffs and fire fighters.

Timmins repeatedly cautioned the public employee representatives that, although nearly all county officials were against Granger–Hunter incorporation, few of them could be counted on in the clinch. Nineteen seventy-eight was an election year and most incumbent county officials would soon become candidates. They would probably hesitate to arouse 14 percent or more of their constituents by appearing too strongly on one side or the other of the incorporation issue. Timmins also warned the unions that the county leadership would not put up money or furnish manpower for the anti-incorporation effort: "All of them will be glad to see you spend your money and mobilize your troops, but you'll be on your own. If you defeat incorporation, everyone in the county leadership will be glad, but there will be no tangible rewards. If incorporation succeeds, it'll be the fault of the unions for not using the right strategy. If there's bad press, the unions will take it in the neck, alone."

For these reasons the county employee unions decided to keep their strategy confidential from the majority of elected officials and to keep their own counsel. Commissioner Pete Kutulus met in a closed-door session with the union leaders on January 3, 1978, and agreed with Timmins's political dynamiting strategy that was outlined at the meeting. Sheriff Delmar L. (Swede) Larson and Fire Chief Charles (Chick) Paris also reviewed the proposed strategy and were fully aware of what was being planned. Their political expertise was drawn on to critique the campaign strategy and to identify potential weaknesses or suggest alternative techniques or ideas. With these three exceptions, the other elected county officials and department heads knew only a few details of the political dynamiting campaign being launched.

The strategy adopted was relatively simple. It called for four task forces (A, B, C, D) to be organized by January 16, 1978. Most were operational within a few days of that date. Each task force was given a set of specific objectives and a series of suspense dates and was organized with several co-chairmen and committee members. Almost everyone on the committee was either a deputy sheriff or a fire fighter. All four task forces were directed by a coordinating committee.

To coordinate such efforts, the county deputy sheriff's leaders (not union officials in this case, but men closely aligned with them) scheduled a private meeting for January 18. About fifty county supervisors and managers were invited. A roll call showed that almost all county departments were represented, many by department heads. Several elected officials attended. At this meeting Timmins explained the plans for defeating incorporation. He used the blackboard to demonstrate relevant property tax computations. Many questions were answered. The group disbanded with an awareness of the need for cooperation. At least two county employees who lived in Granger (not sheriffs or fire fighters) met with Timmins after the meeting. Each doubted that incorporation could be stopped, and neither cooperated in the subsequent union opposition campaign.

All public employees were instructed to carry out campaign assignments on their own time, out of uniform, and without using county vehicles or equipment. With two or three exceptions, this stricture was apparently followed. Several sheriffs took annual leave for several days to carry out assignments. Late in the campaign, however, one female deputy was reported by a citizen for using her patrol car to distribute flyers door-to-door as she was going off shift. The sheriff suspended her at once for several days without pay. The story appeared briefly on one or two television news broadcasts but never received much attention. At least one complaint was received about a sheriff using his office telephone for calls related to the campaign. Nevertheless, the coordinating committee appeared to take great care in instructing union members and in monitoring the distribution of literature. The campaign was low profile in most instances—although many residents knew their neighborhood sheriff or fire fighter even out of uniform.

Legal Opinion on Union Activity

Timmins had anticipated challenges to the "right" of public employees to oppose incorporation or to be involved in such a campaign effort. (At the December 15 University of Utah conference, the issue of public employee rights had come up three times in the question-and-answer period.) To resolve the question before it could become a serious campaign issue, the author requested an opinion from the Salt Lake county attorney, R. Paul Van Dam, on December 29, 1977. An informal response was received on January 17, 1978 which read, in part,

> I have briefly researched the law concerning political activity by government employees and find that in almost all cases, courts uphold laws which restrict partisan political activities by governmental employees. But I have found nothing which restricts governmental employees from engaging in non-partisan or at least non-candidate oriented political type activities in which I believe you and the individuals you represent are engaged. Therefore, even though the section discussed relating to deputy sheriffs [U.C.A. 17-30-22] is extremely restrictive, I believe the Court would not prohibit individual deputies from exercising their right to determine what form of government should prevail in Salt Lake County.
>
> Another issue which comes to my mind from your letter, is whether or not a union or organization can formally engage in the activity which you describe. This issue relates to labor law and while I am not an expert in the field, I am aware of prohibitions against contributing by labor organizations to particular political candidates unless such monies are raised as "free" money as distinguished from "dues" money. I am further aware that dues money of such organizations is often used for efforts to increase voter participation and education of people with the purpose of getting them to the poles [sic] but that such activity is related only to get out the vote efforts and not to support one individual candidate and/or political philosophy or another.

Timmins furnished copies of the county attorney's letter to the public employee union leadership and to the Salt Lake County commission. The issue never became important during the campaign except for one or two references to rights of unions in a few of the later public debates. When incorporation proponents did raise the issue, the strategy was to hold up the county attorney's letter and quote an appropriate line or two and then just drop the issue.

The Opponents Take a Poll

Between the publication of Baker's poll results on December 29, 1977, and January 3, 1978, Timmins interviewed in person or by telephone several dozen county officials, community leaders, church officials, and selected residents in the Granger–Hunter area. He felt he then had a pretty clear picture of the neighborhood and its major concerns. However, he thought a systematic sampling of public opinion would be helpful. Experienced survey personnel were hired, an instrument was prepared, and a survey sample was carefully drawn.

The survey, taken January 3 through 10, was based on interviews with over 300 area residents. Surprisingly, nearly 65 percent of those interviewed opposed incorporation. Fifty-eight percent of those interviewed ranked their concerns or worries in the order listed in the survey instrument: (1) What would the new city really cost residents in taxes? (2) What would happen to levels (or quality) of city services? (3) What would happen to the schools? These three concerns became the key themes in the union's campaign.

The poll also showed strong antagonism in the Hunter neighborhoods to being aligned with Granger. Consequently, campaign literature was especially earmarked for the Hunter (or western) portions of the area. Analysis of the proposed municipal boundaries also showed that one stake (or diocese) of the Church of Jesus Christ of Latter-day Saints (Mormons) lapped over into the central and southern end of the proposed city boundaries. Latter-day Saint statistics showed 60 percent or more of the area was Latter-day Saint in religious affiliation. The poll showed that a majority of residents in the Kearns stake felt closer to Kearns (a neighborhood to the south with strong Kearns High School identification) than to Granger. The opponents' subsequent mailings and door-to-door distribution the week before the election emphasized the separate interests of the southern area and the western, or Hunter, area of the proposed new city. The results of the poll guided the opponents' efforts at persuasion but were not made public.

The Early Stages

During the week of January 7, either Timmins or the consultants with whom he had subcontracted met with tax and revenue specialists, school administrators, fire and police personnel, and county department heads; their aim was to put together an exhaustive position paper. Timmins completed the campaign issues materials on the sixteenth and briefed the full coordinating committee on the seventeenth. By the twentieth materials were being printed, and by January 29 nearly twenty thousand brochures and other pieces of literature were being mailed or distributed door-to-door by off-duty union members.

No front groups were actually organized by the unions, but all campaign literature was printed either without any source name or bore the signature "Granger–Hunter Taxpayers Opposed to Incorporation" or "Citizens Against Incorporation," names suggested by Timmins. However, in a full-page ad placed by one of the union task forces ("VOTE NO" was in 2½-inch high block letters) that appeared twice in at least four suburban weekly newspapers, the copy mistakenly carried the line, "Phone 535-7495." This was the office telephone number for a sheriff's department captain who was coordinating the union campaign. Incorporation proponents never seized upon the gaffe, however, and this use of a government office phone number never became the subject of a critical newspaper editorial or television news story.

The union mailings and ads were aimed at the issues identified in the January 3 poll. At Timmins's suggestion the concern about the quality of the candidates running for mayor and council of the proposed new city was ignored. Thus radio spots, advertisements, and flyers stressed the cost of municipal services, the loss of service levels, and the fear of financing a new school district—but not the qualifications of candidates running for proposed offices. In public debates during the last week of the campaign, however, opponents belittled the candidates' qualifications in every speech. In each instance proponents took the bait and outlined the candidates' qualifications in great detail. Audiences were rarely impressed.

The first public *debate* on January 20 (all other public meetings before that date had presented only the side favoring incorporation) was attended by over 100 residents. Timmins was criticized by one incorporation proponent as ". . . a highly paid front-man who doesn't even live in this area." Timmins admitted he was being paid a high fee, that he didn't live in the area, and that he had been hired to carry out research and analyze data. Randy Baker, administrator for the community council, was similarly challenged by an incorporation opponent. He admitted that he too did not live in the area and that he had been promised a job if the proposed city incorporated.

By the end of this first debate the deputy sheriffs and fire fighters present had lined up several key allies who were to prove valuable in the next seventeen days. One Hunter resident who attended the meeting organized a 35-member neighborhood opposition group, held a press conference, printed a flyer (using the union data) and circulated at least 5,000 copies of it in the Hunter neighborhoods—all before February 7. One woman in the audience was the editor of two key weekly suburban newspapers that subsequently took strong editorial stands against incorporation.

The Role of an Expert Speaker: Dr. Smith

Also attending this first debate was Dr. Paul M. Smith, a consultant employed by the union group. Smith had served as superintendent of several large school districts in California in the 1960s before he retired and became head of a consulting firm in Murray, Utah. Smith was a gifted speaker as well as an experienced public administrator and tax expert. He served as speaker for the union at eleven subsequent public meetings and on seven radio and television programs, the broadcasts being part of the opposition's media blitz during the last ten days of the campaign.

An experienced public debater, Smith recalled later that he found it "easy to force proponents to debate my choice of issues. . . . Each night I'd pick a new issue (for example, the prospective cost of a new school system), and the proponents would have come prepared for the previous night's debate issues. This kept them on the run. I used standard debate tactics, but the proponents were never well prepared on the issues. . . . I felt the audiences tipping more and more my way, night after night." On the other hand, *The Deseret News* of January 26 reported of one debate attended by about 500 people, "Crowd reactions to speakers . . . seemed to indicate a fairly even split between those who want incorporation and those who would rather stay with the county."

Surprise Media Campaign Stresses Taxes

Baker and the candidates for the proposed city council were truly surprised by the dynamiting literature distribution, radio spots, and newspaper advertisements and seemed unaware of the opposition's strength until the first full-page ads appeared on January 26. After the election, Baker told Timmins he was shocked by Timmins's estimate that the unions had spent $15,000 to $20,000 on media. Baker's side had provided him with relatively little money for media advertising to promote the cause of incorporation.

The unions' flyers, radio spots, and ads hit hard on three of the "worry" issues revealed in the poll. For example, a full-page ad (paid for by Citizens Against Incorporation) that appeared in each of the two area dailies, the *Salt Lake Tribune* (morning) and *The Deseret News* (evening) for Monday, February 6, concluded with the following summary:

Three Simple Facts

Your taxes will go up. It is not possible for the new city proposed budget to cover and accomplish even a third of what proponents say it will. Your property taxes will go up just to maintain the present level of services you are already receiving from your Salt Lake County government.

The quality of service will go down. It isn't possible for the proposed city to provide the quality of service you now enjoy as a resident of Salt Lake County.

Your representation will be reduced. Residents of Granger–Hunter-Draper will be trading eleven elected officials for six elected officials plus appointees. Further, creating the new city won't do away with Salt Lake County Government. It will just add one more layer of government and one more tax load on residents who are already over-burdened. Ask yourself if you can really afford such a "representative government."

The top of the ad was taken up by highly condensed statements such as one predicting an estimated $200 property tax increase on an average Granger–Hunter home if incorporation succeeded.

Radio spots were frequent beginning on February 1 and peaked the Monday before the election. These spot advertisements hammered mostly on the tax increase theme and quoted the $200 figure. The radio ads appeared mostly on several key western music or rock music stations in the valley and ran as many as sixteen to eighteen times a day.

One prominent local radio station received complaints from Granger–Hunter businessmen objecting to the union ads. It broadcast an editorial on February 3, condemning the unions for circulating information "that is not entirely correct." The editorial especially criticized as a half-truth the opposition's prediction that incorporation would bring sizable property tax increases. Union members and their families deluged the radio station with irate telephone calls and visits. The reaction by union members was sufficient to get the station's management to run a lengthy rebuttal (prepared by the unions) to its editorial several times on February 6, the day before the election, even though the station management was unpersuaded by the union tax data. The union rebuttal sought to show "why property taxes could go up as much as $200 a year on a typical $40,000 home in Granger–Hunter." The $200 figure was a key element of the dynamiting strategy and was repeated so often in radio spots and campaign literature that during the last days before the vote some newspaper editorials accepted it as an established fact.

Typical homes in Granger–Hunter were then worth about $40,000. Proponents of incorporation had originally stated that the new city could operate on only 10 mills of property tax (plus other tax revenues, of course). The 10 mills was roughly equivalent to the tax burden imposed by Salt Lake County for a few selected services only. The 10-mill figure was adjusted upward almost every day during the last week of the campaign as proponents tried to respond to union opposition charges that the new city would "really need a 35-mill levy to raise adequate revenue for a city of 50,000."

This potential 35-mill property tax increase used by the opposition (based on a $40,000 home appraised at 20 percent of market value) would amount to about $200 more in annual property taxes—an increase above that being proposed by incorporation proponents. The simplistic $200 figure was repeated and repeated in all the opposition literature and advertising. It was a difficult statistic for proponents of incorporation to refute, since anyone with basic arithmetic skills could compute the dollar amount (even without understanding how mill levies were set, what sinking funds were, etc). Compared to the complex budget data of proponents and the complicated mill levies and service fees of the county's budget, the $200 figure seemed easy to grasp.

The opposition was aided by a last-minute statement about tax increases that came from an independent and unexpected source. On February 1 the Utah Taxpayers Association released a statement saying, "If residents of the Granger–Hunter area vote to incorporate, they can expect a significant increase in taxes." The statement used figures that differed significantly from the budget and estimated tax figures of incorporation proponents. The association's release received widespread television and radio coverage and was quoted at length in the two dailies. The Taxpayers Association had publicly endorsed county–city consolidation but had not previously taken a position on proposed incorporations.

The Granger–Hunter Community Council's response to the union's media campaign seemed too late and too modest to counter the impact. Advertisements rebutting the unions' stand on costs first appeared on February 2, five days before the election, and then only in one or two suburban papers. (Most suburban papers were published on Thursdays and hand-delivered over the next day or two.) Perhaps the most telling rebuttal by proponents was an advertisement with a political cartoon showing Granger–Hunter as Red Riding Hood and the union opposition as the Big Bad Wolf in grandmother's clothes. The opposition by public employees was linked in the cartoon with the advocates of major county–city unification (consolidation), urban county, etc. The ad was signed by mayors and officials of several nearby smaller municipalities, all of whom urged a "yes" vote.

The School Issue

The 1977 *Study* by the University of Utah had contained this paragraph:

Potential School District

The Utah code states that all cities of the first and second class are required to have a school district. . . . The Granger–Hunter area potentially qualifies as a second-class city (60,000 to 100,000 population). . . . If the Granger–Hunter area considers incorporation, attention should be given to the school district situation because the area nearly qualifies as a second-class city.

The unions' strategists had planned to make the school district question a key issue during the weekend before election. The idea was to issue at the last minute what Jonas in *Political Dynamiting* had described as the "strategically-timed publication of carefully researched, damaging, difficult-to-answer charges based upon selected excerpts from the truth."

Between January 26 and February 1, Dr. Smith subtly raised the school issue in debates and radio talk shows. He argued that the Granger–Hunter population could already be over 60,000 thus requiring a separate school district. He suggested that residents of the proposed new city might therefore have to finance not only a new city but also a new school system. Proponents countered that the area's population was barely 50,000 and therefore the question of a separate school district was several years off. Further, they argued, state law could easily be amended to eliminate the requirement of a separate school district. Such a bill had just failed passage only because one house of the Utah legislature had gotten bogged down in its last frantic hours. The 1979 legislature would surely pass such a bill, proponents said.

Other public employees had made many calls to radio talk shows on the school issue and had brought up the matter in public meetings. By February 1 it had become such an inflamed issue that a Granite School District board member who lived in the Granger–Hunter area convinced Dr. John Reed Call, superintendent of Granite School District (the state's largest school system), that Call must make a public statement on the issue. Call appeared at a Friday, February 3 meeting—on the very weekend before the election—and delivered an address in which he tried to defuse the whole issue. Call was "angered" when he saw Saturday morning's *Salt Lake Tribune*, which headlined its second section, "Buy Granite District Facilities? Schools Cloud Granger–Hunter Plan." (Call told Timmins later that the *Tribune* distorted the whole thrust of his statement. A reading of his prepared address seems to bear out his criticism. However, it should be noted that the reporter who covered Call's speech had spent three hours before the meeting getting a briefing from Dr. Smith. Smith met with the reporter again immediately after Call's speech. Some leaders of the Granger–Hunter group felt the *Tribune*'s story had been biased and that the daily had "gone out of its way to knife the incorporation from the beginning." The *Tribune* had earlier editorially endorsed county–city consolidation and unification, but it never took an editorial position on the Granger–Hunter incorporation.) As reported, Call's remarks were portrayed as raising the specter of a new Granger–Hunter school district having to "impose a 28-mill tax levy" to "pay off the city's prorated share of [Granite] district's $56 million bonded indebtedness" besides buying school buildings, etc.

Timmins and Smith learned only on February 2 that Superintendent Call would appear at the meeting on Friday, February 3. Knowing basically what he would have to say, the two consultants scurried for two days to get population data to support the dynamiting campaign. Smith picked up the latest population counts from the Salt Lake County Planning Department, the county auditor, and the post office well after 6 P.M. on the evening of Call's address. The *Tribune* story on Saturday added that Dr. Smith and Henry H. Price, a candidate for mayor and spokesman for the incorporation proponents in the debate, "Both agreed no one knows now how many people live in the area. Estimates range from 53,000 to more than 61,000, depending on who is making the estimate. Dr. Smith said he received a report from the U.S. Postal

Service [that very day] indicating there could be 61,000 residents of the area." Smith waved this ostensibly official postal service document in front of the audience and said 61,000 residents should begin to worry about paying for a school system. Smith appeared on all major television channels that evening and again waved this piece of paper. The U.S. Postal Service report was only an unofficial estimate by a postal employee and was handwritten on a plain piece of paper. Smith never showed it to anyone; he just waved it around.

Last-Minute Confusion over the Issue of Public Employee Activism

Complaints about political activism by government employees were not very noticeable in the early days of the campaign. As noted before, County Attorney Paul Van Dam's December 29, 1977, letter to Timmins had been secured to neutralize this issue, should it arise. Van Dam's letter had included a warning, however, that civil service laws applying to deputy sheriffs were much more severe than those that applied to other public employees. "The law," he wrote, "is extremely restrictive in allowing political activities by deputy sheriffs." Earlier sections of this chapter have described occasional activities (such as the use of a public agency telephone number or the preparation and distribution of materials) that might have furnished occasions for proponents of incorporation to make a point of the extent of political activism by public employees. For example, a team of union members (deputy sheriffs and fire fighters) as well as members of the Utah Public Employees' Association met during the weekend of January 21 and designed a brochure. More than 10,000 copies were printed, and some were distributed door-to-door.

During the last two weeks of the campaign a mimeographed flyer (undated and with no reference to authorship) was circulated among county fire fighters. "If Granger–Hunter incorporates," it read, "it will be necessary to initiate the following reduction in force: . . . " It then listed reductions of forty-four fire fighter positions and six officer demotions that would have to be effected in the two county fire stations serving the Granger–Hunter area. "In addition," the flyer concluded, "we will not construct additional fire stations [at two locations in the area]. These two stations would have required thirty-six additional fire fighters, two captains, and four lieutenants." Timmins knew that the flyer had been issued by the Salt Lake County fire chief, Charles Paris. Union fire fighters never made public reference to this matter, and proponents of the Granger–Hunter incorporation raised no public complaints about the propriety of the flyer.

As the week of the election neared, the issue of political activism by public employee unions was raised by Granger–Hunter proponents; rather general complaints were aired along with the argument that it was not proper for unions to become involved in local politics. This offended some residents who belonged to AFL-CIO organizations. The proponents of incorporation had not made a key distinction: The main activism in opposition to incorporation was coming from public employee unions affiliated with *independent* unions and employee associations. The day before the election, the Granger–Hunter Community Council offered its apologies to AFL-CIO unions for what it called a "serious misunderstanding." It added, "We encourage all union members in the community to stay involved, vote . . . and remain active in community affairs."

Post-Mortems on the Election

Several thousand flyers and brochures arguing against incorporation were delivered by mail the Saturday and Monday before the Tuesday election. Approximately sixty radio spots with the same themes were aired during the last three days. At least 5,000 flyers were hand distributed during the last weekend. Full-page ads appeared Thursday and Monday in the dailies and some weeklies.

In the election on February 7, "47 percent of the registered voters turned out to reject incorporation by a 6-to-5 margin," the *Deseret News* reported the next day, noting that "10 to 20 percent is more normal for a special election." Union officials and members celebrated election night returns at a downtown Salt Lake City hotel. Dr. Smith was visible on all the late evening television broadcasts made from the county clerk's office. The morning newspaper said Randy Baker bitterly "criticized the role police and fire fighter unions had played in the campaign." "Unions," he was quoted as saying, "became improper power groups."

In interviews conducted after the election by the author's graduate assistant, some of the candidates for office in Granger–Hunter made similar comments: "We were blitzed." "The union members did us in." "We never anticipated such an organized campaign." "The public employees sandbagged us at the last minute."

Between February 10 and February 20, Timmins surveyed a random sample of over 300 Granger–Hunter residents. One question asked, 'When do you think you (or your neighbors) really made up your minds to vote against incorporation?" Seventy-one percent of the respondents answered, "During the last week."

Another question asked why the respondent or his or her neighbors had voted against incorporation. The responses were

1. Fear of a possible $200 property tax increase: 77%;
2. Object to being joined with Granger: 71% of Hunter residents in sample. Object to being joined with Hunter: 32% of Granger residents in sample;
3. Dislike of the quality of the various candidate(s) running for mayor or council: 69%;
4. Fear of possibly having to pay for a whole new school district in Granger–Hunter: 66%;
5. Fear of a possible loss of quality police and fire protection: 57%; and
6. Fear that we were moving too fast on becoming a city—issue needed more study: 55%.

Timmins, looking back over the campaign, drew two broad conclusions. First, the power and effectiveness of the public employee unions in collusion with county government (especially the elected officials) was impressive, even awesome. The unions far outspent the proponents of incorporation. They were able to muster scores and scores of union members for campaign work, more or less on a volunteer basis. Political finesse and organizational commitment were also impressive. John Rohr wrote in *Ethics for Bureaucrats: An Essay on Law and Values* (New York: Marcel

Dekker, 1978) that public officials are responsible under oath to uphold democratic values—behavior sadly lacking in the county officials described in this chapter.

Second, the campaign seemed to show that Frank Jonas was right. It is difficult for opponents to respond effectively to a political dynamiting campaign. Such an effort is not the kind of "smear" or "lie" or "political defamation" that can be referred to the press, or to a fair campaign practices committee for investigation, arbitration, or rebuttal. The dynamiting campaign is thoroughly researched; and it is deliberately timed to explode during the last few days before the election. To have any hope of effective defense or refutation, opponents would have to have research data, ads, speakers, and flyers ready for instant response.

Baker, looking back from the proponents' side, disagreed with Timmins about the value of the preelection opinion survey and the strategy of framing opposition publicity and arguments in terms of what that survey showed the residents were concerned about: "It was not the issues but the half-truths, not your [Timmins's] strategy but your fear tactics that defeated incorporation." Baker also argued that "the media (especially the big newspapers) conspired with advocates of big [county] government and public worker unions to defeat home rule."

Baker was not the only one critical of the news media. Two weeks after the election, the mayor of Alta criticized "sloppy news reporting" and said that news organizations should "check the accuracy of handouts and statements made at public meetings before they are reported."

Assignments

1. As a class, or in teams, discuss the case and the essentials of a free election. How can political dynamiting be prevented? Can it? What would have been fairer in this campaign? Review the ethics of the various participants and groups. What lessons can be learned? What suggestions would you have for the proponents of home rule the next time?

2. Design a set of recommendations to the state legislature (of your state) for a state fair campaign practices law; if there is already such an existing statute, how best modify it? What steps can best assure ethical behavior, especially in local elections like the one described in this chapter?

Notes

1. See "Property Assessment Levels in Utah—1977," *Utah Foundation Research Briefs* 78-3 (30 January 1978): 1–2.

CHAPTER 8

Political Smear Campaigns

"Smear!" the Senatorial candidate charged. In a hotly contested U.S. Senate race, one candidate had issued campaign literature that hit his opponent pretty hard—not so much with "untruths" as with "half-truths," delicately and deliberately timed to have maximum impact. The candidate making the charge was E. J. (Jake) Garn, who, years later, would become the first (and thus far the only) U.S. senator to fly into space with one of the space shuttle teams. How best can such campaign tactics be handled? How best to change such unfair campaign tactics? One method has been arbitration through the joint efforts of the National Fair Campaign Practices Committee and the American Arbitration Association (AAA). The following case, almost unique in the literature, describes such use of arbitration and shows the strengths and weaknesses of the process. But even more important, perhaps, it raises a number of troubling ethical questions.

The Original Dispute

On October 14, 1974, E. J. (Jake) Garn, mayor of Salt Lake City, filed a charge with the Fair Campaign Practices Committee in Washington, D.C., against Wayne Owens, charging a violation of the fourth article of the Code of Fair Campaign Practices.[1]

Garn, Republican candidate for United States senator from Utah wrote, "I request arbitration under your code and will abide by the findings of your arbitration."[2] Owens, then a United States congressman and Democratic candidate for the Senate, responded on October 21, saying in part, "I request that the Garn complaint be dismissed and that my complaint be submitted to arbitration as soon as possible."[3] Owens also sent copies of his letter and complaint to Common Cause and the League of Women Voters.

This chapter analyzes the arbitration process used in the Garn–Owens dispute and attempts to document the ethical strengths and weaknesses of arbitration as a means of resolving disputes arising during political campaigns.

The requests of Garn and Owens for arbitration on the charges of unfair campaign practices received prominent television, radio, and newspaper coverage in Utah, a state noted for the intensity of its political campaigns.[4] The filing of Garn's complaint with the Fair Campaign Practices Committee soon involved the American Arbitration Association.[5] The procedure for arbitrating campaign disputes has been spelled out as follows:

When a dispute is referred [to the Fair Campaign Practices Committee and thence to the American Arbitration Association] the AAA will arrange for arbitration proceedings in the locality where the dispute arises. Arbitrators will be selected from the 23,000 men and women who serve on the AAA's National Panel. Panel members are highly respected members of their communities, who have a reputation for impartiality and a knowledge of the arbitration process. Arbitrators will have no personal interest in the election of any candidate involved in a dispute over violation of the Code of Fair Campaign Practices. The panel of arbitrators in each particular case will be selected by mutual choice of the candidates from lists submitted to them by the AAA. Once designed, the arbitrators will hear both sides, will decide the issue, and will make a finding, which will be publicized so that the final decision can be made by the voters whose exercise of their franchise is the life blood of our democratic society.[6]

On October 31 and November 1, 1974, the radio and television stations and newspapers in Utah carried the story of the appointment of "a three-man panel of arbitrators . . . in connection with cross complaints of distorted campaign material allegedly used in the U.S. Senate campaign of Representative Wayne Owens and Mayor Jake Garn."[7]

The San Francisco office of the AAA received the Garn letter of complaint on October 24. The following is from a memorandum from Michael F. Hoellering of the AAA to Robert Coulson, president of AAA, dated November 8, 1974:

That same day a list of five arbitrators from Salt Lake City were given to the parties and because of the Monday of October 28 being a holiday, the parties were given till 12 noon, Tuesday, October 29, to respond to the lists. Owens rejected the entire panel requesting that the board be composed of arbitrators outside of the state of Utah. Owens also agreed to pay one-half of the cost of travel expenses of an outside board of arbitrators but, since Garn refused to make any such contribution, the AAA determined that Salt Lake City arbitrators would be utilized. The appointments were made on the afternoon of October 29 and consisted of Reese Anderson, Esq., Chairman, Leonard Russon, Esq., and Professor A. J. Wann, of the Political Science Department of the University of Utah.

Notice of hearing for 2 P.M. on Thursday, October 31, was also given to the parties.

Late on October 29, Professor Wann informed the AAA that he was unable to serve due to serious illness. The next morning professor William Timmins was designated in his place.

The *Deseret News* reported on October 31 that Owens rejected the initial list of five names "because its members were involved in local partisan politics, according to Owens campaign official Peter Billings."[8]

The author's first involvement came by a long-distance telephone call on Tuesday, October 29, from AAA's San Francisco office. In that conversation he was informed of the procedural dilemma that had arisen over Owens's rejection of the list of five arbitrators and the last-minute illness and withdrawal of Dr. Wann. During that telephone call the AAA staff member reviewed the author's AAA data card and discussed whether the author could be neutral and objective as a member of the tribunal. The author noted that he was treasurer of the Salt Lake County Republican

Central Committee[9] and a well-known partisan—indeed, he went so far as to discuss fund-raising efforts then going on in the campaign at county level. AAA noted the problems they were having in finding local (i.e., Utah) arbitrators. He was told that the AAA would check further and advise him if he were acceptable as a member of the tribunal. The next morning, October 30, the author was advised by a telephone call from an AAA staff member in San Francisco that he was being designated as a member of the arbitration panel in place of Dr. Wann.[10] The names of the tribunal were released to the press on October 31.[11]

The other two members of the tribunal were both attorneys. All three were from Salt Lake City. All were reasonably well known in their community. All had some experience in hearing procedures and arbitration. The three arbitrators did not know one another well; they had only a superficial professional acquaintance.

Hoellering's November 8 memorandum continued

> On October 31, Owens filed a document with additional complaints against Garn requesting that the arbitrators be provided with a copy. Counsel for Garn objected to these as untimely and improperly filed.
>
> At an executive session with the board of arbitrators it was determined that the additional complaints would not be received until the parties were heard on this issue, and also that the hearings would be closed.
>
> The hearing commenced at 2 P.M. on October 31, and, after extensive argument the arbitrators reserved decision on the acceptability of the additional complaints. Counsel for Owens requested an adjournment till 4 P.M. on Friday, November 1, because of a necessary trip to Seattle, Washington, and the hearing was adjourned till that time. At the close of the hearings arbitrator Timmins for the first time disclosed (to the two parties) that he was the treasurer of the Salt Lake County Republican Central Committee and it was determined that it was appropriate for him to withdraw. Since the supply of available arbitrators in Utah at this time was exhausted, William Hammond, a member of the panel in Portland, Oregon, was substituted in place of Professor Timmins.
>
> The hearing recommenced at 5 P.M. on November 1. During the brief session on October 31, counsel for Owens accused arbitrator L. Russon of being a die-hard Republican, and Mr. Russon now demanded a stipulation from the parties to accept the findings of the arbitrators, and if they did not like same that they would not smear him in the press because he was a registered Republican. Counsel refused to so stipulate, Mr. Russon declared himself no longer impartial and withdrew as arbitrator from the case.
>
> After these developments were explored by the parties they agreed at 8:30 P.M. that they wished to continue with a three-man board, that Mr. Russon should be replaced by a registered Independent from outside the state of Utah, and that hearings would recommence at 1 P.M. on Saturday, November 2, and would continue until completed.
>
> That evening Leo Lightner, a registered Independent and a labor arbitrator in California, was disignated to complete the board.
>
> On November 2, at 12 noon, the newly constituted board of arbitrators met and Reese Anderson agreed to remove himself and substitute Mr. Lightner as chairman of the panel.

Subsequently, both Garn and Owens "agreed to bury the hatchet" the Sunday preceding the Tuesday election. They issued a joint statement dissolving the arbitration panel, "in view of the difficulty in obtaining an acceptable arbitration panel . . ." and left the determination of the issues "to the voting public."[12] Garn won the election by a large margin on Tuesday.

The hearing sessions were closed, as noted above, but received extensive television and newspaper coverage.[13] In self-justification, the author wishes to comment that he assumed both Garn and Owens were well aware of his background and community activity. Certainly the AAA knew. It was only later, after the fact, that the author learned the details surrounding Owens's earlier rejection of the AAA's list of arbitrators and that the San Francisco office of AAA *had itself selected or reconstituted the tribunal.* Of course, this practice is in full harmony with the published *Fair Campaign Practices Arbitration Rules.*

The *Rules* read as follows:

9. *Appointment from Panel*—Immediately after the filing of the request for arbitration and the answer, the AAA shall submit simultaneously to each candidate an identical list of names of persons chosen from its National Panel of Arbitrators. Each candidate shall have 24 hours from the time of receipt of the list in which to cross off any names to which he objects, number remaining names indicating the order of his preference, and return the list to the AAA. If a party does not return the list within the time specified, all persons named therein shall be deemed acceptable. From among the persons who have been approved on both lists, and in accordance with the designated order of mutual preference, the AAA shall invite the acceptance of three arbitrators to serve and shall designate one of them as Chairman. If the candidates fail to agree upon three of the persons named or if those named decline or are unable to act or if for any other reason the appointment cannot be made from the submitted lists, the Administrator shall have the power to make the appointments from other members of the Panel without the submission of any additional lists.

10. *Vacancies*—If any Arbitrator should resign, die, withdraw, refuse or be unable or disqualified to perform the duties of his office, the AAA shall on proof satisfactory to it, declare the office vacant and shall appoint a substitute from the Panel.

11. *Qualifications of Arbitrator*—No person shall serve as an Arbitrator in any arbitration in which he has any financial or personal interest in the election of either candidate unless the candidates, in writing, waive such disqualification.

12. *Disclosure by Arbitrator of Disqualification*—Prior to accepting his appointment, each Arbitrator shall disclose any circumstances likely to create a presumption of bias or which he believes might disqualify him as an impartial Arbitrator. Upon receipt of such information, the AAA shall immediately disclose it to the candidates. If either candidate declines to waive the presumptive disqualification, the vacancy thus created shall be filled in accordance with the applicable provisions of these Rules.[14]

Long after the close of the 1974 elections, the Fair Campaign Practices Committee issued its 10th biennial report, *Now More Than Ever* . . .[15] The report noted that "Three 1974 complaints went to arbitration, pursuant to the 1968 agreement between FCPC and the American Arbitration Association. All three arbitrations were begun in the two weeks before Election Day."[16] It may be of interest to quote from the report the results of the three cases of fair campaign practices arbitration in 1974:

One (in a New York congressional race) went to a conclusion. The arbitrators heard charges by the original complainant, and denials and countercharges by the respondent, sitting from 11 A.M. to 3:30 P.M. on the Sunday before election. At 7:20 P.M. they and the respective candidates released their determination to the news media. The arbitrators had found true some allegations, and untrue others, by both parties. The original complainant won the election.

The second case, in an Illinois congressional contest, occupied the better part of the weekend before election (starting with a three-hour pre-hearing conference on Friday). The hearing itself began at 10:40 Saturday morning, and by mutual consent, was open to public and press, and televised. The hearing continued until 3:15 A.M. Sunday, recessed until 4:45 A.M. and then went on until 1:45 P.M., when the panel returned to prepare a decision. Three-quarters of an hour later, counsel for both candidates delivered a signed joint motion to withdraw the matter from arbitration. After discussion, the arbitrators accepted the motion and released it to the press.

In the third case—a senatorial race in Utah—the procedure was complicated by one party's demand for out-of-state arbitrators, a possible conflict of interest and consequent substitution of an arbitrator, a challenge to another, and the sudden illness of a third. The hearing, finally begun October 31, went on with recesses until 11:30 A.M., November 3, when the parties submitted a settlement document which the arbitrators accepted and released to the news media.

The Arbitration Process Examined

The author has since interviewed many of the participants in the Garn–Owens dispute. His conclusions are that some changes need to be made in the arbitration process used to resolve fair campaign practices disputes. The balance of this chapter will address these recommendations by means of comments made by participants and the author's own reflections.

Now-Senator E. J. Garn wrote on August 28, 1975,

I believe that a finding by the arbitration committee that Wayne's campaign did, in fact, distort and misrepresent my record, as we alleged, would have certainly had an impact on the margin of victory, making it a much wider margin. I feel that there were a good number of people, in any event, who saw the evidence of the misrepresentations and were influenced to support my candidacy even in the absence of a formal finding by the arbitration panel.

It certainly appeared that Wayne attempted to cloud the real issues of the arbitration proceedings through his complaints about the selection of the panel members. He seemed to be laying groundwork for future criticism of the outcome of the arbitration as biased, if the decision went "against" him. I suppose maybe that's good contingency planning, but I don't think that it contributed to a calm, objective atmosphere in which the arbitration panel could work.

I think it was unfortunate that the people of Utah, who were subjected to the claims and counterclaims of those last few weeks of the campaign, were unable to hear the results of a fair and objective assessment. I am afraid that too many people simply chalked the whole thing up to "politics as usual" and, as a result, were more deeply entrenched in their cynicism of the political system.

With regard to the improvement of the arbitration process, the main point that comes to mind is the need to have the panel composed entirely of individuals from outside the "political community." Political activists are bound to have their associations, preconceptions and prejudices, which will inevitably make them unacceptable to one candidate or another. I'm sure that competent people could be found who could serve as members of an arbitration panel who did not have a long history of partisan political activity, but represented the community values in a larger sense; someone with the perspective of the general public. One further improvement would be to increase the speed with which an arbitration proceeding could be started and a "moratorium" placed on public comment until the matter is solved. In general, I view arbitration as a valid procedure in the resolution of unfair campaign practices disputes, if the preconditions that I've mentioned above can be met. In addition, the timing of the arbitration seems to have a significant impact on its potential effectiveness. As in our case, there was no possibility of reaching a settlement in time to give either candidate an opportunity to respond to the report of the panel. In addition, public comment and speculation was running high. These facts weighted heavily on the decision to suspend the arbitration.[17]

In rebuttal to Garn's views on the possible significance of the outcome of the election, John H. Klas, chairman of the Utah State Democratic Committee, wrote: "[I]t is my belief that the hearing or its by-products had no significant influence on the outcome of the senatorial race."

Klas added,

I have observed that these arbitration procedures and hearings on violations of the National Fair Campaign Practices Committee usually are pretty messy and inconclusive, at best. I would believe that this is the responsibility of both parties to work toward the adoption of some sort of a state fair campaign practices code so as to bring this matter closer to home. I must confess that I feel we have been negligent in the Democratic party in not taking more progressive action in this area.[18]

Kent Shearer, the legal counsel to the Utah State Republican Central Committee, wrote:

I do not believe that the Garn–Owens hearing had an appreciable effect upon the outcome of the election. Owens's attorneys went into the hearing hoping for a draw, through the use of challenges frustrated the hearing, and achieved their objective.

The arbitration would have been more effective had the hearing not been commenced at the "eleventh hour." The Owens's stall would not, then, have been so effective.[19]

Both Klas and Shearer clearly acknowledge that Garn and Owens tried to use the hearing to personal political advantage. That is to be expected, of course, and is certainly not a weakness of the process followed or of arbitration, per se.

In a telephone interview with the author on February 19, 1976, the defeated senatorial candidate Wayne Owens discussed the hearing. (He was then serving an ecclesiastical assignment as a mission president in eastern Canada for the Church of Jesus Christ of Latter-day Saints.) The hearing generates "very unpleasant feelings" even now, said Owens.

Owens admitted that he had not followed the arbitration matter very closely: "It was something originated by my staff, and I was so busy with the campaign—spending twenty hours a day campaigning—that I really took very little or no notice of the details." Owens said he was not personally involved in rejecting the initial slate of arbitrators and never did know who was on the panel "until afterwards—after the election." He had "relied solely on his attorney for legal expertise and guidance in the matter of the hearing." Owens is an attorney himself and felt "an experienced arbitrator ought to have been able to be professionally neutral." He added, again, that he never did pay much attention to the details of the selection of the tribunal or the arbitration process.[20] David Watkiss, Owens's attorney during the campaign, also said:

> The real impact of such a Fair Campaign Practices tribunal is if an award is made quickly and resolved prior to the election. People just don't care afterwards.
>
> I believe in the Fair Campaign Practices process. Indeed, I feel very strongly about it . . .
>
> The real difficulty is in being able to get the neutrals as arbitrators in such political campaign disputes—there are no real "independents" in a campaign. Partisan views develop. Sure, we knew Timmins [the author] was a Republican—we'd done our homework after the American Arbitration Association selected the slate of arbitrators. Frankly, we were tempted to let Timmins stay even after a question of neutrality was raised—we figured Timmins was experienced enough in hearings that he might actually tilt Owens's way to try to be fair.[21] But that's the crucial dilemma: How to get fair people? Members of tribunals *must* have experience in hearing procedures and arbitration. They *must* be people capable of looking at the facts, having a proper perspective, and making a firm decision. Frankly, only a few people are so qualified. I am not sure—and I say this as an attorney with some experience—of the need to have neutrals if seasoned arbitrators are available.[22]

Several questions surface in the Utah Senate race. First, is it unusual for one or both parties to reject the entire slate of proposed arbitrators? Joanna L. Mudrock, staff director for the Fair Campaign Practices Committee in Washington, D.C., wrote:

> The answer to your second question—how common is failure to select an arbitration panel—is not very. Checking our files from 1968, when the American Arbitration Association entered into an agreement with the Fair Campaign Practices Committee to provide an arbitration system for political candidates, I found no precedent for the situation presented by that of Garn/Owens.[23]

Thus the Garn–Owens dispute presented a somewhat unusual situation in the selection of arbitrators. Another not so unusual aspect of the Utah arbitration was its "on the eve of the election" aspect and the additional complaints that were filed. Michael F. Hoellering, vice-president for case administration of the American Arbitration Association in New York City, said,

> [T]he Fair Campaign Practices Arbitration between Mr. E. J. Garn and Mr. Wayne Owens was somewhat unusual due to the fact that hearings did not commence till October 31st, at which time in addition to the complaints filed by Mr. Garn, candidate Owens submitted additional complaints for determination by the arbitrators. This additional submission was ruled upon by the panel which unanimously determined that, in the interest of the voting public of the state of Utah, even though technically the additional complaints had not completely gone through the proper channels, that all issues should be dealt with in the arbitration if the hearings were to proceed. Following this ruling the parties requested a recess and after some deliberation informed the arbitrators that they were in a settlement agreement. The board accepted same and granted the motion to adjourn without any findings from the

arbitrators. No doubt the settlement and withdrawal of the case was due in large part to the short time left before the election was to be held.

It is not unusual for parties of other cases to engage in extensive maneuvering over the makeup of the panel of arbitrators or to disagree as to the issues to be arbitrated. As in the above case such issues are always resolved either by the Association, which frequently designates arbitrators for the parties, or by the arbitrators who determine what issues should be heard, as was the case in the Garn and Owens arbitration. Absent an unworkable time limit or the agreement of the two parties to withdraw the case from arbitration, the case then proceeds to a final determination.[24]

The author believes the following changes would be beneficial to the Fair Campaign Practices Committee's arbitration procedures. First, months prior to each election, particularly major elections for national offices, the Fair Campaign Practices Committee and the American Arbitration Association should carefully preselect panels of available arbitrators in each state or by multistate regions. These slates of names would be carefully screened without time pressures, and training materials and guidelines would be furnished for each prospective panelist by AAA. Indeed, the names of the volunteer arbitrators and biographical information would be furnished to all political parties, the news media, and candidates as the campaigns progress. This obviously presupposes a significant new and stronger role by the Fair Campaign Practices Committee in policing campaigns for national office. Enough names would be preselected in this way to provide all parties reasonable numbers of names for rejection and selection. Funding for such pilot efforts may have to come from Congress or other, private, sources.

Second, the Fair Campaign Practices Committee should seek to encourage like agencies in each state—something like branch offices. Ultimately the political campaign dispute arbitration process will be best administered if handled at the state level. Doing so would expedite and strengthen the hearing panel selection procedure, provide maximum publicity potential in state contests, and have the greatest weight in influencing election outcomes where time is short and tempers hot. Obviously, money and the administrative machinery to implement such decentralized efforts are the difficult parts of the solution, but, although difficult, they are not insuperable.

Last, greater advance publicity is needed—whether the above changes are made or not—to alert all candidates to the Code of Campaign Practices and to alert all parties (especially the public) of the availability of the dispute resolution procedure. Without great cost or effort, such advance notice could go a long way toward educating the public about the use of arbitration to resolve campaign disputes, and clean up the campaign and electoral processes of our great republic as it enters its third century.

Assignments

1. Discuss as a class (or in teams) what went wrong with the resolution machinery and procedure set up by the National Fair Campaign Practices Committee and the American Arbitration Association. What worked? What did not? Does the procedure seem to have affected outcome of the election?

2. What changes would the class (or teams) propose in the Fair Campaign Practices Committee procedures to provide for more ethical campaigns? Debate or discuss these in terms of unintended consequences, costs and benefits, and impacts on electoral campaigns.

3. What other changes would the class propose to ensure improved ethical behavior in political campaigns? What better role could the local press play? What about the role of the political parties? This discussion needs to be hardheaded because pie-in-the-sky solutions just won't work in the harsh reality of a heated political campaign. What good, if any, would the author's proposed specific reforms achieve? What other alternatives are there?

Notes

1. This code article reads, "I shall condemn the use of campaign material of any sort which misrepresents, distorts, or otherwise falsifies the facts regarding any candidate, as well as the use of malicious or unfounded accusations against any candidate which aim at creating or exploiting doubts, without justification, as to his loyalty and patriotism." Quoted from American Arbitration Association, *Fair Campaign Practices Arbitration Rules* (Revised June 16, 1972), p. 7.

"The committee—recognized by both the Republican and Democratic parties—is a private, tax-exempt group established in 1954 to 'help clean up politics.' The committee frequently serves as an intermediary between disputing candidates and goes by the 'Code of Fair Campaign Practices' drawn up by the U.S. Senate." Associated Press news release dated 3 November 1974, quoted in *Salt Lake Tribune,* 14A.

2. Letter from Garn to Fair Campaign Practices Committee, Inc., undated but circa 14 October 1974 (date established from other documents).

3. Letter from Owens to Fair Campaign Practices Committee, Inc., dated 21 October 1974.

4. Frank H. Jonas, ed., *Politics in the American West* (Salt Lake City: University of Utah Press, 1969), pp. 326–379.

5. "Arbitration is the voluntary submission of a dispute by the interested parties to disinterested persons for determination. The techniques of arbitration can be applied to disputes over political campaign tactics using, as a set of principles, the Code of Fair Campaign Practices developed by the Fair Campaign Practices Committee, Inc., which are accepted by most candidates for election to federal and major state offices in advance of their campaigns.

"To achieve expeditious settlement of disputes about violation of the Code of Fair Campaign Practices, the American Arbitration Association has developed Fair Campaign Practices Arbitration Rules. Because of the large number of disputes which can arise about violations of the Code of Fair Campaign Practices, and because it is advisable to have an informed, bi-partisan, organization screen out those which are not suitable for arbitration, the American Arbitration Association will limit its services to those disputes referred to arbitration by the Fair Campaign Practices Committee." Quoted from the foreword in American Arbitration Association, op. cit., p. 1.

6. Ibid.

7. "Owens–Garn Clash in Campaign Charges," *Salt Lake Tribune,* 1 November 1974. See also editorial "Election Probe Begins," in *Deseret News,* 31 October 1974.

8. *Deseret News,* 31 October 1974.

9. The office of party treasurer is elected in Utah by delegates to the biennial county organizing conventions.

10. The author was then associate professor of Public Administration in the Graduate School of Management at Brigham Young University at Provo, Utah. He also taught public personnel and labor relations courses on a part-time basis for the University of Utah's Department of Political Science. (Dr. Wann was chairman of the department.) He had also long been active in public life as an officeholder, candidate, and party worker, including sundry gubernatorial and senatorial campaign committees in Utah over a twenty-year period.

11. See *Salt Lake Tribune*'s story of 1 November, above note 7.

12. "Owens, Garn Call Off Feud on 'Dirty Politics,'" *Deseret News,* 4 November 1974 (Monday).

13. "Arbitration Continues in Senate Campaign Charges," *Salt Lake Tribune,* 3 November 1974, noting the changes in membership on the tribunal.

14. American Arbitration Association, op. cit., pp. 4–5.

15. Washington, D.C., 1975.

16. Ibid., p. 11. "The director of the Fair Campaign Practices Committee said in an Associated Press interview, '. . . [E]lection campaigns seem to be as dirty as ever.' The nonpartisan committee has received 43 complaints about races for the U.S. House and Senate, Executive Director Samuel J. Archibald said Saturday in an interview. Thirteen grievances came in during the last seven days alone. 'We're climbing back into the sludge,' said Archibald. 'All candidates learned from Watergate is how to play dirty politics.' In 1972, the year of Watergate, 'there was the big drop into the political sewer' with 62 complaints, said Archibald. In 1970, the committee counted 50 grievances while in 1968 there were 49 and in 1966 there were 47. Three weeks before Tuesday's election, Archibald released a statement that he had received only 11 complaints about alleged dirty politics. At that time, the committee said it knew that candidates were running cleaner campaigns 'because they realize voters will react against anything that smells of Watergate smear tactics.' But Archibald has since changed his tune—after receiving 32 more grievances at his small office on Capitol Hill. But he doesn't discount what he calls the 'witching hour' type of smear in all this recent flood of filings. This is explained in one of the committee's pamphlets on how to recognize smears. 'Smear artists usually wait for the last minute to launch their most damaging lies.' This way his opponent has little time to counter the charges effectively." Associated Press news release, "Watergate Lesson Fails: Campaigns Still Dirty," quoted in *Salt Lake Tribune,* 3 November 1974.

17. Excerpted from a personal letter to the author from Senator E. J. Garn, dated 28 August 1975.

18. Excerpted from a personal letter to the author from John H. Klas dated 9 May 1975.

19. Excerpted from a personal letter to the author from Kent Shearer dated 2 May 1975.

20. Telephone interview with Wayne Owens on 19 February 1976.

21. In a personal interview on January 20, 1976, A. J. Wann (mentioned earlier as being sick when AAA first called him on October 29, 1974) told the author that he, Wann, urged AAA's San Francisco office to use Timmins despite Timmins's known partisanship since he was experienced in hearings, well regarded locally, and in Wann's judgment "a fair and honest person." Wann is a well-known Democrat.

22. Telephone interview with David Watkiss on 21 February 1976. Notes were read back to Mr. Watkiss at close of interview for verbal verification. Emphasis added.

23. Excerpted from a personal letter to the author from Joanna L. Mudrock dated 30 December 1974.

24. Excerpted from a personal letter to the author from Michael F. Hoellering dated 31 March 1975.

CHAPTER 9

Conflicts Between Political Appointees and Careerists

The Senate had confirmed Natalie as undersecretary, and she accepted her new position feeling she had a clear mandate to make many changes in agency policy and practice. Indeed, her boss, a new secretary in the administration's incoming cabinet, had told Natalie he expected fast change—a new orientation of the agency's traditional mission. Natalie had the grade, the title, the office, and the place on the organization chart, to make changes. Yet, career bureaucrats were blocking her at every turn. They never said no—they just smiled and went on doing things the old way. These career people all were supportive and friendly, to Natalie's face. But nothing really changed. It was more than frustrating. She felt there was an actual *conflict* between her new role and these careerists, some of whose careers spanned several administrations. There was a certain smugness about them, she thought. "Is this called stonewalling?" wondered Natalie aloud. They expect to outlast me, obviously. Well, Natalie thought angrily, we'll see who outlasts whom!

The Sources of Conflict

Certain apparently inescapable differences between career public employees ("bureaucrats," "careerists") and political appointees ("pols," "hacks") frequently lead to conflict. A recent article characterized these differences and conflicts by a clever use of acronyms.

A—**Appointed** for shorter terms, specific time periods
P—**Polar** in policy positions—usually philosophically oriented toward a policy
P—**Partisan**—not always, but usually a political appointment
O—**Oriented** toward short-term goals, options, accomplishments
I—**Insider** information and relationships—loyalty to administration
N—**Need** to be sensitive to needs of elected officials, party in power
T—**Tuned** in to special client groups, political public
E—**Ego** and self-esteem needs often seem paramount
E—**Executive** or management/administrative oriented
S—**Sensitive** to own career, after public service

versus

C—Career oriented, lifetime or long-term commitment

A—Aligned, with long-term, more stable goals, objectives and values of the agency

R—Responsible for policy implementation and usually not the formulation of policy

E—Equilibrist—one who balances himself/herself in unnatural positions and hazardous movements

E—Equanimity or sangfroid—the quality of one who is self-possessed and not easily disturbed or perturbed

R—Responsible to his/her professional work (or profession more than to party or partisan)

I —Inveterate—firmly established by long persistence

S—Sides more with "general public" than with party or administration

T—Tenets (or "doctrines") of good management are held in common and shared with most other careerists

S—Sensitive to needs of merit system, career service and long-term values[1]

The polarity in policy positions is borne out in much recent literature. For instance, note the points raised in the best seller *Megatrends:*

- In politics, it does not really matter any more who is president, and Congress has become obsolete (p. 103)
- Liberal or Conservative, most governors believe the country is too diverse for the federal government's centralized policy making (p. 112)
- We are shifting from a managerial society to an entrepreneurial society (p. 165)
- The new leader is a facilitator, not an order giver (p. 209)
- We will restructure our businesses into smaller and smaller units, more entrepreneurial units, more participatory units (p. 229)[2]

Numerous examples exist in the literature of appointees and their "ego and self-esteem needs" getting in the way of career workers. This author has written of two specific conflicts and their long, legal, lasting outcomes—one involving a career county librarian who runs up against a right-wing county commissioner (see Chapter 3), and the other a young laborer with long hair who conflicts with his middle-aged department head who wears a butch.[3]

Appointee loyalty to the administration in power has often led to corruption of personnel systems and betrayal of the public interest. Examples of the erosion of civil service systems by political appointees or elected officials themselves are widely known. Ban and Marzotto have recently written of one such erosion of the integrity of the federal personnel system when the federal examination process for personnel screening was decentralized as a result of the 1978 Civil Service Reform Act (CSRA).[4]

The literature is likewise replete with evidence of the importance of career employee self-esteem and organizational involvement as sources of motivation for employee performance in the public sector. Too often, appointees belittle or demean the career public servant.[5]

The long-term, career-oriented commitments of careerists can result in bitter conflicts when appointees make policy choices that result in reductions in force (rifs), such as in privatization movements. Just as technical roles can conflict, for example, between budgetary staff and personnel staff, so career and appointee roles can conflict. Simple structural arrangements can often mitigate conflict, however, or at least significantly reduce it.[6] A considerable literature exists on techniques and tools to reduce conflicts—for instance, *Getting to Yes: Negotiating Agreement Without Giving In* (New York: Penguin Books, 1981), suggests strategies such as

- Separating the people from the problem
- Focusing on interests, not positions
- Establishing precise goals at the outset of negotiations, and
- Working together to create options that will satisfy both parties[7]

Both career public employees and political appointees have much common ground. Rather than focus on adversarial relationships, both sides can reduce natural conflicts by a variety of strategies, techniques, and efforts, some of which have already been mentioned.

A recent text edited by N. Dale Wright raises some age-old questions on ethics in our public organizations:

- Must we be ethical as individuals in order to have an ethical society?
- Do good systems produce good people or do good people produce good systems?
- Are there absolute ethical standards to which we as individuals must adhere?[8]

Wright's text would answer these questions for Natalie by saying, "that which goes around, comes around," since "the Founders understood the primary problem of good government to be the problem of the good moral character of the individuals within government."

Assignments

1. What are the *sources* of conflict between careerists and political appointees? To what degree is such conflict healthy? Dysfunctional? What are some of the problems it can cause for both parties?

2. What ethical behaviors should careerists adopt toward political appointees? How about the political appointees' behaviors toward the career public servants he or she supervises? What "code of ethics" should prevail to best serve the broader public interest?

3. Assuming conflict does arise between political appointees and careerists, *who* best should mitigate such conflict? What approach(es) would be best? Why?

4. The class may wish to consider the special ethical issues of the so-called whistleblowers when debating or considering this kind of conflict. How best encourage people to come forward and blow the whistle? Yet, how best protect the whistleblower from reprisal, etc.? How best protect the public manager or administrator? How best serve the public interest in general? The mission of the agency? What is the proper role of the press in such matters?

Notes

1. William M. Timmins, "Relations Between Political Appointees and Careerists," *Review of Public Personnel Administration* 4, no. 2 (Spring 1984): 79; see also same topic in *Public Administration Times,* 15 March 1984.

2. John Naisbitt, *Megatrends* (New York: Warner Books, 1984).

3. Timmins, "The Due Processing of Librarian Layton," *Review of Public Personnel Administration* 3, no. 1 (Fall 1982): 77–82; and Timmins, *Long Hair and the Merit System: A Case Study in Personnel Administration* (Syracuse: Inter-University Case Program, Inc., 1972).

4. Carolyn Ban and Toni Marzotto, "Delegations of Federal Examining," *Review of Public Personnel Administration* 5, no. 1 (Fall 1984): 1–11.

5. See for example, Barbara S. Ronzek, "The Human Factor in the Federal Workforce: Work Experiences, Self-Esteem, and Organizational Involvement Among Public Employees," *Review of Public Personnel Administration* 5, no. 1 (Fall 1984): 43–56.

6. For instance, Timmins, Varley, and Cornia, "Cooperation Between Personnel and Budget Offices During Position Requests and Classification," *State and Local Government Review* 17, no. 2 (Winter 1985): 180–187. See a case study on resolving conflict at the municipal level, in William M. Timmins and R. Dwight Laws, "Politicians vs Public Employees," *American Public Works Reporter* 55 (Fall 1988).

7. Roger Fisher and William Ury, *Getting to Yes: Negotiating Agreement Without Giving In* (New York: Penguin Books, 1981).

8. N. Dale Wright, ed., *Papers on the Ethics of Administration* (Provo, Utah: Brigham Young University, 1988), p. 17.

PART III

Ethics and Public Economics

Four cases on ethical issues in the economics of public finance make up this unique cluster. Faced with all kinds of fiscal pressures now, governments at all levels are becoming productivity centered, privatizing (turning public jobs over to the private sector by contracting out), downsizing, and seeking to attract a new tax base. If you can't do it cheaper, get rid of it, or contract for it, or find new sources of revenue, or become more efficient and productive. A new industry, for instance, means new payroll, new taxes, new jobs, new growth. But when everyone wants the same new building, or factory, or plant (assuming it sounds fine, smells fine, pays its own way, and is legal), ethical practices become important considerations. What about a simple deal to freeze taxes on new construction until the new arts center pays for itself—that's not unethical in return for a $100 million investment, is it? And, are there ethical problems in contracting out jobs if public workers lose their employment? What ethical behaviors do we have a right to expect from managers? Employees? And what about the ethical issues that arise from innovative personnel techniques such as reciprocity provisions, inter-local contracting, and cooperation between government agencies—all methods that bypass traditional governmental personnel administration?

CHAPTER 10

Ethical Issues in Downsizing
Or, Cutting Back

"Downsize," was the challenge! As his director prepared to leave for the district meeting, Mitch knew what the brass wanted. He was expected to cut positions—to eliminate authorized but unencumbered slots. But it wasn't really so simple. Downsizing raised a number of serious ethical questions.

The Case of a Declining Workload

You are the division chief (GS15: $40,832) of a medium-sized district of a federal agency. You have recently become concerned about your staffing: Two months ago the region requested that all future vacancies be closely reviewed in order to reduce current staffing.

Your present authorized on-roll staffing in GS-13 ($29,375) and GS-12 ($24,703) grades is

	Positions Authorized	On Roll
GS-13	16	16
GS-12	20	19

Your workload review of GS-13 assignments indicates that you can fully justify only fifteen positions. The sixteenth position is in question. A review of available workload indicates that at least 25 percent of that position would be spent on GS-13 assignments. In addition, you know that by the end of the current calendar year one of your GS-13 personnel will retire.

Except for this one retirement, your present staff appears to be stable. All of the remaining senior personnel and group managers and key members at the GS-13 level are too young to retire. The highly mobile people have already left the district. You do not foresee any other movement for at least two years.

You do have a potential staffing problem, however, Her name is Theda Black. She is expecting a GS-13 this year. Her supervisor has told you that Theda has been telling some of the other employees that it's only a matter of time and she will be a 13. She has also indicated to several employees that after the last counseling session with her supervisor and branch chief, she was considered the top candidate for the next vacancy. In addition, she has been given responsibility for and has worked on a number of GS-13 assignments since her move to headquarters office. Theda has been a very active person in the district. She was one of the first women professionals hired out of college. She has been used as a college recruiter. She has been an instructor in a district training course for over three years and has been an EEO counselor. She is currently the district's federal women's program coordinator. In this capacity, she staged a very successful Women's Career Day for and with all the other federal agencies in the community.

Theda Black came into the federal agency with a neutral attitude toward unionism. The union's officers have been working to get her actively interested in the union, however, because they believe that she could strongly influence the women in the office, especially the younger technicians and professionals. Theda has been thus far uninterested in their appeals, although (you are told) she has said to others that if management continues to make those "silly" decisions and not meet its commitments to employees, she will not hesitate to become active in the union. Right now, although you are not sure, you would guess that Theda will take any decision on your part to not fill the anticipated vacancy (or reduce the number of GS-13s) very personally.

Theda Black has indicated to you personally that she is not interested in a GS-13 outside of the headquarters city. She stated she has "paid her mobility dues." She has already moved three times within the district between posts of duty. Two years ago she married a local businessman who has custody of his two grade-school children, ages seven and eight.

Some Additional Factors

If you do reduce the number of GS-13s, you will have to reassign the remaining GS-13 work load to another professional. Reassignment could require an additional GS-13 employee to travel to the headquarters office from the field to handle these cases.

Theda Black had received a high quality step increase from her last supervisor prior to her move to the headquarters office.

The feeling expressed by a number of employees to you and your division's branch chiefs is that your district's manager wants to "look good" for the regional director and will automatically cut the number of positions.

You recognize you have done no research to determine who may be better qualified than Ms. Black.

Problem

Your district director has asked you to give her a briefing on your analysis of your division's authorized and on-roll staff for GSs 12 and 13. She is leaving soon for a director's conference sponsored by the regional director, where grade escalation is on the agenda, along with reducing authorized positions.

Assignments

1. Examine in depth the ethical implications of this case in terms of
   a. Responsibilities for position management;
   b. Implications of a multidistrict agreement with a union (what you do may impact other districts under a broader contract);
   c. Potential generation of complaint under EEO laws and regulations; and

   d. The management "integrity" issue—that is, the possibility of management being forced to evaluate an employee's merit based on EEO or union issues.
2. Anticipate the ramifications of an unpopular decision and think through and plan the methods you can use to cope with the consequences. Try not to leave any loose ends—for example, what will be done about remaining work loads, and employees other than Theda.

CHAPTER 11

The Ethics of Tax Incentives and Waivers

"Deal!" critics charged. It was true. The city of Boston had agreed to a property tax arrangement with Prudential Insurance Company that seemed too good to be true to other property owners and developers. The mayor's considered response was to the effect that the city would do the same for any other company willing to spend $100 million in Boston. But the case raises all kinds of ethical issues and interesting questions for local governments, elected officials, big business, the press, the public. What lessons have been learned? What lessons should have been learned?

Before reading this case and discussing it, students should be aware that Prudential's investment in Boston's Back Bay spurred hundreds of millions of dollars in new growth and produced an incredible redevelopment of vast tracts of the city that were once slums and rotting railroad yards. Visitors today could hardly conceive of the change that has resulted. This case could be cited in any argument that the end justifies the means. Yet ethical issues that arose early in the case remain. Public administrators confronted with such opportunities to rebuild their cities may well wish to ponder these issues.

Tax concessions are only one of many kinds of inducements used by cities and states to attract industry. Such concessions are generally condemned because of their nonuniversality in exempting property, the questionable effectiveness of such concessions, and the undesirable social consequences of the tax exemptions.[1]

Other types of inducements by state and local governments are exemption of new plants or industry from property or other taxation, outright gifts of sites, sharing of costs of site preparation or improvements, cash bonuses, loans, provision of buildings or sites at nominal rentals, and guarantees of favorable labor conditions.[2] Several states specifically permit municipalities to make tax concessions to new industries (usually in the form of tax exemption) for periods of five or more years. State laws of this kind are most prevalent in New England and the southern states, and especially among small municipalities.

Such exemptions may be by a formal contract or a written agreement or may be made mandatory by state legislation. Specific action by a municipality without legal authority is a common practice, but municipal officers are seldom held liable for such misappropriation of funds if local opinion favored the concession to attract industry. Specific exemptions may be written into a state's constitution.[3]

This chapter concerns a tax concession between the city of Boston, Massachusetts, and the Prudential Insurance Company of America.

Boston and the Property Tax

A study of politics in Boston painted a portrait of Boston, Massachusetts, as a sick city. The author writes of this aging giant among cultural centers that

> the city has hundreds of narrow congested streets, is dominated by vast areas of broken-down and substandard homes, and is beset by claims and counterclaims of political corruption. Many cities have large slum areas and a history of corruption. Boston, however, leaves one with the feeling that these problems are beyond control. The fantastically high property tax rate ($101 per thousand) is taken by many to be symptomatic of a fundamental disease in the Hub's body politic.[4]

The cause of the rise in the tax rate is not unique to Boston. A decreasing tax base coupled with an increased demand for services and higher costs of providing them (with problems more directly local in character) has pushed tax rates up in many American cities. Some of the causes of the failure of the property tax to supply adequate revenue for the needs of local governments have been frequently discussed.[5] Most of the criticisms of the property tax have been leveled not at the economic aspects of the tax but at failures in administration. One noted tax expert concluded that "the property tax is not beyond recall on its administrative side."[6]

One prime shortcoming of the administration of the property tax is what the National Tax Association called "exemptionitis." The association's considered opinion is that local governments should move toward an exemptionless real estate tax.[7] Mable Newcomer concluded that one primary reason for the decline in the legal tax base was increased legal exemptions.[8] When coupled with the conclusions of the Commission on Intergovernmental Relations that property taxes represented about 1 percent of private property values, it seems evident that a larger property tax could solve many of the financial difficulties now faced by American cities and local governments.[9]

This reasoning is not intended to deemphasize the needs of some local governments for (1) more generous grants from state funds or larger shares of state-collected taxes, or (2) a broadening of local taxing powers. Many writers feel, however, that by strengthening the property tax at its weakest points, local governments can enable it to continue to be a significant—if not the major—source of all local tax revenues.

Taxation and the Prudential Center

The 1960 *Municipal Year Book* stated that Boston, a city already faced with staggering financial needs and burdened with the heaviest property tax rate in the United States, had granted an "assessment freeze," or type of tax exemption, to the Prudential Life Insurance Company for the construction of a vast complex to be called Prudential Center. Under the arrangement agreed upon, ". . . the assessment would be frozen at a level which in effect guarantees an approximate return on capital invested of 7 percent." The exemption, the *Municipal Year Book* also stated, ". . . seems to stem from a conviction that the burden of the property tax is too heavy for certain types of property under certain circumstances and that they should receive special tax concessions."[10] A moderate attitude was taken by the Tax Institute, which said of the tax arrangement between Prudential and the city officials of Boston, "It would be superficial to render a snap judgment of condemnation or approbation. Action should always be judged in relation to existing circumstances and possible alternatives."[11]

In December of 1958 the *Bulletin* of the Boston Municipal Research Bureau commented:

> Boston's property taxes are deterring the normal growth of the city. They are holding construction activity far below normal replacement levels. Only $5 million in valuations were added to the tax roll in 1958 because of new construction.
>
> High property taxes are discouraging systematic programs of urban renewal and desires of individuals to improve old property. Over half of the land assembled through the use of $4 million in federal and city funds in the New York streets section of the South End lies fallow because high property taxes are blocking new development.[12]

The city of Boston was for good reason concerned with stimulating new construction activity. A headline in the 16 May 1959, "Official Chronicle of Boston Municipal Affairs" read "Prudential Clinches 1959 As Record Year." The article said that the first four months of 1959 were the biggest period of building activity of any year in Boston's history. "The overpowering factor," the article continued, "in the 1959 record was the issuance of a $60 million permit for the initial stage of the $100 million Prudential Center now being erected in the Back Bay."[13]

The sliding scale worked out between Mayor Hynes and Prudential officials was ratified on March 18, 1958, will be discussed in more detail. The assessment formula, however, immediately drew a great deal of unfavorable criticism. Many businessmen resented the concession, and other special-interest groups were outspoken in their opposition. The *Christian Science Monitor* in discussing the conference held on the above date reported that "the Mayor [Hynes] emphasized the tax plan was in no way a 'concession' and said the same would be done for any other concern willing to spend 100 million dollars in Boston—or even less."[14]

The Prudential Life Insurance Company was quoted as saying that "to make Prudential Center possible the city of Boston and the Prudential will have to compromise—Boston on taxes, Prudential on return on investment."[15]

Prudential first declared an interest in the site occupied by the Boston and Albany Railroad Back Bay yard and two other parcels of property (totaling nearly 31½ acres) as early as December 1955. The company announced it would consider building a regional office on the site. By early January of 1956 the plans for a $15 million office building snagged over a possible conflict with the proposed route of the Massachusetts Turnpike Authority and the Prudential Company on a toll road route.[16] The easement over which the Boston and Albany and New York Central Railroads proposed to maintain a two-track mainline operation was to be widened to permit a six-lane highway to be built by the Massachusetts Turnpike Authority. The two easements ran diagonally across the property from northwest to southeast. Mayor Hynes at the time of the pact forecast that during the first year of operation the toll road would carry between 60,000 and 70,000 vehicles a day.[17] The mayor also announced at the same time plans for a $5 million convention hall to be erected by the city of Boston on the site.[18]

On January 21, 1957, Prudential made known tentative plans for a $100 million development on the 31-acre site. The project was soon unveiled, revealing a complex of structures that included a 52-story office building, a 25-story luxury hotel, seven commercial buildings, and six apartment houses (providing for 1,750 units). A handout distributed by the company (at a later date) said, "A plaza will be constructed over practically the entire property. This plaza will create a new surface level over the low-elevation site, at a height sufficient to provide clearance for easements running beneath the plaza."[19]

The plans for the Prudential Center included a "ring road" to connect with all adjacent city streets to handle the traffic resulting from the center. The development also incorporated Mayor Hynes's projected municipal auditorium. It is interesting that the proposed auditorium took on increased scale as time passed. The *City Record* for October 24, 1959, showed a picture of the auditorium (facing Boylston Street) and estimated the cost would be $12 million.[20] The particular architectural layout of the development has been altered several times during the years, but the plan has always provided for about 75 percent of the total plaza area to be landscaped as a park. Various amenities to be included were a skating rink, specialty shops, and terraced plazas with pedestrian-scale attractions.[21]

Prudential made it clear from the beginning that this entire project is a commercial venture:

> Our project in Boston is being made strictly for business reasons and for profitable investment. One reason we think it will be profitable is because we count on Boston in particular, and Massachusetts in general, to back up the constructive investment we are making here. We expect more and more of our investments generally to go into New England. We expect that more and more of your investments also will be placed here.[22]

Boston officials on their part made it clear that the city wanted the center. On June 19, 1958, the Board of Zoning Adjustment saw its way clear to approve the height variance of the proposed 52-story building and accommodate the 780-foot structure.[23] A delay in the sale of bonds for the toll road extension by the Turnpike Authority by June of 1958 caused concern, but by June 20 the papers reported this was "cleared up quickly."[24] City officials were more than eager to reach the compromise that the Prudential Company said was necessary if it was to be able to finance the development.

"City officials and company management were agreed that the Center would enhance the appeal of the whole city, with particular benefit to the central business district one mile away."[25] The May 18, 1958, conference in Boston between officials of the city and officials of the Prudential Insurance Company of America (with some business-group representatives invited) disclosed that the development would cost the Prudential nearly 50 percent more "than would be required for a conventional development along strictly utilitarian lines of an equivalent acreage not presenting the special problems of this one."[26] The company publicly stated that the amount of the assessment on the property would be decisive in determining the anticipated tax load, the return on the investment, and thus the feasibility of the entire project.[27]

An earlier conference (January 30, 1957) had discussed only general principles. At that earlier date Prudential had no definite figures, either as to cost or probable income, on which real discussion could have proceeded. An agreement was reached, however, that (1) froze the land assessment at the "present" level (land included the three levels of parking terraces above the easement and the plaza itself); (2) agreed that the later assessments on improvements would be based on economic value (potential income from the projects) rather than other physical value or reproduction cost; and (3) the city suggested that a method of calculating economic value might be by capitalizing net income that would be derived by deducting expenses, depreciation, and a fair return of 6 or 7 percent from gross income.[28]

At the March 18, 1958, conference, Prudential proposed that (1) asssessments be limited to the land (as defined above) until construction started above plaza level, the assessments to remain frozen at the level until such time (as agreed in 1957); and (2) that thereafter taxes increase on a graduated scale for seven years until the full income projected for the development could be received.[29]

Prudential presented figures to show that on the basis of current conditions the expected gross income of the project would leave only a 6 percent or less return on investments, so that after calculation of economic value there would be nothing left for taxes. "Consequently, if the project is to go forward the Prudential will have to accept a very much lower return. This it is prepared to do. . . . "[30] The company officials outlined a proposed timetable for completion of the project extending to (anticipated) full occupancy of the buildings by 1967. Massachusetts law required tax assessment *during* construction. The fact that the project would produce no appreciable income before 1963 and only a slowly increasing amount thereafter until the end of the seven-year construction period, led company officials to state that a tax in excess of 20 percent of the gross revenues would not leave a return on Prudential's investment that could be justified to policyholders or to the regulatory officials that supervised it.[31]

The mayor and city representatives were fully cognizant of these facts. The mayor stated neither he nor the city assessor could give any commitment that would be legally binding for the assessment of future construction. However, they were anxious to assure Prudential that it could proceed and ". . . agreed that Boston was very much in need of the type of development Prudential proposed to build, and that aside from the addition to the ratables which it would represent it would make economic, esthetic, and cultural contributions of great value to the city."[32] Based on the amount of rent ($6 per square foot) Prudential was including as a charge to itself, for space it was to occupy,[33] the city representatives agreed it "appeared to them to be altogether reasonable to conclude that the development would not be economically feasible were the taxes to be in excess of 20 percent of the gross rentals received by Prudential. . . ."[34] The tax agreement devised a "reasonable method of arriving at fair cash value . . . from the standpoint of both the Prudential and the city."[35] The sliding scale increased to no less than $3 million a year after the seven years but was not to be in excess of 20 percent of gross revenues thereafter.[36]

The result of this agreement was that the Prudential officials felt satisfied that construction of the project could proceed, and Boston officials "all agreed that Prudential could safely assume assessments for the periods mentioned in accordance" with the agreement. "All participants . . . signed a memorandum to indicate their concurrence."[37]

On December 10, 1959, the new mayor of Boston, John F. Collins, and Fred Smith, a vice-president of Prudential, announced that the new Mayor had signed the informal agreements which authorized the so-called "Prudential formula" for assessing taxes on the new project. It already had been signed by officials of the administration now ending and by business leaders. Approval by Mr. Collins was one of the assurances that Mr. Smith particularly sought yesterday.[38]

Tax Concessions and Compromises

Early in February 1960, Prudential officials received disturbing indications that the tax concession might be challenged in state courts. A high-level conference of Prudential officials resulted in a call for changes in the state laws and city ordinances.

The strong desire on the part of city officials for the project soon led to a $300 million package plan to ensure by statute a fixed property tax for the insurance company. The *Christian Science Monitor* said of the plan:

> Under the new plan Boston's $100,000,000 Prudential Center has thereby been tied directly to a $200,000,000 plan by the Massachusetts Turnpike Authority to extend the turnpike into Boston and construct parking and other facilities at the project. The turnpike authority will take over the vast, three-level underground garage designed as part of the center—but will lease all "air rights" above the garage to the buildings as originally planned. Instead of paying taxes to the city, Prudential will pay rent to the turnpike authority—which, in turn, will pay a "service charge" to the city equal to what the Prudential would have paid in taxes.[39]

On May 3, 1960, Governor Furcolo filed legislation to permit the merger plan. He also directed that it be sent to the state supreme court for an advisory opinion on constitutionality. The state House and Senate Rules Committee drafted ten questions of constitutionality to accompany the merger plan, stressing *the public purpose of the turnpike extension* as related to the Prudential development site. The court ruled the plan unconstitutional on May 26, 1960.[40]

In 1955 Roger L. Stevens, a developer, had proposed development of the site and had asked for tax advantages under the state's urban redevelopment law (Massachusetts General Laws, Chapter 121A). These laws stated that redevelopment of "blighted" areas as existed in towns and cities of the commonwealth could be spurred by corporations (formed for redevelopment of such areas) being "exempt from taxation and from betterments and special assessments" for a period of forty years with certain regulations imposed.[41] The state supreme court was asked if tax advantages could be given to the developer of the "blighted" site. In its 1955 decision the court decided Stevens's proposal had a private and not a public purpose. As to the area (the site on which Prudential was to later project its vast center), the court ruled that "Neither does the area appear as yet to be blighted in any other sense than the high taxes and declining values retard development—a thing that could with equal accuracy be said of a great many tracts of land in Boston and in other cities in the Commonwealth. . . ."[42]

The proposal of May, 1960, had been sent to the court for an advisory opinion on the construction of tax-exempt public purpose facilities—the multilayer parking garage to be built over the easements and the turnpike extension itself, over which was to be built the Prudential Center with a fixed sum to be paid to Boston in lieu of taxes through the Massachusetts Turnpike Authority. Attorney General Edward J. McCormack, Jr., later stated that in view of the 1955 court decision, it had not seemed feasible in 1960 to approach the court on the basis of *blight* in urging tax concessions for Prudential. "Also," said McCormack in a public hearing, "a theory of urban redevelopment similar to 121A was doubtful because it was not known if that approach could cover other than residential property."[43] McCormack explained that the merger proposal submitted to the court was made under the "theory that the tax exemption would apply to the entire area and the payments agreed upon previously by Prudential and the city of Boston would be for services, etc., and in lieu of taxes."[44]

In quoting the May 1960 decision of the court, the Attorney General pointed out in the public hearing that the court "never passed on this theory" because the court felt the road extension and multistory garage were optional on the city's part and "hence, in the court's opinion, might never be constructed."[45] The court in 1960 indicated it was

> not without recitals as to the future of the railroad yard. This railroad, we know judicially, is maintaining very limited passenger service and has recently sought to withdraw from intrastate passenger service altogether. Its yard, along with the rest of the garage site, lies in the path of the growth of the city, a growth which perhaps should not be long deferred. There may be other facts, too, of which we are not informed, including some coming to light since 1955. They could disclose a condition, the elimination of which would so affect the inhabitants "as a community, and not merely as individuals."
>
> . . . that a corporation confided with the performance of that service might be judicially considered to "perform functions for the public benefit analogous to those performed by various other types of corporations commonly called public service corporations."
>
> . . . such corporations, as has been held in a long line of decisions, may receive favored treatment in the matter of taxation.[46]

McCormack went on to sketch how as a result of the May 1960 decision Chapter 121A was amended to include commercial properties. On August 9, 1960, the court in an advisory opinion approved the new bill's constitutionality. Since an advisory opinion is not binding on the court, McCormack urged the Boston Redevelopment Authority[47] to seek a declaratory judgment to "finally adjudicate all constitutional questions concerning this project."[48]

An earlier editorial by the *Christian Science Monitor* on June 1, 1960, stated that

> in a wise and pointed decision, the Massachusetts Supreme Judicial Court has closed one door on Boston's Prudential Project and virtually invited the legislature to step through another door. . . .
>
> The key question is whether the planned massive civic center fulfills "a public purpose." If it does, a proper constitutional method of building it can be found. If it does not, the court has made clear that marrying it to other public purpose plans cannot justify any relaxation of the constitutional provisions for equality of taxation standards.

The same editorial went on to point out that the "newly opened door" was the proposed broadening of Massachusetts's current limited-dividend redevelopment law to include commercial projects and a more liberal ceiling for dividends. ". . . [T]he ideal tax arrangement," the editorial continued, "must balance the public interest with the company's risk requirements."[49]

The amended General Laws, Chapter 121A, thus met with the approval by the court in an advisory opinion in August of 1960.[50] Considerable worry was expressed by many company officials over the uncertainty of tying the giant center project to urban renewal. Until the state's high court classified the area as "blighted," the development could not be subject to tax concessions. As before, the company needed assurance about future city taxes.[51] On May 4, 1961, Prudential informed the Boston Redevelopment Authority that

> . . . the failure to finance the turnpike extension raised a variety of legal and construction questions for us which cannot readily be answered. We have said that it makes no difference whether a toll road, a freeway, or no road at all goes through our project, but a decision must be made, of course, before actual construction starts whether or not any road is to be accommodated through the tunnel originally designed for the turnpike. We must also know what to do about the Turnpike Authority's easement rights and its legal rights, which are involved in financial and transfer agreements which the Prudential has with the Turnpike Authority, the New York Central Railroad and the city of Boston, and in at least one case, with all three parties.
>
> We do not believe that the access road problem can be solved with certainty within any reasonable period of time. And if we are to proceed with the Prudential Center, we cannot afford a long wait. . . .
>
> We feel so strongly about this that we cannot commit ourselves to proceed with the entire complex at this time, although we do not plan to change the ultimate plans for the Center.
>
> We would like to proceed as soon as the way is cleared by the BRA and the Supreme Court with the construction of the west and center section as planned, but we should hold the east section (containing the apartment houses) in abeyance. . . .
>
> In order to undertake Prudential Center in one major step and one or more smaller steps, it will be necessary to alter our contract with the city to proportion the tax load accordingly . . . our contract with the city should stipulate that the 7 successive increases be prorated, and that the minimum tax on the west and center sections, in 7 years, amount to 20 percent of the projected income, which is approximately $2,000,000. When and if construction of the eastern section is resumed, the same general procedure would be followed, and eventually all or a ratable proportion of the originally projected minimum amount of $3,000,000 will be payable to the city.[52]

The modified building program meant that roughly 64 percent of the project would proceed immediately "once the green light is given to an amended application by the [Boston Redevelopment Authority] and the State Supreme Court" to confirm that the "project is eligible under the 'blighted' area" law for certain tax concessions.[53]

Prudential delayed further construction (the foundations had been flooded to protect against cold weather and to save costs in August 1960) until the state legislature passed new urban redevelopment legislation. Final clearance to start construction again came after the Massachusetts Supreme Judicial Court approved the legality of the new law on December 20, 1961. The Prudential tower and hotel were opened to the public on April 19, 1965.

Property Tax Inducements and Questions

Several interesting points arose during the course of Boston and Prudential's struggle for tax concessions on the site in the Back Bay. Discussion of two of them will
conclude this chapter. The Tax Institute has stated: ". . . it is a rather widely held
belief that the assessments of large corporations in many cities are fixed through a
process of secret negotiations between city and company officials."[54] The
Massachusetts Special Commission on Taxation said that "the common practice among
the states where this class of property [corporate] is subject to the local property
tax is to assess it largely by negotiation between the assessing officials and the taxpayers. Local custom and practice have developed. . . ."[55]

Dr. Mabel Walker has written, "The thing, however, for which communities are
feverishly competing is industry. As one city planner has facetiously said, almost
every community wants a nice taxpaying industrial plant which looks like an art
museum, sounds like a Stradivarius, and smells like Chanel No. 5. Some of the more
sophisticated and discriminating communities prefer research laboratories or offices."[56]
Dr. Walker listed four "tax baits" communities can offer to attract new industries
(plants and offices): (1) the lure of sound fiscal policies, efficient and economical
government, and taxes that are low in relation to the services provided; (2) inherent
tax advantages a community may enjoy through no action of its own (that is, a natural
advantage or one resulting from a favorable state law); (3) tax baits deliberately dangled
before industry—offered openly and without subterfuge and neither covert nor illegal); and (4) those dubious inducements that are widely suspect but seldom if ever
actionable since they are outside the law. Property assessments, Walker noted, offer
the greatest leeway for this last category of tax favors.[57] She noted that these inducements have a will-o'-the-wisp quality, and her article is itself evidence of the
difficulty of pinpointing undercover practices.

In an interesting article, Alan Campbell concluded that

> in this connection the prevailing aversion of businessmen for the corporate income
> tax is almost matched by their strong distaste for local jurisdictions where the tax
> level depends partly on whether the enterprise is in the good graces of the local
> political authorities. The power of those authorities to dispense tax favors is usually
> exercised through the leeway they have in assessing values of property—especially
> personal property.[58]

The Tax Institute noted of the Prudential tax arrangement that "the citizens of Boston
have been taken into the confidence of city officials and are aware of the agreement
reached."[59] But the Boston Finance Commission in 1953 made reference to long-
standing over-assessments and later abatements in Boston and said that

> the injurious effects of manipulated, insupportable assessing year after year upon
> the city's growth and economic well-being must be tremendous. . . .
>
> In addition to scaring off business and industry, "the indirect costs to the city
> cannot be accounted precisely, but in the aggregate must amount to a formidable
> sum. . . ."[60]

Nearly everyone has agreed on how beneficial the Prudential Center will be to Boston.
One only wonders at the "indirect costs to the city."[61]

The Economics of the Tax Concession

The second point arising from the Boston–Prudential tax agreement is the dispute among economists over the merits of the plan. Boston's Assessing Department had been exploring techniques for assessment of new construction on an income basis in order to give an investor (in new building or in extensive capital improvements) a return on investment *proportional* to the return realized by an older, depreciated property.[62] The $100 million Prudential Center was the first major example of the application of the principle of proportional return. The mechanics of capitalizing new construction have been spelled out by Oliver W. Park, then executive director of the Boston Assessing Department:

> In arriving at the assessed value of either a new or an old income producing property, the economic rent for the property must be computed first. This is determined by securing from the owner his statement as to income and expenses, including tax and [operating expense and maintenance] escalator clauses, in as precise detail as possible.
>
> After the economic rental rate has been established and the gross rent computed, an allowance is made for a normal vacancy, ranging from perhaps 2 percent to 10 percent. Since Boston has an unusually low vacancy rate, this should be less than 5 percent in most instances; even though the national averages were above this. . . .
>
> Having arrived at the effective gross rental, a deduction is made for the applicable OE&M after carefully reviewing the expense figures submitted by the owner-manager and comparing the various items with the OE&M experience standards as developed by the Assessing Department for this type of property.
>
> We have now computed the net income available to the owner for: (a) payment of taxes; (b) yield on investment; (c) amortization of investment. An entrepreneur who assumes the risks of erecting a new building at today's high construction costs must be able to realize a reasonable return on his investment each year, plus amoritization, and still have enough left to pay his taxes.
>
> With an older depreciated building, distribution between these three competing allocations is easily accomplished by merely dividing the net income by the sum of (a) the tax factor (10% with a $100 tax rate); (b) the yield factor (6% to 9%); and (c) the depreciation factor (1½%, 2%, or 2½%, on the whole, which may be equal from 2% to as much as 10% on the building value alone).
>
> With a new office building, the yield and depreciation must be allowed on construction costs which may approximate $25 to $30 a square foot, rather than $5 to $10 (depreciated value) a square foot for an older office building. Yet the new office building cannot be rented for more than about $6 a square foot overall, as compared with about $4.50 a square foot overall for a thirty-year-old office building which shows depreciation and has a much lower building value remaining to be amortized.
>
> Therefore, in order to produce a realistic allocation of the net, we must first deduct from the net a reasonable and equitable return (at a rate of, say, 8% for yield and depreciation) on the allowable *cost* of the investment (which will be above its economic value). The remainder is allocated for the tax levy.[63]

Conventional capitalization, it was felt by city officials and Prudential officers, would not provide for yield and depreciation at a tax rate of 10 percent on a basic construction cost of $100 million with a total annual rent of $15 million less operating expenses and maintenance estimated at $5 million. Projected net income before taxes, depreciation, and return would be $10 million. Thus a 10 percent allocation for taxes left no provision for return on investment and depreciation. By using the proportional return alternative, however, the assessor could allow for a return on investment on the net income *before* taxes (proportional to a calculated return on older, depreciated properties) by deducting the proportional return from the net income "*before* provision for taxes so only the remainder amount of that income would be available for tax payment."[64]

Oliver W. Park had written of this method, "City officials decided that the third alternative, the principle of proportional return, was the most equitable to all concerned, and a realistic recognition of the handicap placed on new construction by Boston's high tax rate."[65]

The results of this sort of assessment meant that of Prudential's anticipated net income of $10 million, a proportional return of 7 percent was made (to include return and depreciation without specific allocation of either) that would leave $3 million available for taxes. Under full operation this $3 million comes to 20 percent of gross income. The original tax agreement reached in May 1958 was that after the seven years (during which taxes levied would increase on a sliding scale as detailed above, with an assessment freeze on taxes until construction began above the level of the plaza)[66] the "total assessment would be fixed at such an amount as to produce a total tax not in excess of 20 percent of gross revenues . . ., but in no event less than $3 million per year."[67]

"Somehow," said Park, "Twenty percent of gross income" became the basis for the agreement, and owners of older income properties complained against this apparent tax favoritism. Park pointed out that "the agreement, however, dealt with yield, not with a specific relationship of taxes to income."[68] Prudential has struggled to overcome this complaint of tax favoritism by frequent explanations of the procedure.[69]

Park's remarks in the publication of the National (now International) Association of Assessing Officers drew some spirited replies. The scope of this chapter prohibits extended comment on their analysis of Park's report but an extract from one reply is worthwhile:

> . . . it seems obvious that the $3 million tax bill, which the company has agreed is equitable, has no relationship to the value of the property. . . . In this case, since Prudential has almost a guaranteed return, its property is practically an annuity.[70]

The city of Boston seemed convinced that the advantages accruing from development of the Prudential Center justified moderation of the tax burden—under "public purpose" laws, since subsequent court holdings validated the tax concession—so as to ensure an approximate return on Prudential's investment that would justify the company's investment of more than $100 million.[71]

Assignments

1. Discuss the kinds of tax abatements, rebates, waivers, incentives, etc., that are available; particularly, the under-the-table kind of tools and techniques described in the chapter. Perhaps some sleuthing at the local level would be interesting. Many downtown areas are 70 percent property tax exempt. Who gets these exemptions?

Are they justified and ethical? To whom is the tax burden shifted? How best handle such exemptions and other kinds of tax arrangements? (Recall Woodrow Wilson's famous "open accords openly arrived at.")

2. As a class, or as teams, seek to resolve by consensus whether the tax arrangement between Prudential Insurance Company and the city of Boston was ethical and justified. There will not be a simple, cut-and-dried answer, obviously.

3. What guidelines should public administrators follow who find themselves confronted with ethical choices similar to the one in Boston? Debate or discuss a set of guidelines that could be used to assist you in making such choices.

Notes

1. In contrast, a strong argument for subsidies or inducements to attract industry is given in John E. Moes's *Local Subsidies for Industry* (Chapel Hill: The University of North Carolina Press, 1962). Dr. Moes writes, ". . . [T]he lines of reasoning leading to prevailing adverse opinion are fallacious. . . . In broad outline, the argument [for inducements] is to the effect that when circumstances make the subsidization of industry attractive to a local community, conditions are also such that this type of action will bring the economy as a whole closer to the social welfare optimum as usually defined" (p. 3). Moes's argument for inducements is based primarily on the profitability to the community of subsidization when employment opportunity is needed.

2. As Harold M. Groves has noted, "in most states the exemption of new plants from taxation and more positive inducements such as a gift of a site are illegal but quite common." Harold M. Groves, *Financing Local Government* (New York: Henry Holt, 1939), p. 489 (note).

3. Ibid., pp. 485–486. A current discussion of such exemptions and the effect on the property tax base is given in James A. Maxwell, *Financing State and Local Governments* (Washington, DC: The Brookings Institution, 1965), pp. 149–152.

4. Murray B. Levin, *The Alienated Voter, Politics in Boston* (New York: Holt, Rinehart and Winston, 1960), pp. 1–2. The Boston Standard Metropolitan Statistical Area (SMSA) had the highest median annual real estate property tax as a percentage of median annual housing costs (28.6% as compared to national average of 17.4%). See Table 5-6 in Dick Netzer, *Economics of the Property Tax* (Washington, DC: The Brookings Institution, 1966), p. 106.

5. Well summarized by Louis Schere: "The general property tax has been progressively de-emphasized to the point where it no longer plays an adequate role in the American tax system. Tangible and intangible personal property is substantially exempt, and where not exempt, taxes extend primarily to the questionable categories of business personal property and are readily shifted to consumers. The real estate base has been riddled by excessive homestead exemptions, by governmental, charitable, religious, and similar exemptions, and by a callous and inequitable system of under assessment. Super-imposed on an inadequate base is a complex system of protective rate limitations." Louis Schere, "An Economist's Viewpoint on Tax Policy," *The Annals of the American Academy of Political and Social Science* 226 (November 1949): 172. Strengthening the property tax may also serve to strengthen the federal form of

government. See, Advisory Commission on Intergovernmental Relations, *The Role of the States in Strengthening the Property Tax,* Volume I (Washington, DC: U.S. Government Printing Office, June 1963), p. iii.

6. William H. Anderson, *Taxation and the American Economy* (New York: Prentice-Hall, 1951), p. 153. E. R. A. Seligman, of course, has attacked the tax on its economic aspects, as have others. His justifiable criticisms of the tax are its (a) lack of uniformity, (b) lack of universality, (c) incentive to dishonesty, (d) regressivity, (e) double taxation, and (f) its unsuitability to the present generation ("destitute of theoretical justification"). Edwin R. A. Seligman, *Essays in Taxation* (New York: Macmillian, 1931), pp. 19–32.

7. "Report of the Committee on Property Tax Limitation and Homestead Exemption," *Proceedings of the Thirty-first Conference of the National Tax Association,* 1938, p. 804.

8. Mable Newcomer, "The Decline of the General Property Tax," *National Tax Journal* VI (March 1953): 49. Due wrote, ". . . The property tax is likely to have greater effects than a net wealth tax in influencing business decisions, largely because it is imposed on corporation property, as such, rather than being confined to the net wealth of individuals. The tax lessens the profitability of some marginal projects which will create heavy property tax liability." John F. Due, *Government Finance* (Homewood, IL.: Richard D. Irwin, 1959), p. 405.

9. The Commission on Intergovernmental Relations, *A Report to the President,* June 1955, pp. 102–103. See also, Selma J. Mushkin, *Property Taxes: The 1970 Outlook* (Chicago: The Council of State Governments, October 1965), p. 12 (Table 2-5). A recent article in *Fortune* agreed that the property tax may have all the faults its critics claim, but ". . . it is *not* inadequate as a source and it is very far from exhausted." See "The Great Urban Tax Tangle," *Fortune* LXXI (March 1965): 106.

10. Orin F. Nolting and David S. Arnold, eds., *The Municipal Year Book,* 1960 (Chicago: The International City Manager's Association, 1960), p. 207.

11. *Tax Policy* XXVI (January 1959): 2.

12. Ibid.

13. *City Record* 15 (16 May 1959): 429. Also pointed out was the salient fact that activity would have been $10 million behind the first four months of 1958 had it not been for the Prudential permit.

14. 19 March 1958.

15. Ibid.

16. The road was to be an extension of the toll road from Weston to Boston's South Station with a turnpike interchange at the east end of the easement under the Prudential Center plaza.

17. *Christian Science Monitor,* 3 August 1956.

18. Ibid. The War Memorial Auditorium was dedicated on February 21, 1965 by Mayor John F. Collins. It is a three-story structure with some 150,000 square feet of exhibition area and auditorium facilities. The Memorial is owned by the city of Boston and operated by an auditorium commission. "The War Memorial Auditorium," mimeographed fact sheet (undated) published by Prudential Insurance Company of America, Boston, Massachusetts.

19. "Facts Digest on Prudential Center," 28 April 1960, Boston. An editorial comment by the Tax Institute gushed, ". . . from the standpoint of sheer magnitude the project is breathtaking." *Tax Policy* XXVI (January 1959): 2. The Prudential Center has been called the ". . . largest unified civic and business development in the world. . . ." *Prudential People: Special Annual Report Issue,* Spring 1966 (New Jersey: Prudential Insurance Company of America), p. 9.

20. *City Record* 51: 913.

21. ". . . the generous amount of space devoted to a plaza and the use of a ring traffic artery around the periphery of the project are two features that are currently being given wide advocacy in city planning circles." *Tax Policy* XXVI (January 1959): 2.

22. Carrol M. Shanks (president of the Prudential Insurance Co. of America), *We Believe in New England,* printed address of 31 January 1957 in Boston, Massachusetts, p. 8. Such appeals have been described as "purely strategical moves designed to influence the outcome" of legislative or administrative decisions. See John F. Due, "Studies of State-Local Tax Influences on Location of Industry," *National Tax Journal* XIV (June 1961): 165.

23. *Boston Globe,* 19 June 1958.

24. *Boston Globe,* 20 June 1958.

25. Quote taken from an article by Oliver W. Park (executive director, Assessing Department of Boston), "Equity and the Use of Proportional Return for New Construction," *Case Reports in Assessment Administration* I (September 1959): 51.

26. *Tax Policy* XXVI (January 1959): 4. A review of some of the technical problems involved in sinking footings, etc., in the Back Bay area is found in *Business Week* (11 June 1960): 96–104.

27. A rather full report of this conference is given in the *Christian Science Monitor,* 19 March 1958.

28. *Tax Policy* XXVI (January 1959): 5.

29. Ibid., 6.

30. Ibid.

31. Ibid. Also *Christian Science Monitor,* 19 March 1958.

32. Ibid.

33. Prudential planned to occupy the first eighteen floors of the 52-story building and rent the rest out to others.

34. *Tax Policy,* 6–7.

35. Ibid., 7.

36. Ibid. The exact yearly tax levy is reproduced.

37. Ibid.

38. *Christian Science Monitor,* 10 December 1959.

39. Ibid., 29 April 1960.

40. The decision was not actually read to the State Senate until May 31, 1960.

41. Section 10 of Chapter 121A.

42. Opinion of the Justices 332 Mass. 769.

43. "Statement of Attorney General Edward J. McCormack, Jr., Before Boston Redevelopment Authority Hearing on Prudential Center," State House, Boston, 22 March 1961, p. 1.

44. Ibid., 2.

45. Ibid. This is discussed at length in, Commonwealth of Massachusetts, *Senate Document* no. 634: 1–6.

46. Ibid.

47. In Boston the urban renewal functions of the local planning boards and the state housing board (set forth in General Laws, Chapter 121A) are performed by the Boston Redevelopment Authority.

48. McCormack, op. cit., 3.

49. *Christian Science Monitor,* 1 June 1960.

50. The amended act, *Massachusetts General Laws,* Chapter 121A, as amended through 1960, 652, is printed in *City Record* 52 (25 June 1960): 493–499; and in *Senate Document* no. 634: 7–21.

51. A. S. Plotkin, "The Prudential Center—From Seed to Blossom," *The Boston Sunday Globe* (special advertising section), 18 April 1965, 9.

52. "Letter from the Prudential Insurance Company of America to Msgr. Francis J. Lally, Chairman of the Boston Redevelopment Authority," dated 3 May 1961.

53. *Boston Daily Record,* 4 May 1961.

54. *Tax Policy,* 2.

55. "The Comparative Impact of Corporate Taxes in Massachusetts." *Report of the Special Commission of Taxation,* Part IV (Boston Commonwealth of Massachusetts, 1951), p. 15.

56. Mabel Walker, "Local Tax Competition Within Metropolitan Areas," *Tax Policy* XXV (July 1958): 4. (A detailed statement on such inducements and recent research is found in Benjamin Bridges, Jr., "State and Local Inducements for Industry," Part I, *National Tax Journal* XVIII (March 1965): 1–14, and Bridges, Part II, *National Tax Journal* XVIII (April 1965): 175–192.)

57. Ibid., 4–5. John F. Due has written, however: "The significance of the tax climate image in actual location decisions is difficult to assess. . . . But clearly the figures indicate that relatively low tax rates in themselves cannot protect a state from declining relative growth when other factors are unfavorable, whereas high tax rates and bad reputations taxwise appear not to have very significant effects in the opposite direction." John F. Due, "Studies of State–Local Tax Influences on Location of Industry," *National Tax Journal* XIV (June 1961): 169, 170–171.

58. Alan K. Campbell, "Taxes and Industrial Location in the New York Metropolitan Region," *National Tax Journal* XI (September 1958): 197.

59. *Tax Policy* XXVI (January 1959): 2. Joseph D. Silverherz in his study of assessments noted, "Still another assessor stated a rule which from the foregoing discussion of assessments would seem to be the cornerstone of assessment practice in many localities. He said, 'As long as the taxpayer is satisfied, I'm satisfied.'" Joseph D. Silverherz, "The Assessment of Real Property in the United States," *Special Report of the New York State Tax Commission,* no. 10, Albany, 1936, p. 121.

60. Quoted in Mable Walker, op. cit., 6–7.

61. William Slayton in writing of urban renewal made some lucid observations on tax agreements. He wrote, "In the . . . tax abatement method, however, the subsidy being granted is really hidden, even though it can be estimated fairly well. But it is not looked upon as a cost; it is often regarded as of no cost to the city. Thus,

the relation of cost and benefit is not apparent. If the tax gimmick is, in effect, to be used to finance the city's share of undertaking a redevelopment project, there are much more suitable devices for achieving the same result." William L. Slayton, "State and Local Incentives and Techniques for Urban Renewal," *Law and Contemporary Problems* XXV (Autumn 1960): 796. Robert C. Wood has written of Boston's decline in assessed valuations and rise in tax rates that, "faulty assessment practices and other deficiencies of the property tax as such accounted for some of the difficulty. But . . . the value of tax exempt real estate increased [between 1930 and 1951] by 216 million dollars, an increase of from 19 to 40 percent of total real property value." Robert C. Wood, *Suburbia* (Boston: Houghton Mifflin, 1959), p. 72. Public agencies own 75 percent of this tax exempt property. See an excellent discussion in Wilfred Owen, *The Metropolitan Transportation Problem* (Washington: The Brookings Institution, 1956), pp. 172–174. Experience with tax concessions in Louisiana showed that the cost of the program in terms of lost revenue was out of proportion to the direct results obtained. See Harry W. Wolkstein, "The Unfavorable Consequences of Tax Concessions to Business Location and Development." *Proceedings of the Fifty-fourth Conference of the National Tax Association,* 1961, p. 104. *Fortune* noted that the tax arrangement with the city of Boston ". . . is just another example of Prudential's ability to wait out a deal, as against the average investor's need for an immediate commitment," Robert Sheehan, "That Mighty Pump, Prudential," *Fortune* LXX (January 1964): 102.

62. Based on an article by Oliver W. Park, "The Capitalization Method and the Principle of Proportional Return," *The Realtor* (September–October 1959): 5.

63. Ibid., 5–6.

64. Oliver W. Park, "Equity and the Use of Proportional Return for New Construction." *Case Reports in Assessment Administration* I (September 1959): 51.

65. Ibid.

66. Ibid., 14–16.

67. *Tax Policy,* 7.

68. Park, "Equity and the Use of Proportional Return for New Construction," op. cit., 52.

69. For example, *Christian Science Monitor,* 19 March 1958.

70. Harry J. Loggan and Theodore S. Cady, letter to the editor, *Case Report in Assessment Administration* II (January 1960): 3.

71. An interesting argument has been made in a recent article that tax-exempt property, though removed from the tax rolls, does not represent a loss in municipal assets. The rationale seems to apply to the "concession" on taxes over the Prudential Center. The author writes, "Such properties, especially those of a governmental character, enhance the value of other property and generate other economic values." The author argues that the overall wealth of the community still benefits from a conversion into other forms of wealth. Proponents of the Prudential Center would surely argue that the stimulus to the "New Boston" is worth the loss in resources from the tax deal. See, Ernest Neufeld, "Is Tax Exempt Property a Municipal Asset?" *National Tax Journal* XVIII (December 1965): 415–419.

CHAPTER 12

The Ethical Issues of Privatizing Public Jobs

"Terminated?" Georgiana, the 46-year-old custodial worker cried. She'd worked more than a decade for the county and had planned on retiring in another nine or ten years. Now, she learned to her horror, the county had signed a long-term contract with a private firm that specialized in building maintenance and was laying off everyone on the county's maintenance payroll. Georgiana soon learned the details. The county would honor all accrued leave allotments, but workers would get nothing else—other than blue slips. The company taking over all the custodial duties under the new contract was offering jobs to any former county employee, but at barely above minimum wage and with virtually no benefit package at all. Georgiana was scared—overage and overweight, she was long tenured in a semiskilled blue-collar job and soon to be unemployed in a tight labor market. She had two teenagers to support (no husband) and little education. She learned quickly that her job had been *privatized*. Why would they do this? she wondered. I've received all kinds of awards and bonuses for being one of their best workers.

Georgiana recognized that her job was semiskilled, and she knew it would be easy to replace her. The hiring requirements were not specialized, and the tasks she completed daily were routine. It was more a question of fairness, loyalty, commitment, dedication—those old-fashioned virtues we espouse as a society. Fair treatment did not mean termination. She easily recalled the many times she had worked late to get a mess cleaned up—no thought of overtime pay; the many weekends she had come in for a few hours to set up for legislative hearings and committees—no thought of overtime pay; the holidays she had come in on to set up for parties—no thought of overtime pay (and no invitation either); the dozens of times she had brought in flowers or seasonal decorations bought with her own money. She had given this job a lot more than the official 40-hour workweek.

Privatization can impact on career public employees in five interrelated ways: career disruption and dislocation; morale and productivity; relocation and reciprocity; erosion of civil service and merit systems; and undermining of trust and credibility.

Career Disruption and Dislocation

When a public agency reduces employment by contracting for services to be provided by private workers, career public employees are usually laid off or, at best, positions vacated by normal attrition are not refilled. Reductions in force (rifs) due to privatization can disrupt individual careers and often severely dislocate personal

lives. When a major county government in Utah riffed several hundred social service workers to privatize such services, such disruptions took place. The following
statistics are indicative:[1]

46.1	Average age of riffed workers (in years)
7.5	Average tenure in county service (in years)
4.2	Average period of unemployment before locating new job (in months)
58.0%	Percentage finding reemployment at salary below level of county position at time of rif
86.0%	Percentage who drew down savings, cashed in investments, or withdrew vested retirement savings to cover shortfall (or all three)
23.5%	Percentage who had to move out of state to secure comparable employment
74.0%	Percentage who experienced lengthy depression, serious stress, or had other physical or emotional problems adjusting to rif

Workers interviewed uniformly expressed a sense of "shock," "betrayal," "un-
fairness," and similar attitudes. More than two-thirds claimed they had joined county
service with the intention of staying throughout the balance of their careers. More
than one-half claimed they originally left better jobs or accepted lower pay than they
had earned in former positions to join county service because of perceived security
of tenure and promises of "careers" or "superior retirement benefits," and so forth.
In this survey, the anger of former public workers was significantly heightened
because the jobs they lost were privatized and the private firm, which was the new
contractor, subsequently made an offer to hire many of the riffed workers but at
dramatically lower salaries and with virtually no benefit package.

Perhaps the most revealing statistic of all was that more than 85 percent of this
sample of former county workers stated that they would "never" work in public
service again and would "never" recommend public employment to others. Certainly these feelings of hostility will diminish in time, but the dislocations and disruptions will continue to bear bitter fruit. The grave matter of equity that arises when
career plans are disrupted by privatization must be addressed by its proponents.

Morale and Productivity

In 1982 to 1983 the author interviewed approximately fifty civilian custodial and
craft workers and some midlevel managers laid off from a major federal installation
in Utah when the agency contracted with a private firm to perform work that had
always previously been done by career public employees. The federal agency probably did everything possible in advance to mitigate hardship and shock.

Base officials refused to provide the author with comparative data on before-
and-after productivity measures, and therefore no documented evidence is available
to indicate how (or if) the rif affected productivity. However, former workers and
several supervisors uniformly expressed the following typical sentiments:

• For months before the privatization contract was signed, rumors and stories circulated in ever-growing "hysteria"

- Workers who fully expected to see their positions privatized deliberately slowed down, cut quality, even engaged in sabotage (the author was told some stories of what was done that he hopes were hyperbole)
- Workers anticipating rifs began to use up accrued leave in job searches and to utilize agency facilities (e.g., copying machines for resumes, long-distance calls for job searches) as much as they "dared"
- Even workers (allegedly) who were not to be laid off also "let down" and reduced output in sympathy with friends and colleagues who were being let go because a private firm was taking over
- Hostility and anger were greatest because of privatization; many federal workers had survived budget rifs and work load cutbacks at this same base and had never felt the "hurt" and "outrage" that privatization produced
- Workers who were not laid off (of whom the author surveyed only a small number) alleged that output was down for some months before the actual rifs, even in work areas not impacted directly by privatization and continued long after the private contractor(s) began to function—sort of a continuing lag in morale and productivity by survivors
- Perceptions of continuing workers as to the quality of contractor-provided services were mostly negative, even though management expressed full satisfaction
- Many older workers with significant tenure alleged that co-workers (never themselves) committed serious breaches of integrity immediately after the privatization contract was bid and the contractor(s) announced

Further, using the county example referred to earlier, evidence does exist to show "sympathy cuts" in productivity and a "ripple effect" of negative morale factors among career workers who were not immediately involved in privatization. A key central personnel staff member told the author in a confidential interview that in the division as a whole, sick leave abuse went up, transfers and quits more than doubled, the number of grievances filed significantly increased, and productivity fell (measured by client complaints, etc.) even months after the rifs.

Relocation and Reciprocity

For years private firms have engaged in out-placement in an attempt to assist (usually) executives who are being let go. Government agencies would appear fairer, more concerned, and wiser (in this author's opinion) to set up some formal efforts at assisting workers who are let go because of privatization to find approximate reemployment. This could well include brief training sessions on writing resumes, job-finding techniques and skills, interviewing tips, etc. The author is not proposing that government agencies assume the responsibility of placing each terminated worker, only that a caring, compassionate sense of concern be manifest. For example, careful advance orientation so that rumors can be minimized and efforts by jurisdictions to cooperate on mutual reciprocity provisions can succeed, particularly for civil service employees. Reciprocity provisions have been treated in some detail elsewhere (Timmins et al., 1979) but certainly apply in cases of privatization-caused reductions in force.

Under most civil service and merit systems, candidates seeking employment must compete openly for current vacancies (recruitment and examination) and must rank high enough on civil service registers to be in the top three to top five or "most qualified" categories. If advance reciprocity provisions have been worked out in, say, a metropolitan area, then riffed employees can bypass most civil service procedures and simply be appointed to existing vacancies as close to former job titles and pay grades as can be mutually determined. Virtually all civil service systems permit such reciprocity arrangements if the concerned parties agree to them in advance. Host jurisdictions may receive highly qualified workers for their vacancies in related positions with virtually no costs or efforts. Employees being laid off for any reason can obviously benefit by moving into comparable or closely related positions with minimal disruption or dislocation. But typical civil service procedures require written reciprocity arrangements prior to the critical need, and for this reason public agencies considering privatization should work out reciprocity provisions first through councils of governments (COGs), regional Associations of Governments (AOGs), state leagues of cities and towns or other regional and state bodies, particularly statewide civil service associations, if they exist.[2]

Such reciprocity provisions, important as they are, are not enough, however. Public agencies should set up formal programs to help place public workers being displaced by privatization. The author is also aware of a Utah state agency that replaced some fifty social service workers (in a jobs training area) because of privatization. Because of careful advance planning and out-placement efforts, only about a dozen former state workers were still unemployed thirty days after the private firm took over and only seven were still out of work sixty days later (and several of those had special health or family problems that made efforts at placement more difficult).[3] This is an enviable record, and evidence exists that morale stayed high, productivity did not drop, and hostile feelings were minimal. A humane policy and procedure to assist those being displaced by privatization—or any rif, for that matter—simply makes good sense.

Many of the riffed workers may be excellent candidates for jobs in other units of the agency. It is not uncommon for one state agency, for example, to be laying off workers while another state agency is hiring. Reciprocity provisions may not be needed at all in this kind of situation, but sharing of information and mutual cooperation surely will be. This is but one specific illustration of how a central personnel office or some other group can ameliorate career disruptions and dislocations and maintain morale and productivity, even when some public jobs are lost because of privatization.[4]

A last point on this topic of relocation and reciprocity—the government agency should seek to include in the contracts with the private provider some contractual language on hiring at least some of the displaced public workers. This author's experience to date with privatization suggests that private sector salaries and benefits are so comparatively low as to attract few displaced public workers. This point raises many interesting questions (e.g., how can a private firm hold quality workers at such low wages?) but the only issue raised here is that of humaneness and equity. One of the public agency's efforts at helping riffed workers might be to encourage (or if possible require in the contract) that the private firm hire some percentage of the displaced public employees. Some of the more comprehensive measures already described above will certainly be necessary.[5]

Erosion of Civil Service and Merit Systems

Civil service and merit systems (the terms are used here interchangeably) presuppose stability of public employment and typically do not provide well for rifs—or, if they do, usually provide for such measures as "reappointment registers," rehire "rights," dismissal for cause with appellate rights, and rif rosters (weighted somewhat by seniority and performance). Thus anything that bypasses or supersedes civil service/merit coverages and protections may serve to erode civil service/merit systems.

Contracting public services to private firms patently removes civil service protections (for example, open recruitment for position vacancies; certification of eligibles on the basis of competitive examinations; yes, even veterans' preference; selection on the basis of best [or at least most] qualified). Privatization replaces civil service rules and requirements with something considerably less in terms of employee and general public personnel protections. For instance, employees of private firms are not typically bound by public worker ethics or conflict of interest laws,[6] by nepotism statutes or ordinances or by political activity laws (little Hatch Acts). Privatization opens the door to potential abuses and vitiates many of the reformist laws governing public sector employment passed over the last century since passage of the original Pendleton Act.

This chapter does not discuss other problem areas of privatization such as what an agency does if the private firm goes out of business or if the service level isn't what was promised or if there are no satisfactory bids in the next few years and the city or county has to resume providing a specific type of service. These and a host of related issues bear directly on the issue of erosion of federal, state, and local civil service and merit systems. It took over a century to build these systems. Some of this careful developmental work can be jeopardized by privatization unless costs and benefits are factored into the ultimate decisions on privatization.

Trust and Credibility

Last, our state legislatures and the Congress have over many years developed elaborate systems for public employment. Not all of these systems work well. Indeed, the 1978 Civil Service Reform Act (CSRA) was a major effort to correct commonly perceived problems at the federal level.[7]

Nevertheless, civil service systems and merit systems at state and local levels have generally worked well and are still developing.[8] A measure of public confidence and trust in the integrity of public workers has been built up that privatization may jeopardize. This factor, too, must be built into any cost-benefit formulas used to decide whether to privatize. A century of progress should not be tampered with without the most careful consideration. If the bottom line is calculated using budgeting considerations only,[9] serious errors will be made by privatizing some public services.

Further, promises (implied or actual) have been made by our elected officials and legislatures about careers and the prospects faced by incumbents in the public service. This author is worried about the long-term impacts of privatization on public sector recruitment,[10] selection, and retention. A price may be exacted a generation from now that will be too great to bear. Applicants and employees (especially the best and the brightest) have very long memories. "Career" promises have always attracted and held public servants from sanitation crews to space scientists. The perils of tampering with this reservoir of promises should not be ignored.

This author has suggested five areas of concern in trying to measure the impacts of privatization on career public employees: one of equity to people who accepted career public service employment with good faith, expecting long-term employment based on satisfactory job performance; one of productivity and morale—a ripple effect of long-term impacts even beyond the public employees who are directly affected; one of eroding effects on long-established career systems that have generally served the public well; one that requires proponents of privatization, for example, to provide assistance and relocation assistance to workers being terminated (in part by inter-local reciprocity arrangements); and, last, one of an undermining of long-term trust and credibility by the general public and millions of public workers in the promises made and kept by our elected officials in our executive offices and legislatures.

The author is not opposed at all to privatization. He only suggests that we measure carefully the impacts of privatization on our career public workers and that we be sure of our cost-benefit calculations. All of us know that cost-benefit ratios shift as weights and criteria are manipulated. Privatization is one area of decision making that deserves the most careful ethical assessment because its effects are so profound on our quality of life, our democratic institutions, and our future well-being as a society.

Assignments

1. Discuss the ethical issues of privatization from the point of view of the career public worker whose job is privatized. Do you agree with the author's suggestions (retraining, reciprocity provisions, advance notice, etc.)? Why or why not? Does an employer have ethical obligations to workers under these conditions? If so, what are they?

2. Design a written policy on privatizing public jobs that best serves the interests of the employer, the employees, the private firm(s), and the general public. Subject your policy to debate, cross-examination, cost-benefit analysis, etc.

References

Colby, Peter W. et al. "Civil Service Reform: The Views of the Senior Executive Service." *Review of Public Personnel Administration* 1 (Summer 1981): 75–89.

Timmins, William M. 1984. "Relations between Political Appointees and Careerists." *Review of Public Personnel Administration* 4 (Spring): 79.

———. 1982. "Public Employees and the Exchanging of Gifts." *Public Personnel Administration* 11 (Spring): 61–67.

_____ . 1980. "Contracting for Cooperative Personnel Services." *Public Personnel Management* 8 (September–October): 196–200.

_____ . 1967. "Recruitment Practices in Utah." *Public Personnel Review* 28 (April):
105–110.

Timmins, William M. et al. 1985a. "Conflicting Roles in Personnel Boards: Adjudica-
tion vs. Policy-making." *Public Personnel Management* 5 (Summer): 191–204.

_____ . 1985b. "Cooperation between Personnel and Budget Office During Position Requests and Classification." *State and Local Government Review* 17
(Winter): 180–187.

_____ . 1979. "The Use of Reciprocity Provisions in State and Local Civil Service Systems." *Public Personnel Management* 8 (September–October): 282–286.

Notes

1. Based on confidential surveys with a sample of 120 former county social service employees riffed in 1983–1984 and in-depth interviews by the author with county
personnel staff, division supervisors, and others in administration.

2. There is a National Association of Civil Service Commissioners and Merit
Systems affiliated with the International Personnel Management Association (IPMA)
in Washington, DC.

3. Based on confidential interviews by the author with a sample of displaced
workers and a manager in the program.

4. See related suggestions in Timmins, 1980. Between 1978–1984 Los Angeles
County, California, contracted over 400 privatized contracts valued at $108 million
with a savings of $58 million, which have eliminated more than 2,200 public employee
positions. Average age of public workers was forty years with an average length of
service of ten years. The county claims the "impact has been minimal" because of
the county's vigorous out-placement efforts. These efforts included up-front, early
planning; attrition and widespread use of temporaries; testing and retraining of
employees to be riffed (county ordinance requires 5 percent of the cost savings from
contracting out to be spent on employee retraining); the county's efforts at referral
and placement (employees may be granted up to six months leave of absence without
pay to provide for a continuation of the county's employee health and dental benefit
subsidies during this period; up to one year county-approved retraining with county-
advanced or reimbursed tuition payments; and, if employees resign or retire, one
week severance pay for each full year of county service after at least five years continuous service). Source of data is a letter to the author, dated 27 February 1985,
from the Los Angeles County Personnel Office (mimeographed).

5. Fred B. Pearce, Sheriff of Multnomah County, Oregon (in a letter to the author
dated 21 February 1985) provided typical contract language in Oregon for organized
public employees, as follows:

Contract Work

(1) Unless mutually agreed, the County will not contract out or subcontract any work
now performed by employees by this agreement when such result in layoff of
any bargaining unit employee(s) and the County is unable to find suitable or com-

parable alternate employment for the employee(s). However, this provision shall not apply to contracting out or subcontracting work when such was anticipated and considered as a part of the budgeting process and when the Union Business Representative and/or President have been notified of the specific plan and its probable impact at least thirty (30) days prior to adoption of the annual executive budget or formal Board consideration of budget modifications.

(2) The County further agrees to meet with the Union, at its request, to explore the alternative of work force reduction. The County also agrees that to the extent practicable transfers shall be made to open vacancies and reemployment of employees affected by such action shall occur for as long as they are so qualified in accordance with established layoff guidelines. The Union agrees to assist the County in minimizing the impact of such affected employee(s).

(3) The County further agrees to notify Local 88 Business Agency (AFSCME) and/or President whenever the County contemplates entering into an Intergovernmental Agreement(s) with another public employer. The County also agrees to provide Union with a specific plan and its probable impact relative to Intergovernmental Agreements, when such Agreements are anticipated, at least thirty (30) days prior to formal Board consideration of budget modifications or Board's approval of the annual budget that is to be submitted to the Tax Supervising and Conservation Commission.

6. See a discussion of some of these issues in Timmins, 1982.

7. See, for example, Colby, 1981 and many more.

8. See, for example, Timmins et al., 1985a, and Timmins, 1984.

9. See a discussion of some of these issues in Timmins et al., 1985b.

10. In 1967 this author analyzed a state recruitment program and noted the need to adopt long-term recruitment efforts. See Timmins, 1967.

CHAPTER 13

Ethics and Inter-Local Contracting Arrangements

Kartchner, the city administrator, wanted flexibility. She ran an efficient city operation—three hundred employees, a budget that was well in the black, a new city hall and public safety buildings, a good capital reserve fund, and a reputation as a good boss to work for. She had weathered several elections, including last year's heated campaign.

Cityvale was a good city to administer. But traditional personnel methods did not seem adequate any longer. Kartchner wanted to try new techniques, new approaches, new methods to keep the city efficient and lean, although some of these approaches raised ethical questions in her mind. Take the use of *reciprocity provisions*. She had heard this concept recommended at a recent League of Cities and Towns convention.

Reciprocity Provisions

Following are three examples of the application of the reciprocity provisions she had heard about:

1. A state tax agency assisted a county assessor in completing an extensive reevaluation of commercial and residential properties. To complete the appraisals, state and county employees worked very closely with each other over a period of a year or more. At the end of the period of state technical assistance to the county, several state tax appraisers said they would like to work for the county assessor's office. Supervisors on both sides were willing to approve the personnel transfer. Under a reciprocity provision, the county merit system recognized the merit status conferred on the appraisers earlier by the state merit system, and the state employees were placed in their equivalent grade (and approximate salary step) by the county merit system. No open competition was required by the county since the two appraisers had originally been hired by the state under open recruitment, competitive examination, and selection from a register, and were career state employees.

2. A number of county mental health centers had most of their source of funds and mission absorbed by a counterpart state agency under provisions mandated by the state legislature. The state used a reciprocity provision in its merit system rules and regulations to recognize the merit coverage of the county workers (particularly the social workers and psychiatric workers) and transferred them to positions with state merit system coverage. No open competitive selection was required because

the county merit system was recognized by the state merit system as an equivalent merit system.

3. A small city annexed a mix of residential and commercial property from unincorporated land in the county. Consequently, the county found its staffing needs partially reduced, particularly for deputy sheriffs. The superfluous law enforcement personnel were originally hired by open competitive selection by the deputy sheriff's civil service commission. Since the annexing city had an effective civil service system (with a reciprocity article) for its public safety personnel, the city's civil service commission recognized the comparability of the county deputy sheriff's civil service system and transferred the county deputies, granting them city civil service coverage without open competitive examination at salary grades and steps that were individually negotiated to be as close as possible to their existing grades and steps.

These examples of the use of reciprocity provisions by comparable merit systems confirm the findings of a national survey. The survey, using a random sample of fifty jurisdictions from the International Personnel Management Association's (IPMA) *Membership Directory,* solicited information on the use (or abuse) of such reciprocity arrangements. Over 80 percent (44) of the jurisdictions responded. A typical description of how reciprocity is implemented was included with the questionnaire:

Cooperation with Other Merit System Departments

Section 1—Recognizing Registers or Merit System Status in Comparable Jurisdictions.

Paragraph 1. Upon written request from a department asking for recognition of an appropriate register or County Merit System status for a class of position established under another Merit System operating in conformity with our standards, the County Personnel Director may require any available applicants to compete on an open-competitive basis or he may:

   a. Determine where such merit system operates under standards comparable to our own and obtain specific information or a copy of the minimum qualifications met by the applicant in such other jurisdiction.
   b. Approve the request for a probationary appointment if he has found that:
      (1) Such other merit system operates under comparable standards to our own.
      (2) The class of position in the other jurisdiction is reasonably equivalent to the position to which an appointment is requested under the merit system.

Section 2—Certification to Other Jurisdictions

Paragraph 1. Upon request for certification from any Federal, State, County, or Municipal Civil Service jurisdiction of any employee from a merit system register or of a former employee, the County Personnel Director shall make such certification if the County Merit System records do not show that he is both eligible and available for appointments under the County Merit System.

The results of the survey (see Table 13-1) were impressive because some 32 percent of the sample do have some formal or informal provisions in their rules and regulations and make at least some use of the concept for personnel transfer.

Table 13-1 Use of Reciprocity Agreements

		Total	*Percent*
A.	Formal Reciprocity Agreement now in use (oral or written)	9	22
B.	Limited Informal Agreement (particularly on sharing registers)	4	10
C.	No Oral/Written Agreement (and none anticipated)	23	56
D.	Other Responses ("no merit system," etc.)	5	12
		41	100

This survey drew a number of spirited endorsements of reciprocity agreements as well as several letters highly critical of them. The process is infrequently utilized, but when procedures have been formalized, they provide for several safeguards. Many writers detailed case studies of the use (or abuse) of reciprocity arrangements.

Minnesota's response typified most jurisdictions because that state relied on inter-local agreements and handled transfers on a case-by-case basis. For example, the Minnesota State Department of Personnel operates under a statute which includes the provision that

> the Commissioner may enter into arrangements with personnel agencies of other jurisdictions for the purpose of exchanging and effecting transfers of employees. The commissioner may also join or subscribe to any association or service having as its purpose the interchange of information relating to the technique of personnel administration.
>
> We have long effected the transfer of employees working under merit system jurisdictions under this statute. We have handled these on a case by case basis. . . . We make five to ten such transfers a year.

California's use of reciprocity arrangements includes a unique provision for reinstatement as well as transfer:

> California State Personnel Board: The second program covers approximately 4,000 full-time employees in the State's smaller county public health, welfare, and emergency services departments. This program allows the direct appointment of persons employed in comparable classes in other merit systems. The program also allows the use of eligible lists from other merit systems . . .
>
> > Article 6. Cooperation with Other Merit System Agencies . . . *Certification from Eligible Lists of Other Merit Systems.* At the request of a merit system appointing authority, the State Personnel Board may authorize that appointing authority to use an existing eligible list for a comparable class established in conformity with these standards but under another recognized merit system.
> > 17590. *Transfer or Reinstatement from Other Merit Systems.* Upon the request of a merit system appointing authority, a person who has held permanent status in another recognized merit system shall be eligible for reinstatement or transfer to an appropriate vacant position in the same class, comparable class or in a lower related class in the California Merit System in Accordance with standards established by the State Personnel Board.
>
> Although we do not maintain data on the use of these provisions, we expect that the provisions are used infrequently and primarily for journey-level clerical and Welfare Eligibility Technician classes. Since we encounter few major differences

between our use and selection for these classes and other California merit systems, few problems occur. Salaries for these classes are established by the county boards of supervisors and vary throughout the State.

The Minnesota State Personnel Department uses a form titled "Agreement to Transfer an Employee from Another Governmental Jurisdiction Under Personnel Rule 91e," which details effective dates, salary range, accumulated sick leave, and so forth, and requires signatures of originating and appointed agency officials. The form states that "transferred employees shall be granted all privileges of other employees in the classified service and shall be required to serve a probationary period as outlined in Personnel Rule 97."

Salt Lake County, Utah, requires the initiating department to document all the particulars in a formal letter of request for consideration directed to the three-member County Merit Council. The county personnel director must then verify all details, and the action is approved (or denied) by formal action of the merit council on a case-by-case basis. The procedure is used perhaps six or seven times a year. A careful analysis of the success of these personnel transfers shows that all have proved very successful in the years the provision has been utilized. Both accepting supervisors and employees involved in the transfers were pleased with how well things had worked out.

Most other jurisdictions who responded to the survey likewise used a formal means of completing the transfer of personnel, chiefly providing for verification of established merit coverage and acceptance of accrued benefits, for example, Prince George's County (Executive Order No. 2-1977) details such provisions as status on transfer, notice on transfer, departmental approval, earned sick and annual leave, compensatory leave, new anniversary date, retirement plan, and health and life insurance coverage. These arrangements are then formalized by inter-local agreements. (In Maryland, for example, several forms are used for such agreements.)

The arguments favoring reciprocity agreements can be summarized as follows:

1. Transfer of qualified and competent personnel is facilitated by reciprocity arrangements. Highly skilled personnel (for example, doctors and nurses) are hard to come by and reciprocity provisions expedite hiring key personnel in and between comparable jurisdictions.

2. Loss of valuable personnel is minimized by reciprocity agreements when one jurisdiction is caught in a rif, a shift of program or mission, or a desire to transfer by incumbents. For any number of reasons talented workers may desire or have to leave one public employer. Reciprocity allows greater flexibility in accepting these personnel into another public system without the attendant hazards and delay of announcing a vacancy, recruiting, giving a competitive exam, establishing a register, and so forth. (And, since most systems bring the transferee aboard on probationary status, no real risk exists of unsatisfactory performance or of other unknown factors troubling the employer accepting the transfer.)

3. A significant morale factor can exist. Wherever employees fear potential job loss, there can develop a debilitating condition that hurts morale and thus productivity. Reciprocity arrangements can minimize the fears and concerns of public workers who anticipate the closing of an agency or the reduction of staffing. (In the law

enforcement example used at the beginning of this chapter, reciprocity rules were successful in relocating several officers and deputies. All parties seem satisfied with the outcomes. One twenty-year veteran of a county deputy sheriff's civil service system said, "My greatest fear was having to compete with a bunch of young bucks for a job when the city annexed all that county territory. I just did not want to have to take a written test again." The former deputy has proved to be an excellent city police officer and receives approximately the same pay—but not rank—he previously held with the county.)

4. In an age of shortages of skilled personnel, reciprocity arrangements have great promise of being a fruitful source of talent, especially in EEO-sensitive positions. Remember that reciprocity presupposes the comparability of both the former and new positions—it is not intended as an end run around skills and qualifications.

The arguments against reciprocity run as follows:

1. Such transfers violate the principles of open recruitment by limiting candidates to the transferee(s).

2. The process can be utilized to make end runs around the merit system or civil service system—that is, since no competitive examination is required, there is no guarantee of securing well-qualified personnel. Further, the probationary period is mere window dressing. The accepting agency is favorably disposed toward the candidate or the transfer would never have been carried out in the first place.

3. Employee morale may suffer because employees below the level of the position filled by reciprocal transfer will see their opportunities to rise within the organization eroded.

4. The arguments about flexibility and fruitful sources of talent are the very types of claims always used by those who would weaken the traditional merit principles. All safeguards to the contrary, reciprocity agreements have a risk of being abused and misused.

5. Such transfers may run afoul of promotional provisions in collective bargaining agreements and must be examined in the light of labor-management contracts. (Although no such instances were noted by those who responded to our survey, several raised the issue.)

In summary, formal or informal reciprocity arrangements were used by more than a third of the jurisdictions surveyed. Most jurisdictions have experienced positive results from the limited use of reciprocity. Most restricted use to a case-by-case basis. Almost all transfers were from agencies within state boundaries. In other words, reciprocal transfers are extremely rare across state boundaries, but relatively frequent intrastate. Most used some form of written documentation to regularize the transfer arrangements. And finally, most agencies who used reciprocity were sensitive to the potential abuse of reciprocity transfers but felt the merits clearly outweighed possible hazards.

As Cityvale expanded its fire service district this year to include the new subdivision just being finished, perhaps Kartchner should talk to the county about its surplus fire fighters and lateral them into the new station, without open recruitment.

Kartchner had also attended workshops at the League meetings on contracting for cooperative personnel services. *Not* "contracting out" to the private sector (Chapter 12) but contracting (which includes a variety of cooperative arrangements) with other governmental jurisdictions for personnel services.[1]

How common are such personnel-related contracting arrangements between states and cities, cities and counties, cities and cities, etc.? The author assessed the concept and practice by surveying 110 public personnel agencies randomly selected from the *IPMA Membership Directory.* Sixty-three jurisdictions responded to a detailed questionnaire, a return of 57 percent, which is more than adequate to give some validity to the findings reported here. A number of interesting trends and findings were apparent.

Interjurisdictional contracting can best be described as formal or informal contracting between two or more public jurisdictions for the provision of one or more personnel services by one body for another (or for others). That is, city X contracts with county Y to conduct physical examinations for candidates for X's fire fighters; or, state Z contracts with several cities for the development of valid written examinations for a series of positions in public health; or, city A contracts with city B to program and maintain A's personnel records on city B's computer system; or, state D conducts a salary survey for a number of cities. Numerous other examples could be found. How frequent are such practices and what has been the experience to date?[2]

Of the respondents to the author's mail survey, some 70 percent favor such contracting, while 22 percent do not. (The balance either had no experience upon which to base an opinion or made no choice on the item.) Of those jurisdictions who do now formally or informally rely on another jurisdiction for one or more personnel services, 40 percent use a formal written contract and 60 percent use an informal agreement, most often at least partially reduced to written format, but not legally processed as would be a binding interjurisdictional contract. Many states do not have statutes enabling inter-local contracting, as between cities. The average number of employees among the respondents was 831, with a range from less than 20 employees to over 40,000. The average size of the personnel staff was 8, again ranging from 2 staff to 400 in the personnel operation itself.

Larger jurisdictions strongly favored contracting for personnel services. Among jurisdictions with over 800 employees, over 83 percent were in favor of contracting, and slightly more than half currently participate in such contract services in one way or another. Likewise, the smaller the jurisdiction (and thus its personnel system), the more hesitant or less likely it is to favor contracting and the less experience the personnel staff has had with it. Less than one-fourth of all smaller respondents currently contract for any personnel services.

Four reasons were most often cited by those favoring interjurisdictional contracting. (1) Economic advantages, 50 percent. It is cheaper to have a larger jurisdiction conduct a salary survey rather than have many smaller systems carry out multiple surveys of the same labor market; it is less costly for one jurisdiction to give all the typing and shorthand tests for a group of jurisdictions than to have several systems carry out performance tests of applicants on their own. (2) Better quality of service, 35 percent. For example, a salary survey may be more sophisticated and reliable if done by a particular jurisdiction with broad contacts and experience; or position classification is better performed by experienced staffers in a larger system. (3) Contracting reduces duplication, 19 percent. For example, having one system design or redesign model personnel forms—say, application blanks—can eliminate "reinventing the wheel"; one jurisdiction can design and conduct a basic supervisory training course for several systems as easily as two or more jurisdictions, which would probably largely duplicate the same course objectives, content, and arrangements. (4) The lack of uniquely skilled personnel staff in some public systems, 19 percent. For example, city M contracts with county N to provide help in human resources forecasting because M has no econometricians or personnel skilled in forecasting; or county O contracts with a COG (multicounty) to develop long-range population projections to be used in drafting personnel budgets in the long-range planning document for a metropolitan area undergoing significant regional growth.

Three major reasons were cited in the survey by those who did *not* favor contracting. (1) Political and geographical impracticalities, 50 percent. The separation of two jurisdictions by vast geographical distances would reduce or eliminate contract advantages; or, political opposition by city council P to contractual arrangements with county Q where past friction has colored relationships. (2) The perception that local needs will not be well met by contracting, 33.3 percent. A typical comment was that "no advantage can be perceived in contracting for labor relations" functions, say "at the table negotiations"; or, an offer of state R to city S to conduct its recruitment is rejected because S perceives no need to expand recruitment for its personnel beyond the universe of talent already available. (3) Discrepancy in methods, 20 percent. For example, city T uses a different civil service system than city U does, and U cannot—or will not—reconcile those differences to accommodate a contract for fire fighter agility exams; or, because county V grants veterans' preference and county W does not, the ranking of eligibles for certification is handled differently by each system and thus W chooses not to contract with V, other advantages notwithstanding. Many other individual reasons were cited by those unfavorably disposed to contracting, but the above three were dominant.

Among jurisdictions now contracting (formally or informally) for personnel services, the most common services provided by interjurisdictional contract are testing and examination (52%), recruitment (18%), and salary surveys (18%). Still, given a list of possible personnel functions, respondents indicated much broader contracting interests than is apparent from current practice. For instance, the following percentages of respondents cited strong interest in working out arrangements for cooperative services:

87%   Salary surveys, other benefits, research information
59%   Recruitment services/assistance
57%   Test construction or administration
57%   Test validation
55%   Job analysis, position classification services
52%   Midlevel management training
44%   Executive development

A number of other personnel areas or functions (for example, multi-employer bargaining, human resources planning, impasse resolution and arbitration) received either no comment or very few responses.

Those who favored extending contracting for personnel services even beyond those functions now common suggested the following three major advantages to such extension. Coordination, 36 percent. Contracting would permit effective coordination in, say, recruitment, where job analysis, classifications, certification, and so forth, would require constant and careful coordination to ensure to both parties compliance with system rules and regulations and effective and efficient recruitment. "Economies of scale" was mentioned next by over 27 percent of the survey group and "better quality of personnel services" by nearly 35 percent. Frequent comments were made on this last point, for example, fire fighter training is significantly better for city J now that J has contracted with county K to train J's recruits in K's training facility and with its curriculum and staff.

The chief disadvantage to contracting cited by almost half (46%) of the respondents was the loss of control over one's own personnel system, or some portion of it. For instance, to contract with another jurisdiction for, say, test development and validation is to lose some of the control over the examination process, no matter how carefully the contract is drawn. This disadvantage could be even more pronounced in functional areas such as recruitment and training.

Jurisdictions with some experience with contracting for cooperative personnel services favored long-term contracts. Asked the usual length of such cooperative contracts when they are now participating in such arrangements (or have been previously), respondents stated the optimal length of the personnel services contract to be

38%   3–5 years or longer
34%   1–3 years
28%   0–1 year

One of the most interesting findings of the survey was in answer to question 12, "In your state who would be the logical agency/party to take the lead in stimulating interjurisdictional research and interest in interjurisdictional contracting for personnel services?" Respondents indicated their preferences for initiating agencies (for contract arrangements) as follows:

27%   Leagues of cities
22%   State personnel agencies
14%   Another city or county
13%   State legislatures
12%   COGs (Councils of Government)
10%   Other(s)

To the author it is apparent that state agencies and associations of local governments are perceived as the logical parties to launch cooperative efforts like those described in this chapter.

Jurisdictions with some or a good deal of experience with cooperative personnel services were almost uniformly positive. Few negative incidents were cited. As would be expected, those who favored the concept enough to enter into contract arrangements (formal or informal) seemed to feel that the results were uniformly beneficial. Several respondents noted problems of adequately specifying performance levels, of calculating true costs, of quality control, and of renegotiating contracts after a negative experience. (One city had a very difficult time organizing itself after "getting out of the recruitment business for five years, during which time we had relied exclusively upon a state agency for everything under a contract; and then we had to start all over from scratch when the state expressed no interest in further contracting for services.") Several positive expressions were those of smaller (or poorer) jurisdictions that had received adequate services under such contract arrangements. Indeed, several cities and counties with substantial experience with cooperative arrangements expressed the most positive accounts of quality services, excellent benefit-cost ratios, and improved personnel effectiveness. The respondents' conclusions were overwhelming that when carefully, realistically, and openly entered into, such cooperative arrangements work well, even very well, especially when formalized by contract.

Some Conclusions

Considerable interest is extant in contracting for cooperative personnel services. Larger personnel systems (800 or more employees) have more interest and significant experience—almost entirely favorable. Smaller systems (fewer than 800 employees) have as yet less interest and little experience. Overall, almost 70 percent of the respondents favor such contracting for personnel services, particularly when testing, recruitment, and salary and benefits surveys are concerned. Those systems that favor contracting see advantages in "economies of scale," better quality of service, less duplication of effort, and help when personnel staff is insufficient. Those jurisdictions opposed to contracting with others for personnel services see hazards in political and geographical impracticalities, failure to meet local needs, and discrepancies in methods and techniques involved.

Typically such arrangements are informal (61%) even if reduced to writing, and tend to be for longer periods such as one to three years (34%) or even three to five years or more (38%). Among those who favor contracting for services (a clear majority), the strongest interest in cooperative arrangements lies in salary and benefit surveys, recruitment services or assistance, test construction and validation, job analysis and position classification, midlevel management training, and executive development.

Finally, most respondents felt such cooperative arrangements should be initiated by leagues of cities (or similar associations), state agencies, state legislatures, other (larger) cities and counties, and councils of governments—obviously reflecting a desire, as one response put it, "for larger, more sophisticated systems to reach out and offer help—at cost—to smaller personnel systems who need help but are inadequately staffed and budgeted to get timely assistance."[3]

Perhaps, mused Kartchner, she ought to sign an inter-local contract for testing and selection. Cityvale could never afford its own psychometrician. She was not too interested in contracting for law enforcement or fire fighting, but designing tests and administering a valid testing program was beyond the city's present competency level under any conditions—even a clerical exam could cost tens of thousands of dollars to design and properly validate.

Kartchner had recently been approached to participate in a cooperative recruitment effort. Those offering the service explained it by asking, "Why should a job seeker have to trudge around to ten or more public employers to find out about government job opportunities in her home town? And why should she have to take ten or more similar examinations to be considered for the same kind of job by these same employers?"

These are not hypothetical questions. Job seekers in many localities pointlessly duplicate their efforts. It was not until recent years that enterprising public managers, working together, began doing something about it. One solution was to establish one-stop intergovernmental job information centers. Another was for several governmental units to agree to accept eligibility in one job examination as a valid entry into the same kind of job in all jurisdictions. Still another was to share eligibility lists among different units of government.

Intergovernmental cooperation in hiring practices was stimulated by the Intergovernmental Personnel Act of 1970 (IPA), which in turn, grew out of a recognition that people make the big difference in government performance at every level—and especially at the state and local levels where most public services are delivered. The emphasis of the IPA was on helping state and local governments strengthen their personnel resources through voluntary partnership. Even after Congress ceased funding the program, some efforts continued.

Conflicting laws and procedures can be a problem and so can budget, at least at first. But the fact that innovative joint programs are already working is ample testimony that many problems can be overcome if the desire is there. In the long run, joint endeavors should result in substantial economies, and this possibility alone warrants a careful look at the programs.

The Utah Intergovernmental Personnel Agency Center (UIPA) was funded by a grant from the U.S. Civil Service Commission to the Utah State Department of Community Affairs. The grant funded a new, combined examining program for city, county, state and federal jobs through Utah State Employment Security offices for a broad range of office assistants—clerks, typists, and stenographers, for example. During the first year of operation ten or more public jurisdictions in Utah (federal, state, local, and university) participated in the services of the center. Table 13-2 details the statistics of a typical year of the Utah IPA Center.

The center has received extensive—and favorable—media coverage in Utah as a one-stop shopping center for applicants seeking clerical employment in public agencies. Fourteen offices of the Utah State Employment Service have cooperated in the program by recruiting, accepting applications, administering examinations, etc.

All applicants are required to take a written test covering verbal abilities and clerical aptitudes, and, depending on the job, demonstrate skills such as typing, short-hand, office machine operation, telephone switchboard operation, or data processing operation. In addition, they must also meet the experience or educational requirements indicated for the particular position.

Table 13-2 UIPA Statistics by Participating Agencies

Agency	Typical year		
	No. of orders	*No. of referrals*	*No. of hires*
State of Utah	602	6,214	390
Salt Lake County	164	1,261	146
Salt Lake City	51	375	38
Univ. of Utah	13	26	23
Utah State Univ.	56	300	109
Utah County	18	233	18
Davis County	6	55	1
Weber State	2	8	1
Weber County	5	76	1
Murray City	2	18	1
Total	919	8,566	735

Performance tests are given at the time of the written test to those applying for jobs as typists, stenographers, or secretaries. For the position of typist, applicants must pass a five-minute typing test at a minimum rate of 40 words per minute; for stenographer and secretary they must also pass a stenography test consisting of dictation at 80 words minimum per minute and questions to be answered from the dictation notes. Some higher-level positions require higher typing and shorthand speeds.

Administration of all parts of the written and performance tests requires approximately ninety minutes for typists and two and one-half hours for stenographers. Sample test questions can be obtained from any Utah State Employment Security Office in Utah or from the Federal Job Information Centers in Ogden and Salt Lake City.

Agreeing on Requirements

Before the center was launched, the cooperating jurisdictions had difficulty agreeing on education and experience requirements for the wide range of clerical positions. Ultimately the personnel directors and merit councils agreed on some common "Experience or Education Requirements" as shown in Table 13-3.

Applicants were advised that there could be other positions having the same or similar requirements that might be filled by participating governmental entities from the lists of eligibles resulting from this announcement.

In addition, appropriate training obtained in Job Corps centers, Neighborhood Youth Corps projects, and in other similar manpower development training programs conducted by churches, schools, unions, or other organizations is counted toward meeting the experience or education requirements. The amount of credit allowed for this type of training depends on the scope and intensity of the training and the amount actually completed. Some unpaid experience or volunteer work is credited on the same basis as similar paid experience. This work may have been performed in connection with religious, community, cultural, social services, or professional association activities.

Table 13-3 Experience or Education Requirements

For position of:	The experience or educational requirement is
Clerk Clerk-Typist Clerk-Stenographer Sales Store Checker Cashier Typist Secretary (Beginning Level)	a. Six months of progressively responsible clerical or office experience. To be qualified for typist or stenographer the experience must have included application of the appropriate skill (typing or stenography) as a significant part of the work or b. Graduation from high school
Office Machine Operator Bookkeeping Machine Operator Calculating Machine Operator (Beginning Level)	a. Six months of specialized experience or b. Completion of a specialized course in operation of the appropriate machine plus three months of general experience or c. Graduation from high school
Clerk Clerk-Typist Clerk-Stenographer Typist Secretary (Intermediate Level)	a. One year of progressively responsible clerical or office experience or b. Successful completion of one academic year of study above the high school level in a resident business or secretarial school, junior college, or college
Office Machine Operator Bookkeeping Machine Operator Calculating Machine Operator (Intermediate Level)	a. One year of acceptable experience of which at least six months is specialized or b. One academic year of business or secretarial school or junior college
Sales Store Checker Cashier (Intermediate Level)	Total of 1 year of education or experience as follows: a. Six months of general experience or b. Six months of successfully completed full-time academic study above the high school level plus a. Six months of specialized experience or b. Three months of specialized experience and successful completion of a specialized course of instruction of 50 hours or more in performing duties of the kind to be performed in the position to be filled.
Telephone Operator (Beginning Level)	a. Six months of experience as a telephone operator in a central telephone office or on a switchboard in a business or government establishment, provided that such experience was gained on a switchboard that had at least 25 working lines. This experience may have been on a multiple or non-multiple cord-type switchboard of a "console" automatic electric remote control switchboard or b. Graduation from high school

Table 13-3 Experience or Education Requirements (*continued*)

For position of:	*The experience or educational requirement is*
Telephone Operator (Intermediate Level)	One year of telephone operating experience described in (a) above, which also included some experience in performing long distance or information operating duties
Teletypist (Intermediate Level)	One year of general experience which included one or a combination of the following: a. Experience as a typist, alphabetical keypunch operator or other work which required skill in the operation of a typewriter-style keyboard or b. Any type of experience which provided a knowledge of communications operations and procedures or c. Other types of experience which provided a knowledge of communications equipment operating work or which required skill in use of typewriter boards.
Teletypist (Advanced Level)	1½ years of general experience (see (a), (b), and (c) for Teletypist, GS-3) and ½ year specialized experience which would include experience in operating one or more kinds of the type of communications equipment indicated by title of position
Clerk-Typist Clerk-Stenographer Typist Secretary (Advanced Level)	a. Successful completion of 2 academic years of substantially full-time study in a resident school above the high school level or b. Two years of appropriate experience or c. One year of education and one year of appropriate experience
Cardpunch Operator (Beginning Level)	High school graduation or equivalent
Cardpunch Operator (Intermediate Level)	High school graduation or equivalent plus One year of experience of which six months must be related to the title

Response Time

Response time averages twenty-four hours in most cases. That is, from the time a participating public agency requests a register from the center in Salt Lake City until it is delivered, an average of twenty-four hours elapses. This standard is not always met, but most jurisdictions seem well pleased with response time. Applicants are told that if they receive an eligible rating as a result of this announcement, such eligibility will be for a one-year period unless removed from consideration because of acceptance of a position, failure to reply to official correspondence, or for other reasons. If they do not receive an offer of appointment within the one-year eligibility period, they may again participate in this announcement by recompeting in the examination.

The Job Corps center and Employment Security jointly produced a slide–sound presentation that is shown to all applicants. It reviews job requirements and hiring procedures. The showing is followed by a brief orientation and question-and-answer period, before the examination process is completed (or scheduled).

All jobs are paid at the current monthly or annual salary rate for the position with the particular employing government agency. Information about current rates can be obtained from local offices of the government entity applicants are interested in, and is available and on display at all Employment Security offices around the state. Table 13-4 compares the fringe benefits of the participating jurisdictions. This information is provided in printed format to all applicants.

There is no evidence yet that applicants draw unfavorable conclusions from comparing such data. There has been considerable "market" pressure, however, on some smaller jurisdictions who participate in the services of the center to bring their clerical salary schedules more in line with comparable jurisdictions. When one jurisdiction adjusts its salary schedule for clerical positions, others are acutely conscious of it.

While it is not possible to document all the pros and cons of this new, combined examining program, some major conclusions can be safely made, both positive and negative.

Positive

1. The Utah State Employment Service effort has generally greatly enlarged the universe of talent available to participating jurisdictions.

2. Participation in organizing the center and compromising on operational details has had a beneficial impact on all member jurisdictions. Intergovernmental cooperation and coordination has become a reality. As one personnel director told the author, "Talking together is mutually beneficial. We can all learn from one another."

3. The center has been favorably received by the public as a one-stop shopping center for clerical jobs in the public sector.

4. Using the center has significantly reduced the work load for some of the participating personnel agencies. The personnel director of Salt Lake City told the author that the center has reduced applicant traffic in his office by some 60 percent, thus freeing him and his staff for more important duties than processing clerical applications and administering routine examinations.

5. In general, the quality of applicants certified by the center seems high, perhaps higher than before the center was established. The personnel director of Salt Lake County recently told the author that he receives frequent favorable comment in this regard from county department heads.

6. For individual applicants the center is efficient and convenient. The author randomly interviewed several recently hired state and local employees who uniformly expressed favorable reactions to having been able to take only one test and yet get

Table 13-4 Comparison of Benefits*

	Salt Lake City	Salt Lake County	State of Utah	University of Utah	Federal government
Annual leave	10 workdays first 10 years; 15 workdays over 10 years; 20 workdays over 15 years	12 workdays first 8 years; 18 workdays over 9 years; 24 workdays over 17 years	12 workdays first 5 years; 15 workdays over 5 years; 18 workdays over 10 years	12 workdays first 5 years; 15 workdays over 6 years; 18 workdays over 10 years	13 workdays first 3 years; 20 workdays over 3 years; 26 workdays over 15 years
Sick leave	15 workdays per year**	12 workdays per year	12 workdays per year	12 workdays per year	13 workdays per year
Paid holidays	12 per year	12 per year	12 per year	10 per year	9 per year
Health benefits	Available through group plan	Group insurance with county sharing cost	Choice of plans with state sharing cost	Choice of plans with university sharing cost	Choice of plans with government sharing cost
Life insurance	Available in coordination with group health insurance	Included in group plan	Attractive group rates	Attractive group rates	Attractive group rates
Injury compensation	Yes	Yes	Yes	Yes	Yes
Retirement	Joint contributory system	Entire cost paid by county effective 1/1/73	Entire cost paid by state of Utah	Entire cost paid by university	Joint contributory system

*Other participating governmental entities will have similar or other benefits.

**Employees are given an additional 30 days per year hospital leave, non-accumulative, to be used only when the employee is actually hospitalized.

on many registers. (The author believes most clerical applicants are after a *job* and don't usually care about the supposed differences between the state, county, or city.)

Negative

1. The center has removed considerable control over some personnel matters from participating jurisdictions and vested it in an ad hoc agency clearly tainted by its 100 percent federal funding (even though it is partially staffed on a part-time basis by most of the participating governments). In some jurisdictions there is considerable fear that this will weaken local merit systems or further erode local control over personnel matters.

2. Participation in the center forces member jurisdictions to be in greater competition for applicants. While it could be argued that this is the case anyway (the whole state is a labor market in one sense), smaller jurisdictions express concerns about the long-range impact their participation is having on benefit packages, wage rates, and personnel practices.

3. There is always the fear that if the U.S. Civil Service Commission clerical examination being used is ever successfully challenged in court, all local and state jurisdictions are involved and will be subject to like litigation.

4. To date, the services of the center are chiefly utilized by only three of the participating jurisdictions (see Table 13-2. Salt Lake County, Utah State University, and the state of Utah account for almost 90% of the center orders received and over 85% of the hires).

5. The center's minority recruitment appears disappointing—barely over 3 percent of those hired from center registers are minorities. Most participating jurisdictions cannot rely at present solely on the center for recruitment of minority employees into clerical positions.

The author believes the positive features of the Utah experience outweigh the negative. Observers and practitioners can both benefit from continued study of such efforts at intergovernmental personnel administration.

Kartchner reviewed the ethical questions raised by the three inter-local approaches she had been hearing about—contracting for services, cooperative efforts, and reciprocity provisions. Each bypassed traditional personnel systems. Was this the kind of flexibility she was seeking?

Assignments

1. Interview public agencies in your state who have tried one or more of the three tools or techniques explored in this chapter. How well do they work? Are they being abused? Report back in some detail an analysis of what really happens. Are there ethical dimensions that need to be resolved? Union position on these techniques could be very revealing; talk to some public employee unions.

2. Debate the ethics of each of the three alternative techniques described from the point of view of elected officials, public employees, applicants for employment, and the public's interest. Each method has problems and opportunities.

Notes

1. See Robert D. Lee, *Public Personnel Systems.* (Baltimore: University Park Press, 1979), pp. 121–124, and N. Joseph Cayer, *Managing Human Resources* (New York: St. Martin's Press, 1980), pp. 55–57, for instance. Readers may recognize some aspects of the Lakewood plan in this approach. See John C. Bollens, et al., *The Metropolis: People, Politics, and Economic Life.* (New York: Harper & Row, 1970), pp. 361–363, for details on the Lakewood plan.

2. For the "Future of Contracting Out to the Private Sector," see Cayer, op. cit., 220–221. Inter-local contracting in the area of law enforcement is common, for example. One study showed that several hundred cities in more than half the states use such contracting. See Robert R. Delahunt, *Contract Law Enforcement: A Guide to Program Development.* (Washington, DC, National Institute of Law Enforcement and Criminal Justice, 1978), pp. 7–13.

3. Respondents who cited such favorable experiences included nearly two dozen systems as diverse as Jefferson County, Alabama (County Personnel Board); Pennsylvania Department of Community Affairs (Municipal Consulting Division); and St. Louis County, Missouri.

PART IV

Ethics of Health and the Workplace

This cluster has four controversial cases. In one, a physician in a public hospital must help a family decide whether to withhold life-sustaining care from a comatose, elderly patient. The family is divided over the issue, the courts are indecisive, the physician is being called on to make the decision— do nothing, pull the plug, continue all means possible to sustain life. But who should pay for the choice made?

As more and more women return to work, the need for child care becomes increasingly apparent. Unions, among others, strongly advocate employer-sponsored child care. But this raises troublesome ethical issues. Inadequate child care remains one of the biggest impediments to women's success at work.

Personal honesty is the root of the third case—the ethics of gift giving and exchanging, possible conflicts of interest, concerns, and bosses who lean on subordinates.

Last, legal issues cloud what is at heart an ethical question—the "rights" of smokers versus nonsmokers. Today smokers are clearly in the minority, but what rules should apply on the job? Off the job? A very hot issue.

CHAPTER 14

Bioethics
The Right to Live and the Right to Die

"Suicide," one family member called it. Yet the other members of Marianne's family saw it as only hastening the inevitable.

You are a physician in a public hospital. You see people die every day—some painfully, some calmly. You recognize when there is no hope. This is clearly one of those cases. In some states, medical doctors have been convicted by juries for assisting someone to die (that is, actively doing something to contribute to a patient's death). But in at least one or two recent celebrated cases, juries have exonerated physicians who did more than just "pull the plug." Marianne has been comatose for a long time; brain death is almost certain, vital signs lacking, the possibility of recovery is nonexistent. Some of her family want her to die. Others strongly oppose any change in care—just go on as we're doing. Yet the costs are escalating at a horrendous rate because the kind of care Marianne needs is terribly expensive. A decision is being called for.

Marianne, incurably ill and advanced in years, before lapsing into a coma had simply refused any further extraordinary medical care. She asked only to be allowed to die in dignity—sedated for pain, kept clean, handled with gentleness. But take away all the tubes, respirators, and monitors. Let Nature (or God) take its course. The outcome would be the same, only much sooner. Marianne did not ask for help in dying (say, a shot to stop her heart), only that extra means not be taken to keep her alive. Her sons and daughters had at one time concurred—but who would actually make that decision? Such a decision poses very difficult ethical questions for all concerned.

Bioethics in American Life

Bioethics is a relatively new discipline that deals with the ethical and philosophical questions surrounding biological and medical advances, including such life-and-death decisions as care of the terminally ill. Administrators are involved at every policy level and at every organizational stage. Ultimately, everything involving life involves ethical behavior.

Recall, for instance, the long court battle in the mid-1970s over whether to disconnect a young coma victim, Karen Ann Quinlan, from her life support systems. She was then weaned from her respirator and lived for years in a New Jersey nursing home. Her weight later stabilized at some 70 pounds; she was fed through a tube in her nostrils.[1]

Or the court decision in Roman Catholic Brother Joseph Charles Fox's case, ". . . that a guardian of a terminally ill, comatose patient had the right to terminate extraordinary measures that keep the patient alive, but only within the bounds of strictly defined procedures."[2]

Or the recommendation of the President's Commission for the Study of Ethical Problems in Medicine and Biomedical and Behavioral Research, which recommended in 1981 that all fifty states adopt its proposed Uniform Determination of Death Act, which stated that death be defined as the "irreversible cessation of all functions of the entire brain, including the brain stem."[3]

Or the contrasting Dawson and Taschuk cases in Canada in 1983: The Supreme Court of British Columbia refused the Dawsons' request that their severely retarded son not be given a lifesaving operation; another Canadian hospital apparently ended the severely brain-damaged Taschuk girl's life with an extremely high dose of morphine.[4]

Or finally (though this in no way exhausts recent bioethical dilemmas), recall the case of Mrs. Elizabeth Bouvia, a lifelong victim of cerebral palsy who lost her court battle in late 1983 to be allowed to starve herself to death with dignity and was force-fed by the hospital until a later court decision ordered the feeding stopped if she voluntarily cooperated.[5]

Such cases and the ethical and moral conflicts they engender are extremely difficult to resolve and produce painful dilemmas for medical professionals, hospitals, patients, and families.

The Hippocratic oath (in which a doctor pledges to "do everything to help the patient to the best of [his] ability and judgment and do no harm") and present medical ethics offer too few guidelines in today's high-tech, complex, and troubling world of medical practice. Dr. Robert M. Veatch, medical ethics professor at Georgetown University, proposed the following ways of moving "toward a new code of medical ethics":[6]

• Patients should recognize that each doctor has his own personal beliefs on basic issues and should find out what these are before emergencies arise. For example, if a patient is hopelessly ill, how much treatment does he want? Does he want to be told about a fatal illness? A woman should discuss abortion and what would happen if she gave birth to a severely deformed infant.

• As much as possible, patients should write out what they would want done in specific situations. For yourself, consider a "Living Will." (Write Concern for Dying, 150 W. 57th St., New York, NY 10107.)

• Doctors should promise to keep in confidence all told to them by patients unless breaking confidence is required by law or becomes necessary to protect another individual from harm.

• Doctors should give patients complete information concerning diagnosis, treatment, and prognosis, including alternatives, and should allow patients to participate in decisions about their own health care.

• Doctors must address the question of "sanctioned assisted suicide."[7]

Given this brief—and inadequate—introduction, let us now look into some of the issues that arise in bioethics.

Death is treated differently in America than it is in many other countries. For instance, Americans often abandon the dying—leaving them isolated and alone, albeit in hospitals, nursing homes, or hospices. We sometimes forget that health-care personnel are not any different around dying people than the rest of us. Nurses who treat dying people often feel helpless, stressful, depressed, and uncomfortable, for instance. We typically shelter our children from death and illness—old people and the sick are placed in hospitals and nursing homes. Children rarely get to see death firsthand. In fact, professionals usually care for our dying, not family members in most cases.

There are few logical policies that typically guide us in death decisions: For example, the patient is or should be the primary decision maker concerning treatment while dying. Unfortunately, however, the patient is often ill-equipped to make such decisions at such a time. Thus the dilemma becomes how to judge what is really best for a dying person (e.g., the decision about the use of drugs during a person's final days). There is often a legal or emotional barrier between support people and the dying person, and the question arises of how to deal properly with these barriers. And, as already suggested, we are usually "afraid" of death in American society, or at least uncomfortable with it. But if the patient is unable to make decisions, then the decision falls to those best equipped to protect the patient's best interests, be they spouse, parent, children, or guardian. And sometimes the community must act if the family doesn't or won't act in the best interest of the dying or ill person.

We need to develop adult attitudes toward death. That is, acknowledge that we, too, can be afraid or uncomfortable around the dying. Don't hide from it. We shouldn't hide from death, pretending that death is not a reality.

Health-care professionals should avoid treating dying people the same way they treat people who will get better or who can be rehabilitated. Treating the dying requires special skills—sensitivity, compassion, understanding, and especially a willingness to get involved on a personal level. Further, adults should be able to read and understand consent forms, and hospitals should translate them into ordinary, nonlegal English so that meanings are clear. We need a *care* mentality, as distinct from the *cure* mentality.

But changes are taking place among our professionals. For instance, for many years nurses served patients best by carrying out the orders of the physicians—at least that was the old nursing code. But the newer Geneva Code stresses roles of other health-care professionals and is the new *model* of nursing care. But the new code has created conflict and friction between physicians and nurses. For instance, a patient can now ask a nurse how she feels about an M.D. and she can answer truthfully. Thus in the 1980s the nurse is more a partner in health care and is much more independent now than in the past.

So although we live in an age of change, megatrends, and high technology, our emotions are age-old. We can extend life, but we cannot eliminate death. We can prevent and cure many diseases and correct many ills, but some of life's most debilitating illnesses are still beyond our reach.

Further, confronted with limited resources, we must make hard choices. But we are a moral and ethical society. It is not right to leave health-care professionals, patients, and families alone to make these ultimate decisions, especially under the complex circumstances and trauma that sometimes exist.

Many helpful recommendations have been made, some of which are referred to in this chapter. One specific proposal, however, will be stressed above the others: *bioethical committees* in hospitals and health-care facilities. Such committees are also called medical moral committees or medical ethics committees.

Bioethical Committees in Hospitals

A hospital bioethics committee is a committee that seeks to (a) raise ethical consciousness; (b) sponsor educational programs for all levels of hospital personnel; (c) raise needed questions (not make decisions) on difficult dilemmas; (d) suggest policy guidelines for adoption; and (e) advise the administration on ethical issues.[8]

The first issue that bioethics committees should raise and discuss is *code* or *no code*. In U.S. hospitals, patients being entered are coded ("respiratory failure"), but this *can* be brutal, cruel, and unethical. There is a need to develop *supportive care policies* even for noncoded patients ("code blue" or whatever no codes are called). Code policy should be rewritten to say, *"take care of sick, injured, and dying."* The care given may be different—but we must develop this *care* mentality, rather than only a *cure* mentality. This is part of the educational process that a bioethics committee can encourage in a hospital. Such committees can develop *uniform criteria on dying:* Our society has at different times defined death as cessation of functions in the lungs, in the heart, and in the brain. We can use the Harvard criteria on death, Cornell criteria, Minnesota criteria, St. Louis criteria, or whatever. These criteria are all different and obviously affect hospital responses. But the *norm we seek should be to respect the dignity and worth of the patient as a human person.*

Since there are so many codes for nurses, for trustees, for physicians, etc., a hospital bioethical committee may want to write its own code, although to reach a consensus is a very challenging exercise. Many professionals urge that hospitals translate such codes and policies into local languages (e.g., Spanish). For instance, one system found the word "love" had seven meanings in Chinese (and that hospital had many Chinese staff and patients). Too often we assume everyone has the same values, culture, and belief systems, so precision in definition and translation is vital.

A typical model for the composition of a hospital bioethics committee suggests two configurations, a large committee, and a small committee, depending on needs and desires. Composition or membership might well be as follows:

Large model
One administrator plus one other
  administrative person
Three physicians
Three nurses
One LPN
One social worker
One clergy
One supportive services (security,
  dietary, etc.)
One trustee

Small model
One administrator
One physician
One nurse
One social worker
One clergy
One trustee

As with most committees, the bioethics bodies must address organizational questions such as chairpersons, minutes, agendas, meeting times and places and frequency of meetings, and so forth. But the key is to meet *before* difficult choices must be made and get a feel for the discussion process and the complexity of the ethical and moral questions and issues. Then when trauma demands a decision, the committee is in a position to offer help, as already suggested.

Assignments

1. Discuss the ethical dilemmas that confront persons, families, medical doctors, staffs, hospitals, and the general public in making decisions such as those described in the chapter—on withholding life support, no extraordinary means of supporting life, and orders not to resuscitate. Do not look just at the litigation and legal issues, which are important. More important are the philosophical issues that health care and society must confront.

2. Try to acquire "do not resuscitate" (DNR codes) policies and procedures from nearby hospitals that are willing to cooperate. (These codes are sometimes considered highly confidential.) Analyze them from the perspective of this chapter and the discussion in (1) above.

3. As a personal line of inquiry, do extra research on such bioethical issues as organ and tissue donation, living wills, and related topics.

Notes

1. A typical news story on Quinlan was "Karen Ann Quinlan . . . " *New York Times,* 29 March 1979, C14.

2. "Ending Life-Sustaining Aid is Upheld by Appeals Court," *New York Times,* 28 March 1980, B1.

3. "U.S. Panel Proposes Uniform Law Saying Life Ends at Brain's Death," *New York Times,* 10 July 1981, 1, D14.

4. "Life, Death, and the Law," *Maclean's* 96 (18 July 1983): 41. See also "Doctor's Dilemma: Treat or Let Die?" *U.S. News and World Report* 93 (6 December 1982): 53–56; "Why Doctors' 10 Worst Dilemmas Are Yours Too," *Good Housekeeping* 195 (July 1982): 191–193; "Do Not Go Gentle into That Good Night," *Time* 120 (20 December 1982): 88; "Life and Death and the Law," *Newsweek* 101 (21 March 1983): 52; "When to Preserve Life?" *World Press Review* 30 (June 1983): 56; George F. Will, "Protection of Babies, Too, Is Civil Rights Responsibility," national columnist in *Deseret News,* 16 November 1983, 4A; "Burn Victim Lends Support to Right-To-Die Theory," *The Arizona Republic,* 27 July 1983, E6.

5. See "The Most Painful Question," *Newsweek* CII (16 January 1984): 72.

6. *Good Housekeeping* 195 (July 1982): 192.

7. See, Lynn D. Wardle, "Sanctioned Assisted Suicide," *Issues in Law and Medicine* 3 (Fall 1987): 245–265.

8. Some hospitals now utilize resident "ethical philosophers" to help raise and answer these ultimate questions.

CHAPTER 15

Child Care and Ethical Issues

"Children?" Manny wondered. His personnel director had just outlined a detailed proposal for an agency-sponsored, on-site child-care center. The city agency would operate a care center for fifty preschool-age children, all offspring of agency workers, in several rooms on the ground floor of the agency building. Manny had to admit the projections on reduced worker absenteeism, increased productivity, and reduced employee turnover all looked pretty hardheaded. But should the agency really be caring for small children? Who would design the menus? Who'd furnish the meals and snacks? Who'd staff the center? What about sick kids? And the liability issue? Manny wasn't sure he wanted to get into all this. But the personnel director made a good case—she'd done her homework!

Some 45 percent of all women with children under age six are now working. Many employers are under enormous pressure to provide day-care centers or other alternatives for the care of preschool-age children.

The Importance of Day Care

In 1981 the U.S. Commission on Civil Rights concluded that lack of child care or inadequate child care

- Prevents women from taking paid jobs—the "double bind situations that face many women; they cannot afford child care unless they have a job, but they cannot get a job unless they have child care."
- Keeps women in part-time jobs, most often with low pay and little career mobility—the "negative features of part-time employment combine to create an isolated class of workers, predominantly women, who are cut off from high wages, prestigious occupations, benefits, and career mobility."
- Keeps women in jobs for which they are overqualified and prevents them from seeking or taking job promotions or the training necessary for advancement. Studies in New York City, Boston, and Oregon report several case studies which provide such evidence.
- Can conflict with women's ability to perform their work. Some evidence exists to show a cause–effect relationship between job performance and satisfactory child-care arrangements.
- Restricts women's participation in [public] employment and training programs—such as WIN, CETA, and so forth.

• Restricts women from participating in Federally supported education programs—such as programs supported under the Adult Education Act and the Vocational Education Act.[1]

The commission stressed that equal opportunity for women in employment and education has been a federal goal since the 1960s, as various legislation, executive orders, and judicial decisions indicate, but that "as a matter of public policy, the extent to which the need for child care constitutes a barrier to equal opportunity for women has received relatively little attention, even though many people have urged increased . . . support of child care."[2]

In 1978 the U.S. Department of Health, Education, and Welfare completed a National Day Care Study. The study found that "almost 52 percent of the country's 24.4 million families with children under thirteen have a work-related need for some form of day care."[3] The Commission on Civil Rights ended its 1981 report by saying,

> It is clear from this review that the United States has no cohesive or well-articulated Federal child-care policy. Instead it has an assortment of Federally supported programs established for varying reasons—educational needs of children, social services needs of parents, labor force needs of the economy—that parents use, nonetheless, so that they can take paid work or prepare for work. This assortment of programs is targeted, for the most part, to low-income families; it comprises a system that is inadequate to meet the current or projected need for child care.[4]

The day-care issue has been widely treated—for example, the popular 1980 movie *Kramer vs. Kramer* addressed the male side of the problem—and has produced a growing body of literature.[5] Day-care programs have become an increasingly common part of the employment process, even a bargaining item at the negotiating table with unions.[6]

Day Care in the Public Sector

How common are day-care programs with public employers? The author randomly selected fifty agencies listed in the International Personnel Management Association's (IPMA) *Membership Directory* and wrote to each, enclosing a questionnaire on provision of day-care services. Thirty-nine agencies responded (a 78% response). The deliberately small sample elicited two examples of sophisticated day-care programs— New York State and the United States Air Force. Some of the characteristics of these two programs are cited here, along with a number of other general findings.

A day-care facility called the Children's Place at the Plaza was set up at the Empire State Plaza (a New York State office building complex) in Albany, New York— the first center in the country set up by a state government for state employees.

The Children's Place was the result of negotiations between the New York Civil Service Employees' Association (the state's largest public employee union) and the governor's Office of Employee Relations. The state established the day-care center as Empire State Day Care Services, Inc. The center is mandated to "open and operate child-care centers at state facilities throughout [the] state for children of state employees." The center is operated by a board of directors composed of state officials, legislators, and others. By mandate, the center "must be self-sustaining"—

the state "provides space, renovations, and maintenance." The center had an early budget of approximately $160,000 a year.

Funds to begin operation in 1979 through 1980 came from a U.S. Health, Education, and Welfare research and development grant for "operating an on-site infant and toddler center." The center has been self-sustaining since then. Parent fees pay all operation costs.[7]

The Children's Place at the Plaza has a capacity for 100 children, ages eight weeks through kindergarten. The center is virtually full and there are long waiting lists. The center offers four major programs:

1. Breastfeeding—mothers may return to work and continue to nurse their infant during breaks;
2. Full-day kindergarten;
3. Mainstreaming—provides for up to 10 percent of enrolled preschoolers to have handicapping conditions. Children are integrated with regular program but receive special attention as well; and
4. Children visits—New York State Museum, located in plaza; attend performance at Empire State Youth Theater Institute on premises; firehouse and other field trips within walking distance.

The center operates daily, Monday through Friday (except on state holidays) from 7:00 A.M. to 5:30 P.M. and uses eight classrooms, a small gym, and staff office space in a renovated office building. An outdoor playground is equipped with swings, climbing structures, and other outside playground equipment. The staff includes twenty-one teachers and two administrators along with auxiliary staff (CETA workers and college students) and some volunteers. The children receive one hot lunch and two snacks daily. The meals are provided by contract with the firm that services Empire State Plaza cafeterias.

The center uses an advisory committee made up of parents to recommend any changes in policy or program to the board of directors. All parents become members when they register a child in the center.

In 1980 Welfare Research, Inc., completed an external evaluation of Children's Place and reported the following findings (based on a small sampling):

• The Children's Place has had some effect on women's job status. Forty-five percent of the women who responded reported the center enabled them to either remain employed, become employed, or return to work sooner than would otherwise be possible.

• Thirty-five percent of the state-employed women reported the center had an impact on their ability to work or continue to work.

• Seventy-three percent of the parents reporting reduced absenteeism were state employees.

• Eighty-one percent of the state employees reporting reduced absenteeism were women.

• Forty-seven percent of the respondents strongly agreed or agreed their work productivity has improved since their children have been at the center.

• Eighty-three percent strongly agreed or agreed that they worried less about their children.

- There is a demand for on-site day care, based on the large numbers of children on waiting lists and telephone calls inquiring about available slots.

- Fifty-two percent chose the Children's Place because of its location and convenience to their workplace; another 41 percent chose it for the perceived program quality they felt it would offer.

- Eighty-eight percent agreed that they had observed positive effects in their children since their enrollment at the center.

- Forty-two percent strongly agreed that employers should help subsidize child-care costs.

- The largest percentage of children served at the Children's Place are white.

- The median affordable tuition two-parent families indicated they could pay is $45 per week. For single parents, the highest affordable tuition is $40 per week.

- Forty-four percent agreed or strongly agreed that monthly tuition is a hardship on the family budget.

- Ninety-two percent of the parents strongly agreed or agreed that the center's current operating hours are satisfactory.

- For 70 percent of the respondents, transporting their children to the center was not a problem.

Since this early beginning, many other day-care programs for public employees have been started in the Empire State. For instance, the New York State Office of Mental Health has 38,000 employees—51 percent female. The associate commissioner reported that (as of 1981) "a cooperative effort between New York State management and . . . three major public employee unions representing state staff is underway, which will establish a uniform procedure for starting day-care centers and provide seed money for start-up costs." The Office of Mental Health will pay part of the cost, will locate the facilities at work site(s), will not operate the centers themselves, but will contract facility operation to someone else, and will offer an educational program to children (as opposed to just tending). The Office of Mental Health "has employees in forty locations around the State [of New York] with most employees located on the campuses of our 33 psychiatric centers." The office now has "two operational day-care centers" which are "certified, independently operated, day-care centers on facility grounds," which meet "all licensing . . . [and] mandated liability insurance" standards "promulgated by the New York State Department of Social Services or the City of New York for Center within its jurisdiction."[8]

Until the Empire State adopts some uniform policy, the New York State Department of Civil Service advised the author that

> New York State does not have a uniform day-care policy. We are aware that in several State work locations space has been provided for day-care centers. However, the majority of these day-care center arrangements have been made locally between employees and the State agencies, facilities, and campuses involved. The programs and policies of these day-care services therefore vary widely.[9]

A private sector example may help public administrators better understand how a model day-care program functions. The Stride Rite Corporation of Boston, Massachusetts, established the Stride Rite Children's Center in 1971 and has developed what many see as a model program.[10] (See Exhibits 15-1 and 15-2.) The company explains the following:

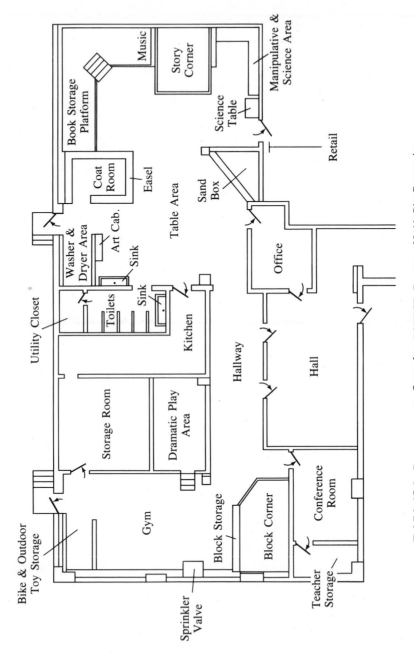

Exhibit 15-1 Day-care center floor plan. SOURCE: Courtesy of Stride Rite Corporation

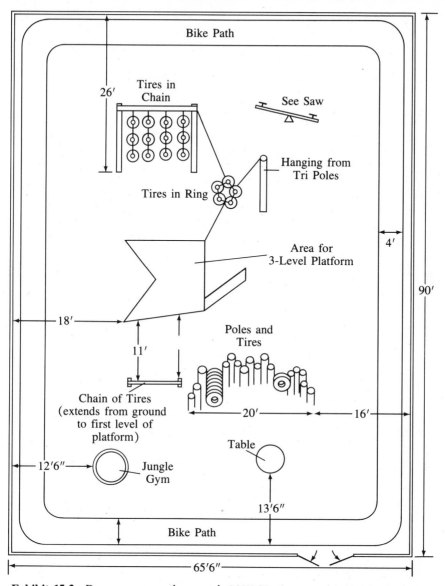

Exhibit 15-2   Day-care center playground. SOURCE: Courtesy of Stride Rite Corporation

How We're Set Up and Financed

The Center occupies what was office space on the first floor of Stride Rite's Boston plant. To create an atmosphere for proper development, the original area was renovated and equipped at a cost of approximately $25,000.

Initially set up to enroll 25 children, the Center was allotted 1,882 sq. feet. Now, with up to 50 children attending, the Center covers 3,397 sq. feet in one large, open learning environment. The Center was designed with strong emphasis on the functional. It includes a kitchen, a cubby room, a bathroom, an office, a small laundry, gym, and open classroom space.

Soon after the Center opened, the staff, working jointly with parents, designed and built an outdoor playground on an adjacent lot. It measures 65.6 × 90 feet.

Start-up costs and annual funding have been supplemented by government subsidies and non-financial sources of support.

A federal program reimbursed 75 percent of the cost of installing the kitchen. A contract with the Massachusetts School Lunch and Nutrition Bureau provides a cash reimbursement which pays for about 70 percent of the cost of the food program.

Few of the learning materials at the Center are purchased commercially. In addition to large amounts of scrap from the factory, the staff uses designer samples, bottle caps, textures, and a lot of imagination to keep costs at a minimum.

Because the Stride Rite Corporation wanted the Center to serve the community as well as company employees, arrangements were made with the Massachusetts Department of Public Welfare to fill a portion of the available seats. The cost of running the Center is approximately $65 per week per child. A contract with Department of Welfare allows $57.50 per week for 23 community children. The tuition for Stride Rite employees is 10 percent of their salaries.

Personnel and Staffing Policies

The Center now employs ten staff members and a number of volunteers. There are also student volunteers and a part-time cook who prepares all the meals eaten at the Center.

From the day it opened, staff turnover has been minimal. The interest and dedication of the staff is the prime contributor in program stability, trust, and confidence of the parent, and a high degree of credibility within the community. Recognizing this commitment, the Center does provide benefits as well as the opportunity to participate in management decisions.

Each employee receives medical insurance, a week off every four months in addition to ten legal holidays and sick leave. Each employee also joins in decisions concerning addition to the staff, curriculum, and policies.

Personnel costs are reduced somewhat by cooperating with high school intern projects and teacher training programs at local universities. Contracts with the federal "New Careers" program fund tuition and a portion of the salary for professional training.

Further professional training is available to staff through university vouchers and federal title training monies.

Reflecting its enrollment, the Center employs both men and women, blacks and whites.

The Value of Industry-Sponsored Day Care

During the past four years, Stride Rite has found the Children's Center to be a valuable investment. Day Care is undeniably an important factor in attracting and keeping desirable personnel.

Equally important, the Center has proven the feasibility and advantages of industry-sponsored day care. Stride Rite feels programs of this kind are superior to either government or profit-directed centers in terms of both education and cost.

In short, the Center has been of significant value to Stride Rite, the participating parents and children, and the community. It has provided educationally-oriented day care for children of employees and community families. It has also resulted in national recognition of both Stride Rite and the case for industry-sponsored day care.

The United States Air Force, Randolph Air Force Base, Texas, was one of the respondents to the author's initial survey. Dr. Beverly Schmalzried of the base personnel center advised that child-care centers for civilian and military personnel were "offered at 122 Air Force bases; with preschool programs at 11 [bases]." These programs/centers "served [1982] over 18,000 children per day in child care centers, 9,000 in preschools." Further,

> [C]hild care programs are offered at Air Force bases where the commander determines a need exists and the resources are available. Air Force child care centers offer a range of comprehensive child care services. The base program usually includes infant, toddler, preschool and school age (after school/summer) care. In addition to full-day and part-day care for these age groups, many bases offer a part-day preschool program. The full-day and part-day programs usually include meal service and snacks. Many centers participate in the United States Department of Agriculture (USDA) Child Care Food Program. Many centers remain open during evening and weekend hours for the convenience of parents.
>
> Child care centers are part of the Air Force Morale, Welfare, and Recreation (MWR) Program under the management of the chief, MWR division at each base. Each center has a child care director who reports to an MWR supervisor. The child care centers are staffed by child caregivers, selected and employed expressly for the purpose of providing care and enrichment programs for children.

The Air Force provides child care "to assist members in discharging these responsibilities. The services are provided to help personnel enjoy the challenges of mission accomplishment and a high quality of life, secure in the knowledge that their children are being well cared for when they are at work and play."

Dr. Schmalzried also wrote that, "in the past two years, high priority has been placed on providing headquarters-level training for child care staff," including hiring of trainers, training sessions for center directors, training newsletters, audiovisual training libraries, topical guides, and books furnished to base centers.

In addition, she wrote that the Air Force has "new initiatives completed or underway to improve or expand the program," including a "24-hour service . . . tested at Cannon Air Force Base, New Mexico, and Hahn Air Base, Germany"; "before- and after-school program for 6- to 12-year-olds tested at four bases"; "2-week advanced course for 25 child care directors at the University of Texas"; and "alternatives for the care of mildly ill [children] have been studied."

Schmalzried noted that the Air Force expects an increased demand for the service to continue because

- Economic conditions are forcing both spouses [civilian and military] to work,
- The improved quality of care in Air Force centers [attracts enrollment of eligible children],
- There is a slight increase in the numbers of single parents and military couples [with children], and
- Air Force centers are reasonably/affordably priced.

Because of these factors, the Air Force is "working on several fronts to increase capacity and improve service [of] child care needs . . . in both the civilian and military environment." Bergstrom Air Force Base in Texas "has been selected as the Air Force model center."

A number of the other respondents to the author's survey indicated great *interest* in day-care centers but *none* has "any current plan(s) to offer some form of day care." For example, the Personnel Director for the Health Department of Lexington, Kentucky (238 employees), wrote that "we recently considered this possibility [of establishing a day-care center] but our budget is being cut next year and we did not . . . pursue it further."

The State of Utah "is considering providing day care at cost to the state employees because [a] survey indicated affordable day care is a prime concern for working parents."[11] This 1982 survey in Utah had some interesting implications.

In mid-1982 a Utah group, Utah Issues Information Program, published a statewide child-care survey, "Who's Taking Care of Our Kids?" Over half of those now working who currently use child care utilize child-care centers. Sixty-eight percent of the unemployed parents surveyed answered that they would work if child care were available (of this group nearly three-fourths had household incomes of $10,000 or less). Sixty-nine percent of the unemployed AFDC parents (parents receiving welfare under Aid to Families with Dependent Children) *would* go to work, the survey reported, if child care were available. And 77 percent of the respondents indicated they *would* use a program if it were offered by their employer. Finally, when the respondents were asked if there was an organized child-care center in their area, and, if so, did they use it, 13 percent responded that there was no facility, 26 percent did not know, and 61 percent knew of an organized child-care facility in their area. Of the parents who knew of a child-care center, 58 percent used the facility. The 164 people who knew of child-care centers in their area and did not use them gave the following as major reasons:

1. Too expensive (91)
2. Inconvenient (31)
3. Inappropriate program for age level (29)
4. Wrong hours (25)
5. Transportation problems (17)
6. Location (15)
7. Disliked the people giving care (12)
8. Other (122)

Responses in the "other" category included "no program offered for the child's age group," "no room in the program," "child too young or too old for center care," and "the child/provider ratio inadequate."

According to the survey report, Utah's governor is seriously interested in day-care programs for state workers.[12]

In mid-1982, the author randomly selected 106 working women with children in four public jurisdictions (Salt Lake County, Sandy City, State Office of Personnel Management, and University of Utah) and administered a detailed questionnaire based on questions in the 1981 U.S. Commission on Civil Rights report quoted in this chapter. He received 69 responses (a 65% return rate). Although this particular survey is part of a broader research effort, several of the findings can be reported here independently.

Table 15-1 summarizes responses to the author's survey of these working women (who have children) and confirm the findings of the U.S. Commission on Civil Rights as concerns public employees and the need for day-care facilities:

Table 15-1 Survey of Working Women

1. Respond to "Obtaining adequate child-care is a major problem for me."

	S. L. County	U of U	Office of State Personnel	Sandy City	Total
Strongly agree	6 (27%)	4 (21%)	5 (33%)	2 (15%)	17 (25%)
Agree	3 (14)	5 (26)	1 (7)	3 (23)	12 (17)
Somewhat agree	3 (14)	1 (5)	3 (20)	0	7 (10)
Somewhat disagree	1 (5)	0	3 (20)	2 (15)	6 (9)
Disagree	6 (27)	6 (32)	1 (7)	3 (23)	16 (23)
Strongly disagree	1 (5)	1 (5)	1 (7)	1 (8)	4 (6)
No response	2 (9)	2 (11)	1 (7)	2 (15)	7 (10)

2. Respond to "My present child-care arrangement is a continual source of stress for me."

	S. L. County	U of U	Office of State Personnel	Sandy City	Total
Strongly agree	1 (5%)	2 (11%)	2 (13%)	0	5 (7%)
Agree	3 (14)	3 (16)	3 (20)	4 (31%)	13 (19)
Somewhat agree	4 (18)	2 (11)	0	1 (8)	7 (10)
Somewhat disagree	0	2 (11)	3 (20)	0	5 (7)
Disagree	8 (36)	4 (21)	4 (27)	4 (31)	20 (29)
Strongly disagree	3 (14)	4 (21)	2 (13)	1 (8)	10 (14)
No response	3 (14)	2 (11)	1 (7)	3 (23)	9 (13)

3. Respond to "Child-care related stress affects my working ability."

	S. L. County	U of U	Office of State Personnel	Sandy City	Total
Strongly agree	3 (14%)	4 (21%)	4 (27%)	0	11 (16%)
Agree	2 (9)	3 (16)	3 (20)	2 (15%)	10 (14)
Somewhat agree	4 (18)	1 (5)	4 (27)	3 (23)	12 (17)
Somewhat disagree	1 (5)	2 (11)	0	1 (8)	4 (6)
Disagree	8 (36)	6 (32)	2 (13)	3 (23)	19 (28)
Strongly disagree	2 (9)	1 (5)	1 (7)	1 (8)	5 (7)
No response	2 (9)	2 (11)	1 (7)	3 (23)	8 (12)

4. Were you ever prevented from taking a paid job because adequate child-care was not available?

S. L. County	U of U	Office of State Personnel	Sandy City	Total
5 (23%) yes	6 (32%) yes	4 (27%) yes	7 (54%) yes	22 (32%) yes
17 (77) no	12 (63) no	11 (73) no	6 (46) no	46 (67) no
	1 (5) no response			1 (1) no response

Table 15-1 Survey of Working Women (*continued*)

5. Have you ever had to take a part-time job when a full-time job was available, *just* because of child-care requirements?

S. L. County	U of U	Office of State Personnel	Sandy City	Total
5 (23%) yes	5 (26%) yes	4 (27%) yes	4 (38%) yes	19 (28%) yes
17 (77) no	12 (63) no	11 (73) no	8 (62) no	48 (70) no
	2 (9) no response			2 (3) no response

6. If yes, would you work more hours now if different child-care arrangements were available to you?

S. L. County	U of U	Office of State Personnel	Sandy City	Total
4 (18%) yes	3 (16%) yes	2 (13%) yes	3 (23%) yes	12 (17%) yes
8 (36) no	4 (21) no	3 (20) no	4 (31) no	19 (28) no
10 (46) no response	12 (63) no response	10 (67) no response	6 (46) no response	38 (55) no response

7. Have you ever taken a lower paying job than you were qualified for, *just* because it fit better into your child-care arrangements?

S. L. County	U of U	Office of State Personnel	Sandy City	Total
8 (36%) yes	8 (42%) yes	4 (27%) yes	6 (46%) yes	26 (38%) yes
14 (64) no	10 (53) no	11 (73) no	5 (38) no	40 (58) no
	1 (5) no response		2 (15) no response	3 (4) no response

8. Have you ever given up a chance for advancement at work because your child-care arrangements kept you from:

a. Working extra hours?

S. L. County	U of U	Office of State Personnel	Sandy City	Total
5 (23%) yes	9 (47%) yes	7 (47%) yes	6 (46%) yes	27 (39%) yes
12 (55) no	7 (37) no	6 (40) no	7 (54) no	32 (46) no
5 (23) no response	3 (16) no response	2 (13) no response		10 (14) no response

b. Having necessary time flexibility?

S. L. County	U of U	Office of State Personnel	Sandy City	Total
7 (32%) yes	8 (42%) yes	10 (67%) yes	6 (46%) yes	31 (45%) yes
11 (50) no	8 (42) no	4 (27) no	7 (54) no	30 (43) no
4 (18) no response	3 (16) no response	1 (7) no response		8 (12) no response

Table 15.1 Survey of Working Women (*continued*)

c. Taking necessary training?

S. L. County	U of U	Office of State Personnel	Sandy City	Total
8 (36%) yes	9 (47%) yes	6 (40%) yes	7 (54%) yes	30 (43%) yes
12 (55) no	9 (47) no	8 (53) no	6 (46) no	35 (51) no
2 (9) no response	1 (5) no response	1 (7) no response		4 (6) no response

9. Have child-care arrangements ever reduced the time and effort that you could give to a job?

S. L. County	U of U	Office of State Personnel	Sandy City	Total
12 (55%) yes	10 (53%) yes	11 (73%) yes	11 (46%) yes	44 (64%) yes
10 (46) no	8 (42) no	4 (27) no	4 (15) no	30 (35) no
	1 (5) no response			1 (1) no response

This chapter will not fully summarize demographic data and other findings of the author's Utah survey.[13] But it is interesting (and obvious) that female public workers confront the same problems with child-care as female workers in general.

Forty-five percent of women with children under age six are now working. A response to this demographic fact is the rapid and recent growth of day-care (or child-care) facilities for children of working mothers. Lack of adequate child care penalizes women workers and acts as a serious bar to upward mobility and equal employment opportunity.

For a number of socioeconomic reasons cited in the chapter, this author concludes that day-care centers and child-care programs will be increasingly common as a feature of public employment and dealing with their operation and maintenance will be one more skill required of public personnel directors. The public sector can learn a great deal from private sector initiatives in child care, but there are also several outstanding public sector models to study and learn from.

Assignments

1. A fruitful topic for class (or team) discussion is the ethical issues surrounding child care provided by government agencies for workers—the impact on working mothers, children, families, society providing the home environment for toddlers, etc.

2. From the data presented, what ethical problems does inadequate child care cause for working women (Table 15-1)? Lack of promotional opportunity? Training difficulties?

3. Consider inviting an operator of a child-care center to the classroom for a structured interview, along with a consumer—that is, someone with a child (or children) now attending such a center. What are the advantages? The disadvantages? The problems? How best solve the problems? Ask about ethical issues, such as whose

children are enrolled? Whose excluded? By what criteria? What role do parents play in designing the curriculum? What about religious diets?

4. As a class exercise, design a care center for preschoolers for a company or an agency where a class member or spouse works (and, of course, where the boss is willing to cooperate). Include square footage, admission criteria, hours of operation, curriculum, role of parents, sick child policy, salaries for staff, criteria for center employees, etc. Numerous ethical issues will emerge that must be resolved.

Notes

1. U.S. Commission on Civil Rights, *Child Care and Equal Opportunity for Women* (Clearing House Publications no. 67, June 1981), pp. 9–14.

2. Ibid., 8.

3. Abt Associates, *Children at the Center: Summary Findings and Their Implications* (Cambridge, MA: Abt Associates, 1979).

4. U.S. Commission on Civil Rights, op. cit., 51.

5. For examples of excellent guides and how-to-do-it manuals:

Empire State Day Care Services Corporation; *On-Site Day Care: State of the Art and Models Development* (Albany, NY: Empire State Day Care Services Corporation, 1980).

————— . *On-Site Day Care: Bibliography* (Albany, NY: Empire State Day Care Services Corporation, 1980).

Emily Herbert, Jackson, et al., *The Infant Center: A Complete Guide to Organizing and Managing Infant Day Care* (Baltimore, MD: University Park Press, 1977).

Dorothy June Sciarra, *Developing and Administering a Child Care Center* (Boston: Houghton Mifflin, 1979).

Marion O'Brien, et al., *The Toddler Center: A Practical Guide to Day Care for One- and Two-Year Olds* (Baltimore, MD: University Park Press, 1979).

Stevanne Auerbach, *The Child Care Crisis* (Boston, MA: Beacon Press, 1980).

6. See the following for a brief history of day care in the United States and the AFL-CIO's official attitude toward day care: Joyce D. Miller, "The Urgency of Child Care," *American Federationist* 82 (June 1975): 1–8. See also, "Day Care: A State Labor–Management Incentive," *Quality of Work Life Review* 1 (Number 2): 5–6.

7. Letter to author dated 28 July 1981, from M. McCormick, Empire State Day Care Services Corporation.

8. Letter to author dated 29 July 1981, from T. Sharkey, New York State Office of Mental Health (Albany).

9. Letter to author dated 7 May 1981, from N. Fitzgerald, New York State Department of Civil Services (Albany).

10. See, "Stride Rite Children's Center: How We Do It." March 1981 (Boston, MA).

11. "Day Care Necessary for Working Mothers to Survive," *Salt Lake Tribune,* 31 May 1982, and response from Utah Office of Personnel Management in author's survey.

12. Ibid.

13. Of the total respondents, 35 percent were under 30 years of age and 74 percent under age 40; 44 percent were married; 1 percent were black, 4 percent American Indian, 9 percent Hispanic, 4 percent Asian; 71 percent held jobs in classes/grades below supervisory levels; 25 percent were high school graduates and 68 percent had post-high school training; and 47 percent had family incomes below $20,000 a year. Thus this sample is sharply *unlike* the group(s) surveyed by the U.S. Commission on Civil Rights, et al. (being largely female public workers, white, and better than average education), yet the findings were consistent throughout.

CHAPTER 16

Public Employees and the Exchanging of Gifts

"Again?" Lois thought. A year ago the deputy director had petitioned everyone in the department above a certain pay grade level for a voluntary contribution for an anniversary present for the director and his wife. Both of them were popular with most employees, particularly top staff, and the director's wife always attended retreats, seminars, annual picnics, and so forth. She was a charming woman, and few had complained too loudly about the handsome sets of matched luggage presented at a staff meeting to the attractive couple on their twenty-seventh anniversary. But, here it was a year later and the deputy was back again—this time for the boss's *birthday*, of all things. The director had suggested a set of golf clubs and bag that would cost in excess of $1,000, so all top personnel were asked to be generous. Lois wondered if this request was ethical and correct—hey, the director received a salary many times hers. Where should the line be drawn on gift giving? Was it voluntary? True, she held a position as a political appointee, serving at the pleasure of the department head. But he hired her for her technical skills, not her patronage.

She reflected that every year the agency encouraged wholly "voluntary" contributions to the United Way campaign, the American Cancer Society, and so forth. Considerable effort went into assuming 100 percent participation throughout the agency. Lois knew the director took great pride in the plaques he hung in his office, showing his agency's level of support of these worthwhile efforts.

Lois did not know if her department even had a rule or a policy on gift giving. She was certain there were rules against accepting gifts from vendors or suppliers or taking any kind of gratuities from those the agency served. But how about bosses and workers? Or co-workers? On reflection, Lois realized she and other co-workers had sometimes traded gifts when someone was retiring, getting married, had a grand-child, and so forth, but usually these were small gifts among close friends. Was there a difference between these exchanges of inexpensive presents and golf clubs on the director's birthday?

Students of ethics soon realize that integrity and honesty are concepts that may get a little fuzzy on specific application. Lois wasn't accepting presents from clients she served in her official capacity. Was there an integrity issue here? A recent book on ethics concluded "that organizational ethics is dependent on personal ethics. In other words, we must become better people if we are to have better organizational governance. Good systems do not produce good people: rather good people produce good systems."[1]

In any typical government agency, employees may commonly exchange gifts or small presents at special times such as Christmas (or other holidays), weddings, baby showers, and personal birthdays. Should such gift exchanges be prohibited? Or regulated? Some dispute exists as to how these questions should be answered.

A Survey on Gift Exchanging

The author conducted a national survey of government agencies on the question of employee gift exchanges. This chapter reports the findings.

A random sample of one hundred agencies were selected from the membership directory of the International Personnel Management Association, and these one hundred jurisdictions were mailed a cover letter and questionnaire. Sixty-nine agencies responded (a very good rate of return), although for various reasons only sixty-seven responses were usable. Table 16-1 shows the profile tabulated from the responses to the survey.

Table 16-1 Respondent Profile

Jurisdiction	Number	Percent
Federal Agencies	12	18
State Agencies	22	33
Counties	7	10
Cities	18	27
Other(s)*	8	12
Total	67	100%
Populations served	Number	Percent
(Clients)		
under 10,000	4	6
10,001 to 100,000	13	19
100,001 to 500,000	14	21
500,001 to 1,000,000	10	15
over 1,000,001	26	39
Total	67	100%
Number of employees in jurisdiction	Number	Percent
under 100	5	8
101 to 500	19	28
501 to 1,000	7	10
1,001 to 5,000	17	25
5,001 to 10,000	4	6
10,001 or more	15	23
Total	67	100%

*School districts, research bureaus, and various special district governments.

Of the sixty-seven respondents, forty-one, or 61 percent of the total, do not have "any personnel policies or rules that govern the giving and/or exchanging of gifts between employees" (e.g., wedding gifts, birthday gifts, Christmas gifts, baby shower gifts). However, twenty-six jurisdictions, or 39 percent of the total respondents, do have such policies or rules.

Obviously, this figure is somewhat skewed in that twelve federal agencies (from the U.S. Army to the Tennessee Valley Authority) responded. Even taking all twelve of these responses out of the survey still leaves fourteen jurisdictions who do have such policies, some 21 percent of all respondents. Indeed, a number of agencies have specific rules to cover precisely the kinds of situations cited in the original survey questionnaire. Some examples will be quoted.

A number of respondents were opposed to any stated policy on employee gift exchanges. For instance, the Administrative Services Director of the city of Baldwin Park, California, wrote that "gift giving/exchanging is a personal matter between employees . . . not mandatory, [but] individual choice." The city manager of Oregon City, Oregon, wrote, "I think [such a written policy opposing or controlling gift exchanges] would be a case of over-ruling. Should a policy be made to restrict an employee's right to choose whether or not to give? You might as well restrict all giving if you limit their right to give to fellow [*sic*] employees."

While the above criticism may be a bit overstated, a few others expressed some qualified support for such a measure, while still stating general opposition to the principle involved. The personnel officer of the Juniata Valley Office of Mental Health and Mental Retardation (Lewiston, Pennsylvania) wrote

> We do not have a problem with such an issue. I could see, however, where there could be resentment developed among employees because some may receive gifts from each other and others may not. Policies such as this may be a good precaution to prevent a problem such as this from developing. . . . I do not believe you could legally deny an employee the right to give or receive a gift from a fellow [*sic*] employee.

A Scottsdale, Arizona, respondent suggested a common theme in answering the question, "Should there be policies and rules governing the giving and/or exchanging of gifts between employees in your agency?" The city personnel director said, "Not until any problems occur. Any policy or rule should be reactive to the specific situation." The personnel director of Flint, Michigan, answered the same question saying that he did not worry ". . . as long as such gifts do not involve city property, do not cause a conflict of interest, or do not affect [employees'] ability to do their job[s]." The personnel officer for the Ohio State Reformatory (Mansfield, Ohio) went a step further. He strongly opposed such a policy or rule, "as long as the gift giving does not interfere with normal work routine. The more written policies you have, the greater your legal obligation is."

Others objected to the administrative burden of such a policy or rule. The assistant city manager of La Verne, California, argued that "rules such as these [gift exchanges among employees] are unenforceable. I believe that management can set the example by not getting involved in so-called 'business' luncheons, vendor gifts, etc." The employment officer of the City and County of Denver, Colorado, went even further. He felt such policies were "debatable." Among some employee units, birthdays, showers, and the like are considered social/morale activities. Also, some employees are close friends who would resent impositions on what they consider their personal rights. "Further," he added, "generally speaking, one should probably not attempt to legislate common sense. Furthermore, businesslike relationships need not be sterile ones. Should problems occur with an individual or unit, these can be handled individually through the normal supervisory process." This same idea was expressed by the personnel director of the North Broward Hospital District (Fort Lauderdale, Florida), who said, "Special occasions depend upon personal relationships and should not be regulated."

Many jurisdictions felt absolutely "no need" for such a policy. The Wake County personnel director (Raleigh, North Carolina) said simply, "There is no problem with regard to this issue [here]." The personnel director of the town of Greece, New York, said, "All gifts of this type (weddings, birthdays, etc.) are voluntary . . . and rules/policies are unnecessary." A state personnel officer in Cheshire, Pennsylvania, said, "This agency has no problems in this area. Gifts are normally given only when an employee retires." And the director of personnel, City of Norfolk, Virginia, put it succinctly: "There is no need for such a policy." An even stronger position was taken by the personnel officer of the Poway Unified School District (California) who stated, "What individuals do in their own personal lives is not, and should not be, anybody's business but their own."

The director of personnel, New York State Parks and Recreation (Albany), wrote, "The exchange of gifts between employees does not constitute a conflict of interest," and thus should not be regulated as would gifts from vendors, and so forth. One personnel official in Hyattsville, Maryland, warned, "We've got to get away from thinking that we have to address every problem, regardless of importance, with a new rule!"

Smaller jurisdictions commonly were less concerned than larger ones, however. For instance, the personnel director of Chicopee, Maine, said, "As far as I can see, there is no harm done [in letting co-workers exchange gifts] and our worker morale has never been higher. Of course, with fewer than one hundred workers, everyone knows each other; as a result, abuses are uncommon." A personnel official for the state of Washington noted strong conflict of interest rules and regulations in the state, but insofar as regulating employees exchanging gifts, "We find no need at this time."

The 39 percent of responding jurisdictions who do regulate employee gift exchanges had a wide variety of policies.

The personnel administrator for the Office of Management and Finance in the Louisiana State Department of Health and Human Resources (Baton Rouge) felt that whatever the policy "should be" it should not be,

> . . . more restrictive than provided for in the [Louisiana] Code of Governmental Ethics. The exchanges taking place within the agency are among work groups and friends in celebration of special events, such as Christmas, retirement, weddings, etc. Such gifts are and must be voluntary and according to state law, and cannot be used to influence agency business.
>
> All public employees, regardless of their governmental jurisdiction, are governed by a state code of ethics which is part of the state statutes. The code prohibits any compensation for services rendered in the course of employment other than that received by the employee from his agency, and prohibits the acceptance or solicitation of anything of economic value as a gift or gratuity from any person who conducts

activities regulated by the employee's agency or who has interests which may be substantially affected by the performance or nonperformance of the public employee's official duty.

The chief of the Legislative Reference Bureau of the state of Wisconsin wrote that Wisconsin state agencies are

regulated under Sections 19.41–19.59, "Code of Ethics for Public Officials," of the 1979 Wisconsin Statutes. These statutory provisions are administered by the State Ethics Board. Section 19.45 (3) of the statutes prohibits public officials from receiving anything of value that might influence the actions of the official. In checking the Wisconsin Administrative Code, we did not locate anything further in the Ethics Board provisions [as governing employee gift exchanges].

The Wisconsin statute 19.45 on "Standards of Conduct (for Public Employees)" provides for typical and general prohibition on gifts or favors as follows,

(3) No person or organization may offer or give to a state public official, directly or indirectly, and no state public official may solicit or accept from any person or organization, directly or indirectly, anything of value if it could reasonably be expected to influence such state public official's vote, official actions or judgement, or could reasonably be considered as a reward for any official action or inaction on the part of such state public official.

It is interesting that a very positive response was received from the director of the Institute of Industrial Management of the Osaka, Japan, prefectural government. He wrote that in Japan,

we have the particular habit [of] exchanging gifts in mid-summer season and [at] year-end. And the gifts are usually given from subordinate persons to supervisors in these cases. So the letter of [the] Vice-Governor is issued prior to the season in which [he] instructs employees to take self-disciplinary action [regulation] in sending or receiving gifts. There are no specific rules on wedding gifts or birthday gifts (which are usually given from superiors to subordinate persons).

The personnel director for the East–West Center of the University of Hawaii (Honolulu) enclosed Policy Number 5402E on "Acceptance of Gifts," which provides that,

B. Policy
  1. An employee is prohibited from soliciting or accepting, directly or indirectly, any gift, gratuity, favor, entertainment, loan, or any other thing of monetary value from a person who has, or is seeking to obtain, contractual or other business or financial relations with the Center, conducts operations or activities that are regulated by the Center, or has interests that may be substantially affected by the performance or nonperformance of the employee's official duty.
  2. An employee is prohibited from soliciting contributions from another employee for a gift to an employee in a superior official position.
  3. A superior official is prohibited from accepting a gift presented as a contribution from employees in a subordinate position.
  4. An employee is prohibited from making a donation as a gift to an employee in a higher official position.

C. Interpretations of Exceptions to Policy

    1. Acceptance of or donation for a voluntary gift of nominal value when made on a special occasion such as marriage, illness, retirement, birthdays.

    2. Cases of obvious family or personal relationships (such as those between the parents, children or spouse of the employee and the employee) when the circumstances make it clear that it is those relationships rather than the business of the employee concerned which are the motivating factors.

    3. Acceptance of food and refreshments of nominal value on infrequent occasions in the ordinary course of a luncheon or dinner meeting or other meeting, or on an inspection tour when an employee may properly be in attendance.

    4. Acceptance of loans from banks or other financial institutions on customary terms to finance proper and usual activities of employees, such as home mortgage loans.

    5. Acceptance of unsolicited advertising or promotional material, such as pens, pencils, note pads, calendars, and other items of nominal cash value.

    6. Acceptance of inexpensive "exchange" gifts from persons whose cultural heritage is known to foster such an exchange and where nonacceptance would be construed to be an insult or would be an act of discourtesy to the giver.

    7. Acceptance of expensive gifts of obvious cultural or artistic value by the employee when such gifts are not construed to be gifts to the individual employee, but are given to the East–West Center. Such gifts will be placed in an EWC exhibition or given other appropriate use within the Center.

A personnel officer for the U.S. Government Printing Office in Washington, D.C., cited "GPO Notice 655.1, dated February 23, 1973" which reads in part,

> (5) No soliciting of contributions is allowed without approval of the Public Printer. Department/Service heads may permit voluntary contributions for flowers or gifts for employee weddings, serious illnesses, departures, or death in immediate family.
>
> The maintenance of collection records by name or by organizational unit is strictly prohibited in order that no employee or group of employees feels compelled to donate to any other employee or official. Contributions for a retiring employee may not be solicited until his application for retirement has been submitted and the date of his retirement is known. In the case of employees, GS-16 and above contributions may not be made until the employee is permanently off the work site. Donations made for any purpose are expected to be nominal and completely voluntary.

A base personnel officer from a U.S. Army program (civilian) at Ft. Monroe, Virginia, cited federal employee regulations in,

> Section 7351 of Title 5 of the United States Code [which] prohibits (1) an employee from soliciting contributions from another employee for a gift to an employee in a superior official position, (2) a superior official from accepting a gift presented as a contribution from employees receiving less salary than himself, and (3) an employee from making a donation as a gift to an employee in a higher official position. Voluntary gifts of nominal value when made on a special occasion such as marriage, illness, or retirement are not prohibited.
>
> These restrictions are intended to require that employees avoid any action which might result in or create the appearance of using public office for private gain, giving preferential treatment to any person, losing complete independence or impartiality, or affecting adversely the confidence of the public in the integrity of the

government. In sum, the policies and rules are intended to preclude conflicts of interest among employees.

Another respondent, a personnel branch chief from the Tennessee Valley Authority (TVA) (Knoxville) also cited Title 5 of the United States Code as governing such practices in the vast TVA. A General Accounting Office (GAO) respondent noted the agency has its own similar rule. Smaller employers may have established policy, but it is often unwritten. An example is Oregon City, Oregon, where the officer responding to the author's survey wrote that the city had an unwritten policy that city employees do not accept gifts from outsiders and that giving or exchanging of gifts between employees in the city is restricted "only to the fact that all [such] gifts must be voluntary."

A city of New York personnel officer cited, "New York City Personnel Policy and Procedure 705-77 [which] prohibits accepting gifts, including those between employee and supervisor." He then added, "However, gifts among peers or colleagues are not specifically prohibited, and I feel that it is a poor practice [i.e., exchanging gifts] but one that might best be left to the discretion of the employees concerned."

Many survey respondents acknowledged detailed state statutes (or local ordinances) governing gifts from outsiders but which did not specifically apply to or include provisions for employee gift exchanges. For instance, a personnel officer for the Kansas Department of Human Resources (Topeka) quoted the Kansas code on "Ethics" (46-237), which is a very typical statute. It is entirely silent on employee gift exchanges but covers other circumstances and allows exceptions as follows:

> No state officer or employee or candidate for state office shall accept, or agree to accept, any economic opportunity, gift, loan, gratuity, special discount, favor, hospitality, or service having an aggregate value of one hundred dollars ($100) or more in any calendar year from any one person known to have a special interest, under circumstances where he or she knows or should know that a major purpose of the donor is to influence him or her in the performance of his or her official duties or prospective official duties. Hospitality in the form of food and beverages are presumed not to be given to influence a state officer or employee in the performance of his or her official duties or prospective official duties, except when a particular course of official action is to be followed as a condition thereon.
>
> Except when a particular course of official action is to be followed as a condition thereon, this section shall not apply to (1) any contribution reported in compliance with the campaign finance act; or (2) a commercially reasonable loan or other commercial transaction in the ordinary course of business.

The most detailed and carefully worded statute cited by a survey respondent also does not specifically mention public employees exchanging gifts, but would clearly apply to any abuses or concerns about the sundry practices possible. The Washington State Code, Title 42: 8.200–210, reads

> (1) No state employee shall receive, accept, take, seek, or solicit, directly or indirectly, any thing of economic value as a gift, gratuity, or favor from any person if such state employee has reason to believe the donor would not give the gift, gratuity, or favor but for such employee's office or position with the state.
>
> (2) No regular state employee shall receive, accept, take, seek, or solicit, directly or indirectly, any thing of economic value as a gift, gratuity, or favor from

any person, or from any officer or director of such person, if such state employee has reason to believe such a person: (a) has or is seeking to obtain contractual or other business or financial relationships with such employee's agency; (b) conducts operations or activities which are regulated by such employee's agency; or (c) has interests which may be substantially affected by such employee's performance or nonperformance of official duty.

(3) Exceptions to the provisions of this section made by regulations issued pursuant to [statute] in situations where the circumstances do not lead to the inference that the official judgment or action of the state employee receiving, directly or indirectly, the gift, gratuity, or favor was intended to be influenced thereby.

Except in the course of his official duties or incident thereto, no state employee shall, in his relationship with any person specified in the succeeding sentence, use the power or authority of his office or position with the state in a manner intended to induce or coerce such other person to provide such state employee or any other person with any thing of economic value, directly or indirectly. This section shall apply to relationships with any person or any officer or director of such person from whom such state employee, if he were a regular state employee, would be prohibited by [statute].

Summary

Sixty-seven (of one hundred) public personnel agencies responded in a random sample survey on practices covering public employee exchanges of gifts. Twenty-six (39%) do have written policies covering such practices, and forty-one (61%) do not make provisions. Many respondents to the survey felt a policy or rule governing exchanges of gifts between employees is totally unnecessary—even superfluous. Common sense should dictate behavior, many felt. Others argued that such behavior belongs outside agency controls. This attitude was especially common among smaller jurisdictions. This chapter summarizes the findings of the national survey and quotes from several model statutes. Indeed, the author ran a chi-square analysis on the survey findings. No significant relationships were found between having a policy on employee gift exchanges and other variables on the survey (for example, whether the jurisdiction was federal, state, or local), except that a very significant positive relationship was found between a jurisdiction's size (clients served and number of public employees) and whether or not the agency had a policy on employee gift exchanges. Smaller agencies have apparently not yet confronted abuses or problems among employees. Some of the larger, more sophisticated personnel systems have adopted written policies governing (and restricting) exchanges of gifts between employees—especially in a supervisor–subordinate relationship. Most written policies clearly permit such gift exchanges but anticipate abuse by prohibitions typical of broader employee ethics and conflict of interest laws.

Assignments

1. Should there be a policy on exchanging gifts in Lois's department? Why or why not? Discuss or debate the issue thoroughly.

2. Assuming there *should* be such a policy, develop (as a class or by teams) a written *model policy* based on the case examples.

3. Analyze unforeseen or unintended implications or consequences of such a written policy. Could the policy be a "cure worse than the disease"? What dysfunctional behaviors might result from such a policy? Will the policy result in more ethical behavior? Discuss. Consider inviting one or more experts to critique the policy and these questions.

Notes

1. N. Dale Wright, Ed., *Papers on the Ethics of Administration* (Provo, UT: Brigham Young University, 1988).

CHAPTER 17

The Ethics of Smoking Versus Nonsmoking at Work

"Ridiculous!" muttered Charlie, with real venom. He was standing outside on a patio of his state government office building, smoking a cigarette. Charlie had worked more than a decade as a senior data specialist for the state's data processing center. Yes, he was a smoker. He *liked* to smoke. He's smoked since early high school. And he'd *continue* to smoke. But a few months ago the state legislature passed a stiff indoor clean air act and here Charlie was—out in the cold, having a smoke. The entire office building had been declared a no-smoking facility (hallways, restrooms, offices, meeting rooms, foyers, storage rooms, cafeteria), and for Charlie and workers like him who smoked, that meant going outside the building to have a smoke. Charlie was really angry today. The weather was most unpleasant, and Charlie hadn't taken time to dress warmly. It robbed him of the pleasure he derived from his smoking. Charlie reflected that smokers have rights, too. Health fanatics were imposing their values on everyone else. Charlie wondered what his legal rights were on this issue. Could he file a grievance through his union? What if he insisted on his right to smoke in his own small office? Maybe he could buy some kind of a smoke-filtering device. Anyway, it was more than a minor frustration, Charlie thought, as he glanced at his watch and saw his break time was up. He quickly lit up one more smoke—better have another one, he thought; it was a long time until the next break.

Smoking on the Job

In the last few years, a heated controversy has arisen over secondhand smoke (or side-stream smoke) in the workplace and the costs of smoking versus nonsmoking among employees. The author conducted a smoking/nonsmoking survey of International Personnel Management Association (IPMA) and National Public Employee Labor Relations Association (NPELRA) agency members randomly drawn from the IPMA membership directory and NPELRA membership roster and reports the findings as follows.

The American Tobacco Institute and other pro-smoking groups have waged a carefully modulated campaign for some years now, appealing to "reason" and "goodwill" in resolving disagreements between smokers and nonsmokers. This campaign has been countered by clean indoor air acts passed or strengthened by some thirty-six states[1] and by aggressive and sometimes strident campaigns by "nonsmoker rights" groups. Many public agencies have begun studying the smoking/nonsmoking issue or have taken various other action steps.

The costs of smoking have been articulated as follows:[2]

It costs employers an average of $4,600 more per year to keep a smoker, rather than a nonsmoker, on the average payroll. The cost breakdown is as follows:

$1,820 in lost productivity. This represents thirty minutes a day for smoking breaks and smoking rituals such as lighting up and puffing.

$1,000 in damage from cigarette burns and extra cleaning maintenance for smoke pollution.

$765 in lost time due to the average smoker's increased chance of illness and early death.

$230 in medical care. Heavy smokers use health care at least 50 percent more than nonsmokers.

$220 in absenteeism. Smokers are absent 50 percent more often than nonsmokers (or nearly 2.2 days more per year).

$86 for the effect of smoking on the health of nonsmokers working nearby.

$45 for accidents due to loss of attention, eye irritation, coughing, etc.

$45 in increased fire insurance.

The secondhand smoke issue has drawn champions from both sides. Many argue that passive smokers (those who breathe the smoke expelled into the air by smokers) suffer from the same ailments known to plague smokers, though to a lesser degree. Advocates of smoking argue that research findings are too preliminary and feel that both sides should proceed with caution before infringing on one group's "rights" when cooperative efforts will usually solve the problem better than heavy-handed tactics that favor nonsmokers over smokers.

Businesses and government agencies at all levels are confronted to some degree with the problem. One respondent to the author's mailed survey wrote, "The smoking/nonsmoking issue is not a problem for us" (Asheville, North Carolina). But in many other jurisdictions the issue *has* become a problem. In fact, more than 38 percent of the survey respondents now have "formal or informal personnel policies and procedures on smoking versus nonsmoking at work," and a few more are developing such a policy. This group includes public agencies (towns, cities, counties, school districts, states, several federal agencies) with fewer than 100 public employees as well as those with more than 140,000 public employees, from coast to coast.

Survey Methodology

This chapter will not attempt to resolve the medical[3] or legal[4] issues surrounding smoking/nonsmoking in the workplace (some notes and bibliographic references do give more detail, however). It does report on the findings of the national survey by the author and gives in some detail the policies and procedures of a number of public agencies who responded.[5]

Of the 175 survey instruments mailed out, 145 usable responses were received for a response rate of 82 percent. In addition, dozens of respondents wrote letters or commentary and more than a score enclosed copies of policies, statutes, memoranda, and so forth. Many comments were extremely positive about the survey itself— obviously it aroused great interest.

The complete survey and results are reproduced in the Appendix (pp. 171–175). Some 38 percent of the public agencies surveyed do have "formal or informal personnel policies and procedures on smoking versus nonsmoking at work." Based on the data in the Appendix, of those responding "yes,"

41.4%   give nonsmokers incentives/advantages in lunchroom, dining room, cafeteria or snack room seating or eating arrangements;

24.1%   give nonsmokers incentives/advantages in office/space assignments;

20.7%   give nonsmokers incentives/advantages in group life insurance, disability protection and/or other nonmedical or health plan insurance provisions;

6.9%   give nonsmokers incentives/advantages in recruitment or initial selection for employment; and

7.0%   give some other form(s) of incentives/advantages to nonsmokers (training, lower health plan premiums, and so on).

Of the respondents answering "yes" on the survey, some of the most common (over 75 percent) policies or procedures were:

11.7%   Respondents have a state law that covers at least some smoking policies;

11.4%   Respondent's agency includes specific references to policy (on smoking versus nonsmoking) on the smoking/no smoking signs or posters displayed in working areas, meal areas, restrooms or lounges, or other work sites (other than where safety is a factor);

8.0%   Respondent's agency segregates smokers and nonsmokers in work areas/work stations or office/room assignments;

8.0%   Respondent's agency provides or makes available programs (counseling, therapy groups, other formal means of employee assistance) to help employees stop (or cut down) on smoking;

7.1%   Respondent's agency supports by internal promotion such yearly efforts as the Great American Smoke-Out sponsored by others as a national campaign;

6.5%   Respondent's agency segregates smokers and nonsmokers in eating or dining areas;

6.5%   Respondent's agency segregates smokers and nonsmokers in meeting rooms, conference rooms, training rooms, and so forth;

6.5%   Respondent's agency provides "smokers' rooms" or a segregated, set-aside room (or rooms) where smokers are requested to go to smoke;

5.9%   Respondent's agency includes specific references to policy on smoking versus nonsmoking in the "employee handbook" and/or "policies and procedures manual."

4.9%   Respondent's agency includes specific references to policy on smoking versus nonsmoking in new employee orientation.

The smoking/nonsmoking issue obviously leads to conflict between workers in the office and necessitates some forms of intervention by management.

34.8%   Had an incident come up between smokers/nonsmokers where management or supervisors had to intervene;

24.4%   Designed an office or structured an office layout at least in part because of the smoking/nonsmoking issue;

17.0%   Studied the smoking/nonsmoking issue while looking at ways to contain health-care costs;

11.9%   Made any kind of agency internal study or research effort over the smoker/nonsmoker issue;

8.2%   Had an arbitration or grievance case over nonsmoking/smoking; and

1.5%   Had been involved in litigation or court case with an employee over the smoking/nonsmoking issue.

A number of interesting examples were cited by respondents of smoker/nonsmoker incidents, grievances, union relationships, or office layouts. Some of these cases are quoted as follows.

More than 77 percent of the survey respondents were nonsmokers (although some 25 percent of them were *former* smokers who had quit, one as recently as seven weeks ago, others more than twelve years ago). These nonsmokers gave these primary reasons for not smoking: health reasons (44.2 percent); "messy" reasons—smell, stains, burns, etc. (25.2 percent); cost factors (17.5 percent); religious reasons (4.9 percent); others—"never started," "didn't like the taste," "my children convinced me not to," etc. (7.3 percent); and agency incentives and advantages (0.9 percent).

Interestingly, 22.7 percent of the survey respondents themselves *were* smokers (78 percent smoked cigarettes; 9.3 percent smoked cigars; 9.3 percent smoked pipes; 3.1 percent used chewing tobacco). Smokers identified their own belief systems about the smoking/nonsmoking conflict as follows:

41.3%   I am personally willing to work/dine/visit in areas set aside at work for smokers;

33.3%   Problems in the work area between smokers and nonsmokers can best be solved by reasonable people conferring and compromising and not by mandatory agency personnel policies and procedures;

12.7%   Whether or not an employee smokes is none of the employer's business (allowing for safety reasons, of course, such as fire hazards, danger around explosives, and so forth);

9.5%   The entire secondhand smoke controversy is overblown (no pun intended) and is not an issue where I work;

3.2%   Nonsmokers should *not* be given any agency incentives or advantages (e.g., segregated dining areas, insurance advantages, etc.).

A number of smokers added written comments. One cigar smoker said cigars stink so badly that even *he* doesn't like to smoke them in an enclosed space; others were quite outspoken about what they perceive as a majority (nonsmokers) trampling on their (minority) rights. Several written comments expressed great reservations about restrictions on use of tobacco off the job. Such restrictions were seen as a radical invasion of personal rights and privacy. In contrast, a number of nonsmokers added strong commentary about banning or restricting smoking in the workplace and secondary smoke—comments such as, "It's about time"; "This is an issue whose time has come"; "We can measure the cost savings"; "I'm tired of being a passive smoker"; and so forth. Not all written comments (on either side) showed polarization, but some expressed feelings and values that were quite strong.

A number of the individualized responses by several jurisdictions are cited below. They illustrate how public agencies are coping with the many issues raised in the survey.

Survey Findings

The city of Virginia Beach, Virginia, has had at least one "incident come up between smokers/nonsmokers where management/supervisors had to intervene" and has "designed an office or structured an office layout at least in part because of the smoking/nonsmoking issue." The city "segregates smokers and nonsmokers in work areas/work stations" and in "office/room assignments." The city "provides or makes available programs (counseling, therapy groups, other formal means of employee assistance) to help employees stop (or cut down on) smoking," and includes specific references on the issue in new employee orientation.

The city of Virginia Beach requires all uniformed employees in the fire department to sign a binding contract with the key clause "[*Employee name*] agrees that upon employment, he/she will not smoke nor utilize smoking material considered as dangerous within the framework of controlled substance statutes on or off duty. This condition to be in effect during the entire tenure of the employee."

In a telephone interview with the author, the fire chief stressed that this is a condition of employment only for new fire fighters, but will be enforced (up to and including discharge for noncompliance). He noted that the city completed a survey recently where more than 80 percent of the fire fighters identified themselves as nonsmokers and favored such a tough new policy. Obviously a double standard of compliance will exist where old-timers who are "grandfathered" in will be allowed to smoke sometimes and new hires will not. The nonsmoking provision will uniformly apply to bunk areas, dining room, etc., but smoking will be permitted for old-timers in general work areas of the stations. The fire chief admitted he has "drawn some bad press (along with much positive press commentary)" and has been called a "fascist dictator" by some detractors. Virginia does not have a public employee collective bargaining law, but the chief said his "recent employee survey showed more than three-fourths of the 80 percent supporting the nonsmoking policy were union members [International Association of Fire Fighters], so the new policy is not an issue with the union itself."

The Skokie, Illinois, fire department also requires new hires to sign an agreement (see box).

A personnel officer for Oklahoma City, Oklahoma, wrote, "This city's fire department has a nonsmoking policy for first-year recruits. After one year they are free [again] to smoke. One recruit was terminated because of [violation of] this policy. He filed suit in our district court. The judge dismissed the case. The employee then filed with the EEOC. They found no probable cause [for his charge of discrimination]."

Hampton Roads, Louisiana, has a nonsmoking policy for new fire and police (sworn) personnel, a policy recommended by the city attorney.

Fire Department Condition of Employment Agreement

I, _____ , acknowledge that by accepting employment with the Village of Skokie Fire Department as a Fire Fighter/Paramedic, I am agreeing to the following condition of employment: From my date of hire, I will not smoke, chew, or use any tobacco product(s) on or off duty during the entire tenure of my employment; if I do smoke, chew, or use any tobacco product(s) at any time during the entire tenure of my employment, I will be subject to dismissal for cause. I understand this condition; agree to it; and accept such a condition of employment with the Village of Skokie.

_____   _____

Signature   Date

Typical of many smaller cities is the written policy of the city of Oakland Park, Florida (with 281 employees). Florida passed a Clean Indoor Air Act in 1985. This city provides for mediation of disputes between smokers and nonsmokers by immediate supervisors, but does not provide any elaborate detailing of procedures or means of enforcement. The city's policy reads in part:

> In work areas, where space is shared by two or more persons, an effort shall be made to accommodate individual preferences to the degree prudently possible. When requested, supervisors shall make a reasonable attempt to mediate a settlement and/or separate persons who smoke from those who do not.
>   Employees may designate their private offices as smoking or nonsmoking areas. Visitors to private work areas will honor the wishes of the host.
>   In City-owned vehicles, smoking shall be permitted only when there is no objection from one or more of the occupants.
>   Employees and visitors are expected to honor the smoking and nonsmoking designations and to be considerate of nonsmokers in their vicinity.

A written response by Oakland Park on the survey shows the city attempts to resolve conflicts by courtesy, consideration, and good will, but (as quoted above) still stipulates that when "accommodation is not possible, the rights of the nonsmoker should prevail." The response added that, "majority rule" has been the policy to date, and "a vast majority are nonsmokers." The city office building has only one small lunchroom that seats perhaps twenty persons, and nonsmokers have not complained about smoking there because it is "recognized that the lunchroom is the only place smokers can go, because virtually every office area is off-limits now, unless there is a supervisor who smokes who will let an employee smoke in the supervisor's own office."

The city of Salem, Oregon, has about 1,500 municipal employees. The city is covered under a state law on smoking, and implemented the following policy in 1983 (revised several times since):

Smoking in City Facilities

General Discussion

The purpose of this letter is to establish a policy regarding smoking in city facilities which provides a smoke-free work environment for employees.

Policy

Smoking is prohibited in all city buildings, except as listed below. Smoking is also prohibited in city equipment where any occupant objects.

Smoking is permitted in:

- The City Hall restaurant, except where posted otherwise.
- Engine bays of all Fire Stations.
- Any completely enclosed room which can be designated by the Department Head to be used exclusively for smoking.

Industrial injury claims have become extremely costly for many communities in recent years, especially for fire fighters. As a consequence, Salem's civil service commission amended its civil service rules in 1983 to prohibit smoking on or off the job by fire fighters (because of city liability under Oregon's Occupational Disease Law) as follows: "Fire fighters appointed after March 9, 1983, must not smoke tobacco either on or off duty during their term of employment."

Salem's fire-fighter rule naturally attracted considerable press coverage and controversy. The city's personnel director strongly endorsed the policy for fire fighters on cost containment grounds alone. In a telephone interview on February 10, 1986, he told the author that controversy has now largely died down and only two incidents have recently arisen—neither involving fire fighters.

In a related incident, Salem's police chief designated one small room as an exclusive smoking room under the city's general smoke-free policy. Unfortunately, the room's ventilation system drew the smoke into several other offices and nonsmokers objected. The police chief ultimately banned smoking entirely for police department employees in the building. Another incident involved complaints by nonsmoking employees in the public works department in Salem about the more frequent breaks taken by employees who smoke. The result was a restriction of smoke breaks to the lunch hour and the two coffee breaks.

The personnel director of Fort Dodge, Iowa, wrote that "because of the pension related liability issue, we have discussed smoking as it relates to Police/Fire Personnel." Several other jurisdictions also made similar comments about considering the no smoking issue for uniformed personnel because of the liability risks.

One suburban school district with 3,600 employees (classified and teaching), Davis County, Utah, based its no-smoking policy in all school buildings on a state statute prohibiting smoking in school and other public buildings—a law typical of most school systems in the United States. The district's policy handbook includes this very general statement:

No Smoking in School Buildings

A. Smoking in school buildings is prohibited by law. This regulation applies to students, teachers, maintenance personnel, administrators, visitors, personnel who rent school facilities, etc. The law has as its basis the necessity to prevent fire and/or explosion and their attendant effect on personnel, equipment, and buildings.

B. In view of the fact that students are prohibited from smoking on or near school grounds, it is respectfully requested that all school district employees refrain from smoking on school grounds as well as in school buildings.

The district's personnel director (who completed the survey instrument) modified his answer on item 3 ("Your agency segregates smokers and nonsmokers in eating or dining areas") by adding, "Smoking [is] not allowed in dining areas." This district *has* studied the smoking/nonsmoking issue as a means of containing health-care costs, and includes the issue in employee orientation and training.

As do most states, Utah regulates use or possession of tobacco products by minors (see UCA 76-10-105 making such "Possession of . . . Tobacco By Minors" a criminal offense). Utah has designated compliance officers in each school district (usually a vice-principal) who enforce the nonsmoking policy on school grounds and in buildings. Accommodation in most general public buildings among public employees in Utah has been achieved by designating smoking/nonsmoking areas in cafeterias and so forth, but smoking is strictly prohibited in school buildings.

Ramsey County, Minnesota (with over 5,000 employees), has had a smoking policy for many years (under Minnesota's Clean Indoor Air Act) but has recently begun to enforce the provisions of the act more rigorously for several reasons. For example, moves into several new county office buildings have "forced employees to redefine work areas" and "come to grips with our preferences and dislikes"; "a number of incidents have arisen between smoking/nonsmoking employees which have forced supervisors to invoke provisions of the act—which requires the preference of even *one* nonsmoker to be favored"; and because the county "made [an] internal study or research effort over the smoker/nonsmoker issue which led to greater emphasis on the enforcement of provisions of the earlier law." The ordinance defines floor areas, ventilation systems, complaints, appellate procedures, and so forth. It is of interest, however, that in one of the new county office buildings, the Human Services Department has established a policy that "contains provisions that are beyond the minimum requirements established by the Minnesota Department of Health and the Minnesota Clean Indoor Air Act," as follows:

> Smoking is prohibited throughout all CHSD leased space, except locations specifically designated as smoking permitted areas. Nonsmoking areas include all offices whether occupied by one person or several, all open office areas, hallways, corridors, interview booths, conference rooms, restrooms, file areas, and storage rooms. Portable ashtrays are banned from all nonsmoking areas.
>
> Smoking is permitted in specific designated and posted areas in waiting rooms, lounges, lunchrooms, and shops. Employees are expected to confine smoking to normal rest breaks or lunch periods. Leaving a work area at any other time to participate in a break is not allowed. Nothing in this policy shall be construed to conflict with smoking prohibitions imposed by the Fire Marshall or other law, ordinances or regulations.

This departmental policy (which also provides for enforcement, penalties, and appeals) embraces an area that drew spirited comment by many others on the survey instrument itself, that smokers "get many more breaks and time away from their work area than nonsmokers"—that is, smokers leave their work areas more frequently than the normal two breaks per work shift.

This same issue surfaced in a number of other places as well. The office of the deputy superintendent of the Oregon Department of Education (Salem, Oregon) issued a memorandum on November 7, 1979, to all staff that addressed the department's policy on smoking breaks:

Supervisors shall allow smoking breaks for their employees which will be subtracted from the time designated for lunch. Also, employees needing more smoking time may take additional breaks by extending their working hours beyond the normal starting and ending times to ensure an eight-hour working day.

Madison, Wisconsin's response to the survey checked virtually every item on the instrument. The respondent, a chief of employee relations in one of the departments, noted that

when the Wisconsin Clean Indoor Air Act [1983 Wisconsin Act 211, Non-Smoking Law] first passed in February 1983, the complete issue was clouded with "rights" issues. After three years under the statute the air has cleared. We had a confrontation with union representatives who defended smokers' rights—the next day nonsmoking union members demanded their rights be defended. This created political problems within the union itself.

Pasadena, California, gives nonsmokers "incentives/advantages" in lunchroom or cafeteria eating arrangements and separates smokers/nonsmokers in dining areas; "supports by internal promotion such yearly efforts as the 'Great American Smoke-Out' sponsored by others as a national campaign"; "provides or makes available programs . . . to help [city] employees stop (or cut down on) smoking"; "segregates smokers and nonsmokers in work areas/work stations or office/room assignments"; "segregates smokers and nonsmokers in meeting rooms, conference rooms, training rooms, and so forth"; "includes specific references to policy on smoking versus nonsmoking in pamphlets on health plans, medical coverage, employee fitness, employee assistance programs, etc."; and the city posts signs in meal areas, restrooms, working areas, etc., all in compliance with a municipal ordinance.

The survey showed efforts by several jurisdictions to help employees stop smoking for health reasons even where no other particular efforts were underway. Galesburg, Illinois, set up a stop-smoking clinic in cooperation with a local hospital, for example. Many such programs were reported.

The California State Personnel Board regulates approximately 144,000 public employees. In 1982 the California assembly passed a nonsmoking ordinance which provides that

each state department shall either adopt the existing policy of the State Personnel Board on smoking, or adopt their own policy on smoking which addresses the rights of nonsmokers to a smoke-free environment in formal meetings, informal meetings, and work stations, and which allows for administration of the policy and for the resolution of conflicts regarding the policy.

Many departments of California state government have now adopted their own no-smoking policies under this law. For instance, the Contractors State License Board in Sacramento issued this bulletin to "all CSLB Headquarters Building Employees" on January 6, 1986:

Subject: Headquarters Building No-Smoking Policy

After considerable thought, analysis, and debate, a no-smoking policy has been developed for CSLB Headquarters building staff. The evidence that "secondary smoke" in most environments is hazardous to a nonsmoking individual's health has become overwhelming. In addition, some people have allergic reactions to cigarette smoke. We ask that all employees abide by this no-smoking policy.

Effective January 13, 1986, there will be no smoking in the headquarters work areas. Smoking is acceptable in the break room; we are attempting to obtain purchase approvals for equipment to clear the smoke in this room. Those offended by smoking should plan to minimize their time in the break room until the equipment is purchased.

We recognize that this new policy may not be easy for some. We hope that supervisors will be flexible in the next few weeks to allow employees a few extra minutes to step away from work areas (to the break room or outside) if they just must smoke. This is for a transition period only and should not continue indefinitely.

I appreciate your cooperation in designing a healthier work environment.

Summary and Next Steps

The author received 145 responses to a mailed survey (or 82 percent of the total sample). Of this number, 38 percent of the public agencies (cities, counties, school districts, state agencies, and several federal agencies) do have smoking/nonsmoking policies. Over 41 percent of the agencies with smoking policies segregated smokers and nonsmokers in dining or lunchroom areas; over 24 percent segregated smokers/nonsmokers in office or space assignments; over 20 percent favored nonsmokers in life and disability insurance programs. More than 75 percent of those agencies with smoking policies included some form of reference to smoking in policy manuals, included the topic in orientation and training, provided stop-smoking or therapy groups, or otherwise engaged in a wide variety of other activities involving the smoking issue procedures. Over 34 percent of the total number of respondents have had an incident between smokers and nonsmokers that required management intervention, and more than 24 percent reported designing an office or structuring an office layout at least in part because of the smoking/nonsmoking issue. Some public jurisdictions now restrict hiring to nonsmokers, including a few agencies that ban or restrict smoking by their employees even off the job. Many other units are now studying the smoking issue or plan to. Over 77 percent of the survey respondents were nonsmokers (a fourth of them, however, were *formerly* smokers). Most of them did not smoke for health reasons and "messy" reasons (smell, stains, burns, etc.)—rarely because of incentives/advantages offered by management (0.9 percent). Of the 22.7 percent of respondents who were smokers, more than three-fourths smoked cigarettes, and over 18 percent smoked pipes or cigars. Over a third of the smokers felt conciliation, compromise, and reasonableness could best solve workplace problems between smokers and nonsmokers. A number expressed very strong feelings about the erosion of smokers' "rights."

A number of cases were cited in the chapter of how various jurisdictions are handling problem areas such as designating restricted areas, signs, smoking breaks and relief periods, room ventilation, employee assistance programs, hiring contracts, and disability claims. Some law cases bearing on the issue were also cited, and a number of studies on the costs and hazards of smoking and secondhand smoke were referred to.

In general, it appears that public jurisdictions, along with private industry, will move at an accelerating pace toward a smoke-free society in the years ahead.

What are the recommended next steps if a public agency decides to institute a nonsmoking policy? Although a full discussion of them is beyond the scope of this chapter, the following basic steps (the first letters spell the word "restrict") have been suggested:

R—Review the Research:
The first step to successful nonsmoking policy implementation is a comprehensive understanding of the rationale behind the introduction of smoking restrictions and a review of the many possible alternatives.

E—Employee Involvement:
Stringent smoking restrictions will present a hardship to certain employees because of their addiction to nicotine. Participatory management, which involves employees in policy development and implementation, is the key to success.

S—Strategic Plan:
Resolution of any problem in a corporate environment requires the development of a strategy—clean indoor air policies are no exception.

T—Time for Transition:
As with any change, people need time to make the required adjustments. Organizations need different timetables for policy implementation based on differences in employee populations.

R—Reduce Exposure to Smoke:
It is possible to get so involved with policy development that an organization loses sight of the goal of the policy—a smoke-free workplace.

I —Incentives for Employees:
Many employees use the reduced opportunities to smoke at work as an incentive to quit smoking. Assisting these efforts is a wise corporate investment.

C—Clear Communications:
A lot of time, energy, and resources go into the tobacco industry's efforts to keep people smoking. Any counter-education effort needs to be sophisticated in its message and delivery.

T—Take a Bow:
Organizations that have successfully implemented stringent smoking policies tend to attract very favorable media attention.[6]

Appendix—Survey Responses

1. Does your employer have any formal or informal personnel policies and procedures on smoking versus nonsmoking at work?

   a.   55 yes   90 no

   38%   If "no," please go to item 4 below; if "yes," please complete all the other questions below.

2. Please check all that apply at your agency:

   a.   1   3.5%   Nonsmokers are given incentives/advantages in agency group health plans or medical coverage (lower premiums, better coverage, whatever);

   b.   6   20.7%   Nonsmokers are given incentives/advantages in group life insurance, disability protection and/or other insurance provisions;

   c.   2   6.9%   Nonsmokers are given incentives/advantages in recruitment or initial selection for employment;

   d.   1   3.5%   Nonsmokers are given incentives/advantages in selection for promotion, executive development, mobility training, or other forms of training programs;

   e.   7   24.1%   Nonsmokers are given incentives/advantages in office/space assignments;

   f.   12   41.4%   Nonsmokers are given incentives/advantages in lunchroom, dining room, cafeteria, or snackroom seating or eating arrangements;

3. Please check all that apply at your agency:

   a.   38   11.7%   There is a state law that covers at least some smoking policies;

   b.   23   7.1%   Your agency supports by internal promotion such yearly efforts as the Great American Smoke-Out sponsored by others as a national campaign;

   c.   4   1.2%   Your agency tries to segregate smokers/nonsmokers when assigning workers to travel together or to go with each other on field assignments;

   d.   26   8.0%   Your agency provides or makes available programs (counseling, therapy groups, other formal means of employee assistance) to help employees stop (or cut down on) smoking;

   e.   21   6.5%   Your agency segregates smokers and nonsmokers in eating or dining areas;

   f.   26   8.0%   Your agency segregates smokers and nonsmokers in work areas/work stations or office/room assignments;

   g.   15   4.6%   Your agency segregates smokers and nonsmokers in lounges or rest room facilities;

   h.   21   6.5%   Your agency segregates smokers and nonsmokers in meeting rooms, conference rooms, training rooms, and so forth;

i.   8   2.5%   Your agency segregates smokers and nonsmokers during breaks or rest periods;

j.   21   6.5%   Your agency provides "smoker's rooms" or a segregated, set-aside room (or rooms) where smokers are requested to go to smoke;

k.   15   4.6%   Your agency has installed improved ventilation or filtering systems to reduce the problem of so-called second-hand smoke;

l.   2   0.6%   Your agency (like a lot of the airlines) has a posted "Cigarettes only! No pipes or cigars" policy;

m.   16   4.9%   Your agency includes specific references to policy on smoking versus nonsmoking in new employee orientation;

n.   8   2.5%   Your agency includes specific references to policy on smoking versus nonsmoking in at least some training courses of workers and supervisors;

o.   19   5.9%   Your agency includes specific references to policy on smoking versus nonsmoking in the employee handbook and/or policies and procedures manual;

p.   13   4.0%   Your agency includes specific references to policy on smoking versus nonsmoking in at least some issues of the employee newsletter or other agency communications to workers;

q.   11   3.4%   Your agency includes specific references to policy on smoking versus nonsmoking in pamphlets or literature on health plans, medical coverage, employee fitness, employee assistance programs, etc.

r.   37   11.4%   Your agency includes specific references to policy on smoking versus nonsmoking in smoking/nonsmoking signs or posters displayed in working areas, meal areas, restrooms or lounges, or other work sites (other than where safety is a factor);

s.   1   0.3%   Your agency has a specific policy on chewing tobacco (applying to spitting, spittoons, etc.);

4. Are you personally a smoker, or do you use tobacco?

a.   32   22.7%   yes
     109 77.3%   no

If "no," go to 5 below; if "yes," do you (check all that apply), then go to 6 below:

b.   25   78.0%   smoke cigarettes
c.   3   9.3%   smoke cigars

d.	3	9.3%	smoke a pipe
e.	1	3.1%	use chewing tobacco
f.	0	0.0%	use tobacco snuff
g.	0	0.0%	use other tobacco products (please specify)

5. If you do not smoke or use tobacco, what are your personal reasons for not doing so? Check all that apply:

a.	91	44.2%	Health reasons
b.	36	17.5%	Cost factors
c.	52	25.2%	"Messy" reasons (smell, stains, burns, etc.)
d.	10	4.9%	Religious reasons
e.	2	0.9%	Agency incentives/advantages (e.g., lower cost for medical coverage)
f.	15	7.3%	Other

6. If you do smoke (see 4 above) please check all comments below that apply (your
   own belief systems, as it were):

   a. 8   12.7%   Whether or not an employee smokes is none of the em-
                   ployer's business (allowing for safety reasons, of course,
                   such as fire hazards, danger around explosives, and so
                   forth);

   b. 2   3.2%   Nonsmokers should not be given any agency incen-
                   tives/advantages (e.g., segregated dining areas, insurance
                   advantages, etc.);

   c. 21 33.3%   Problems in the work area between smokers and
                   nonsmokers can best be solved by reasonable people con-
                   ferring and compromising together and not by mandatory
                   agency personnel policies and procedures;

   d. 6   9.5%   The entire secondhand smoke controversy is overblown
                   (no pun intended) and is not an issue where I work;

   e. 26 41.3%   I am personally willing to work/dine/visit in areas set
                   aside at work for smokers;

7. Has your agency ever (check all that do apply):

   a. 0   0.0%   Discharged a worker over the smoking/nonsmoking
                   policy?

   b. 11 8.2%   Had an arbitration/grievance case over smoking/non-
                   smoking?

   c. 23 17.0%   Studied the smoking/nonsmoking issue while looking at
                   ways to contain health-care costs?

   d. 2   1.5%   Been involved in litigation/court case with an employee
                   over the smoking/nonsmoking issue?

e.	47	34.8%	Had an incident come up between smokers/nonsmokers where management/supervisors had to intervene?
f.	33	24.4%	Designed an office or structured an office layout at least in part because of the smoking/nonsmoking issue?
g.	16	11.9%	Made any kind of agency internal study or research effort over the smoker/nonsmoker issue?
h.	3	2.2%	Other

Assignments

1. As a class, or in teams, discuss the smoking on the job issue. Reach some kind of group consensus on the best way to handle such concerns, especially the ethical issues.

2. Research your state's Indoor Clean Air Act, if any. How is it being applied? Enforced? What are typical practices in your state or community?

3. As a class, or in teams, draft a model smoking on the job policy that satisfies the ethical issues raised by 1 above and fully satisfies the legal issues (if any) of 2 above.

4. This topic lends itself well to a debate between smokers and nonsmokers, possibly drawn from class members themselves. Assuming debate rules are followed by participants, a debate could prove to be most enlightening to advocates of each position.

Notes

1. William M. Timmins, "States Legislate Indoor Clean Air Acts," *Public Administration Times* 9 (15 February 1986): 3.

2. National Public Employer Labor Relations Association, *Newsletter* 8 (31 January 1986): 6.

3. See C. Everett Koop, "Is a Smokeless Society by 2000 Achievable?" *Archives of Internal Medicine* 145 (September 1985): 1581.; Everett R. Rhoades, et al., "Smoke Free Facilities in the Indian Health Service," *New England Journal of Medicine* (12 December 1986): 1548; Jonathan E. Fielding, "Smoking: Health Effects and Control," *New England Journal of Medicine,* 313:491–498 and 313:555–561 for several examples.

4. See, for example, *Shimp v. New Jersey Bell Telephone Company* (1976), 368 A.2d 408, and *Vickers v. Veterans Administration* (1982), 549 F. Supp. 85, for two related cases.

5. One hundred seventy-five questionnaires were mailed out based on random selection from IPMA's 1985 Membership Directory and NPELRA's 1985 Membership Roster. A total of 145 usable responses were received for a response rate of 82 percent, considered very satisfactory. All the materials quoted hereafter were supplied by survey respondents.

6. William L. Weis, *Toward a Smoke-free Work Environment* (Seattle: Fresh Air for Non-Smokers, n.d.) See also, Leah L. Woodruff, "Life Insurer Plans for a Smoke-free Office," *Business and Health,* November 1984, 22–23; Rhoda Nichter, *Guide to a Smoke-free Workplace* (New York: Group Against Smoking Pollution, n.d.); American Cancer Society, *Model Policy for Smoking in the Workplace,* n.d.; American Lung Association, *Creating Your Company Policy: Freedom from Smoking at Work* (1985); United States Public Health Service, *No Smoking: A Decision Maker's Guide to Reducing Smoking at the Worksite* (Washington, DC, The Washington Business Group on Health, 1985); and American Lung Association, *Taking Executive Action: Freedom from Smoking at Work* (1985).

References

Books

American Cancer Society. *The Dangers of Smoking, the Benefits of Quitting.* New York, 1982.

Califano, Joseph A., Jr. *Governing America.* New York: Simon & Schuster, 1981.

Diehl, Harold S. *Tobacco & Your Health: The Smoking Controversy.* New York: McGraw-Hill, 1969.

Fritschler, A. Lee. *Smoking and Politics.* Englewood Cliffs, NJ: Prentice-Hall, 1969.

National Institute of Drug Abuse. *Research on Smoking Behavior.* Washington, DC: U.S. Government Printing Office, 1977.

Skinner, William Iverson. *Tobacco and Health (The Other Side of the Coin).* New York: Vantage Press, 1970.

Sobel, Robert. *They Satisfy.* Garden City, NY: Doubleday, 1978.

Timmins, William M., and Clark B. *Smoking and the Workplace: Questions and Answers for Human Resources Professionals.* Westport, CN: Greenwood, 1989.

Troyer, Ronald J., and Markle, Gerald E. *Cigarettes: The Battle Over Smoking.* New Brunswick, NJ: Rutgers University Press, 1983.

Whelan, Elizabeth M. *A Smoking Gun (How the Tobacco Industry Gets Away with Murder).* Philadelphia: Stickley, 1984.

Winter, Ruth. *The Scientific Case Against Smoking.* New York: Crown, 1980.

Articles and Related Publications

American Council on Science and Health. "Cancer in the United States: Is there an Epidemic?" 1983.

Bock, Fred G. "Nonsmokers and Cigarette Smoke: A Modified Perception of Risk." *Science* 215: 197, 1982.

Cameron Charles. "Lung Cancer and Smoking," *Atlantic* 197(1): 71–75, 1956.

Cascio, Wayne F. "Costing the Effects of Smoking at the Work Place." In *Costing Human Resources: The Financial Impact of Behavior in Organizations,* pp. 80–97. Boston: PWS-Kent, 1987.

Christen, Arden G., and Glover, Elbert. "Smokeless Tobacco: Seduction of Youth." *World Smoking and Health* (Spring 1981): 20–23.

Foote, Emerson. "Advertising and Tobacco." *Journal of the American Medical Association* 245(16): 1667–1668, 1981.

Garfinkel, Lawrence. "The Impact of Low Tar/Nicotine Cigarettes." *World Smoking and Health* 5(2): 4–8.

Hymowitz, Norman. "Personalizing the Risk of Cigarette Smoking." *Journal of the Medical Society of New Jersey* 77: 579–582, 1980.

Little, Clarence Cook. "The Public and Smoking: Fear or Calm Deliberation." *The Atlantic* (December 1957): 74–76.

Lilienfeld, Abraham M. "The Case Against the Cigarette." *The Nation* 194(13): 277–280, 1962.